READING OLD BOOKS

Reading Old Books

WRITING WITH TRADITIONS

Peter Mack

PRINCETON UNIVERSITY PRESS

PRINCETON & OXFORD

Published by Princeton University Press
41 William Street, Princeton, New Jersey 08540
6 Oxford Street, Woodstock, Oxfordshire OX20 1TR

press.princeton.edu

Library of Congress Control Number 2019931722
ISBN 978-0-691-19400-4

British Library Cataloging-in-Publication Data is available

Editorial: Ben Tate and Charlie Allen
Production Editorial: Jill Harris
Jacket Design: Layla Mac Rory
Production: Merli Guerra
Publicity: Alyssa Sanford and Katie Lewis
Copyeditor: Cynthia Buck

Jacket art: Raphael, *The School of Athens*, c. 1509–1511.

This book has been composed in Miller

Printed on acid-free paper. ∞

Printed in the United States of America

10 9 8 7 6 5 4 3 2 1

For Vicki Behm

CONTENTS

THIS BOOK SEEKS TO UNDERSTAND the ways in which literary tradition has been and can be useful. It argues that literary tradition provides essential imaginative resources for writers and readers. Writers use earlier books for plots, for phrases, for ideas to copy or contradict, for moral support, and for lessons in becoming better writers. This book investigates how writers learn from and use their predecessors, and how readers use the idea of a literary heritage, in order to argue for the importance of tradition to readers and writers. We need to be critical of how, and why, the word "tradition" is used by writers or critics, but we cannot allow that necessary wariness to blind us to the ways in which writers make use of earlier texts to make meanings and to create new works. Nor can we afford to ignore the role of reading earlier texts in helping us understand new writing.

In the introduction, I investigate the history of the word "tradition," the ways in which over the last 160 years the word has been applied to literature, and the opinions of a range of sociologists, historians, philosophers, and critics on the use and value of tradition. Some of my sources for this introductory discussion were suggested by a critic's part in establishing the significance of literary tradition (Sainte-Beuve, Eliot, Leavis); others by people with whom I discussed my ideas (Gadamer, Adorno, Ferrante, Hobsbawm and Ranger, MacIntyre, Shils), and still others by my reading around the subject. Late in the day I remembered that E. R. Curtius had some interesting things to say on traditions and canons.[1] In the introduction, I emphasize the importance of studying the process by which the later reader or writer uses the older text, the freedom which the writer enjoys in choosing both a text to follow and the way in which to exploit it, and the different uses which readers and writers make of tradition. For one can best understand how tradition works by studying a later writer's use of an individual text. The requirement that a writer (or reader) should somehow possess a particular tradition whole is too demanding and tends to obscure that writer's use of other national and cultural traditions.

In the case studies which follow, I use detailed investigation of particular texts to try to understand a range of different ways in which tradition, usually represented by one or more older books, has proved helpful to different kinds of writers. I chose the user texts partly because they were already known to me (Chaucer, Spenser) and partly because they illustrated interesting or difficult relationships with tradition (Petrarch, Gaskell, Ngũgĩ). I wanted to investigate the role of tradition at later historical periods as well as in the earlier periods I usually work with, and I needed to include examples of writers who seemed to be highly original and who used texts and ideas from outside their own language and culture. I wanted to write about some books I have long admired and others I have come to know relatively recently (Tasso and Gaskell are for me recent discoveries), as well as about books on which I had not previously written much. My non-English examples favor Italian because that is my second language and because English authors make especially fruitful use of Italian texts in the Middle Ages and the Renaissance.

These studies investigate the nature of the relationship between each writer and the prior text or texts which he or she is using. They ask what tradition opens up for a new text and what it closes down. They aim to illustrate a range of ways in which reliance on particular previous texts or on a vaguer notion of tradition promotes or supports effective new writing. I hope that these studies demonstrate a range of different ways of using tradition fruitfully, but I do not imagine that they exhaust the possible types of productive relation between tradition and writing. The limitations of my knowledge and of time precluded a more comprehensive historical approach to this vast topic, yet the focus on a few texts has advantages for showing the ways in which individual readers and writers use traditions.

In chapter 1, I start from the proposition that Petrarch founded a European tradition of writing love poetry which has to some extent obscured his own poetic achievement, and I investigate the ways in which he wrote great poetry by filling poetic structures borrowed from the troubadours with ideas and phrases from Latin poetry and Dante. I aim to rescue Petrarch's poetry from the assumptions of later readers of the Petrarchan tradition by showing that his poetic greatness is inseparable from his reading of Latin, Italian, and Provençal poetry. Petrarch also makes many illuminating comments on how writers use their reading. Chaucer was later acknowledged as the founder of the English poetic tradition, but, as I argue in chapter 2, he improved his own writing by translating a minor work of Boccaccio and adapting the lessons he learned from reading Boccaccio, first to the transformation of *Troilus and Criseyde* and later to *The Canterbury Tales*. In chapter 3, I examine the ways in which Ariosto, Tasso, and Spenser wrote epics out of their predecessors' works. Ariosto started from Boiardo but privileged shock and surprise. Tasso combined a more unified structure based on Homer with emotional episodes adapted from Ariosto. Spenser adapted Ariosto to create his own loose form of unity, while borrowing and reinflecting episodes from Ariosto and Tasso in order to express his own ideas. In chapter 4, I investigate Elizabeth Gaskell's writing on the almost new subject of the living conditions of industrial workers in Manchester and their alienation from the millowners; she wrote not only on the basis of her personal knowledge of Manchester living conditions but from her reading of Shakespeare, Carlyle, poetry, and the Bible. Gaskell's reliance on the encouragement of other writers when she was attacked prompted her to offer support to later women writers, both privately through her letters and publicly through her biography of Charlotte Brontë. In chapter 5, I examine Ngũgĩ wa Thiong'o's use of his knowledge of the Bible, English novels and plays, and Gikuyu folktales, proverbs, and traditions to write a new kind of comic novel about the government and development of an African nation after decolonization. Ngũgĩ addresses the uses, both repressive and liberating, of Western and African traditions in the postcolonial state.

This book was written out of the experience of teaching and discussing literature at the University of Warwick. I thank the Department of English and its then-chair, Maureen Freely, for the study leave in 2016–2017, which enabled me to draft the book. Individual chapters owe a great deal to colleagues at Warwick with whom I have taught and discussed texts, ideas, and authors: Catherine Bates, Paul Botley, Gloria Cigman, Gill Frith, Simon Gilson, John Goode, Tony Howard, Derek Hughes, Ed Larrissy, Neil Lazarus,

Jennifer Lorch, Paul Merchant, Pablo Mukherjee, John Rignall, Carol Rutter, John Stokes, Rashmi Varma, Christiania Whitehead, William V. Whitehead, Sarah Wood, and Martin Wright. Some of them have also read chapters for me. As I leave the department I am especially conscious of what I owe to my colleagues and students. I am very conscious of my debts to my teachers at the Warburg Institute, especially Michael Baxandall, J. B. Trapp, Charles Schmitt, and D. P. Walker, and to the institute's incomparable library. I am grateful to friends around Leamington and in the wider world who have suggested books and given me critical readings of individual chapters: Charlotte Brunsdon, Robert Conn, Gordon Fyfe, Lawrence Green, Andrew Hadfield, Daniel Javitch, Neil Kenny, Steven Mailloux, Nicholas Mann, Kees Meerhoff, Nicola Miller, both David Morleys, David Norbrook, John North, Walter Stephens, and David Wallace. I am warmly thankful to Maria Devlin McNair, Carolyn Steedman, and Marjorie Woods, who gave me close critical readings of the entire text, greatly to its benefit. I have been greatly helped by the anonymous readers for Princeton University Press, who made valuable detailed suggestions for improving the text. Within Princeton University Press, I thank Ben Tate, Hannah Paul, Jill Harris, Cynthia Buck, Al Bertrand, and Charlie Allen for their responsiveness, promptness, and kindness.

As usual, nothing would have been possible without the unwavering support and kindness of my wife, Vicki Behm, our children, Johanna and Mike, William and Naomi, Emily, and Rosy, and our grandchildren, Sophie, Bella, and Sam.

READING OLD BOOKS

Ideas of Literary Tradition

THIS BOOK INVESTIGATES THE ROLE of tradition in our understanding and teaching of literature. As soon as you start to look into the question of literary tradition, one very surprising fact emerges. Whereas modern readers sometimes think of literary tradition as something which goes back to the origins of literature, in fact people have spoken about literary traditions only in the last 160 years. For once, we can say exactly when the term was first used. On 12 April 1858, Charles Augustin Sainte-Beuve gave a lecture at the École Normale Supérieure in Paris entitled "Qu'est-ce-que c'est la tradition littéraire?," which he published as one of his *Causeries du lundi* that same year.[1] Early in the twentieth century, in 1919, T. S. Eliot could begin his lecture on "Tradition and the Individual Talent" by saying, "In English writing we seldom speak of tradition."[2] Since the 1940s literary scholars seem to have used the phrase "literary tradition" almost continuously, though there has been less use since a peak about twenty years ago. Of course, the practice of using the past in order to write new texts originated long before 1858, but people used different words to discuss it, words like "imitation," "models," "inheritance," and "borrowing." These words mostly placed more emphasis on the writer's choice and agency, whereas "tradition" seems more monolithic and coercive.

Almost equally surprising is the wide discrepancy in the valuation of the word "tradition" by different authors. For some modernists, postmodernists, and presentists, tradition is the enemy of original thought and therefore significant literature must be regarded as an attack on traditional modes of thought and expression. In sociology it is customary to treat "tradition" as the opposite of modernity or rationality. T. W. Adorno, who, as we shall see, saw tradition somewhat differently, famously wrote about the proper way of hating tradition, as if that was some sort of ethical imperative for modern thinkers and writers.[3] Tradition often represents the old-fashioned, such as a habit of musical performance which falsifies the composer's intention by incorporating anachronistic practices. In that case, the early music movement set out to sweep aside centuries of accumulated tradition in favor of authentic performances on early instruments.

But are there ways in which writers and readers can and perhaps must use tradition? Robert Conn has shown how, in the early twentieth century, Alfonso Reyes attempted to create a distinctive profile for Latin American literature by reorienting its connection with tradition. Reyes emphasized a combination of native literary traditions, Greek rather than Latin models, and a revised approach to the literary heritage of the Spanish language in order to create a distinctive role for Latin American writers and intellectuals within modern global literature, even as he was negotiating the difficulties of his own political position within and outside Mexico.[4] Arnold Schoenberg, by general consent the most revolutionary innovator in twentieth-century music, claimed that he had "written new music which being based on tradition is destined to become tradition."[5] The contemporary Italian writer Elena Ferrante insists that good writing emerges from a knowledge of literary tradition, even when that tradition seems hostile to or ignorant of what the writer wants to do.

> Writing is also the story of what we have read and are reading, of the quality of our reading, and a good story, finally, is one written from the depths of our life, from the heart of our relations with others, from the heights of the books we've liked.[6]

She makes the argument that the writer must know literary traditions and be able to alter and add to them, particularly in relation to women's writing, which she sees as obliged to confront both male literary tradition and the specificity of female experience.[7] For her the literatures of the past, high and low, are a great resource, but also one which must be enlarged and changed in order to address important neglected female issues, especially around motherhood.

> We, all of us women, need to build a genealogy of our own, one that will embolden us, define us, allow us to see ourselves outside the tradition through which men have viewed, represented, evaluated and catalogued us—for millennia. Theirs is a potent tradition, rich with splendid works but one that has excluded much, too much, of what is ours. To narrate thoroughly, freely—even provocatively—our own "more than this" is important: it contributes to the drawing of a map of what we are or what we want to be.[8]

For Ferrante, while the male tradition is imposing and rich and can hardly be ignored, the responsibility of the woman writer is to create a female tradition which will enable further thought and writing by better defining what women are and what they want to be.

In this introduction, I discuss the ways in which the related notions of tradition and literary tradition have been used and analyzed. I begin by showing the complexity of the word's meanings and associations through a survey of its uses, based firmly on the *Oxford English Dictionary* and the work of Harry Levin. Then I consider the influential literary approach to tradition in the work of the first French and English critics to exploit the term, Sainte-Beuve and T. S. Eliot. Next I describe the generally negative approach to tradition in the sociological tradition, to which Adorno's somewhat different views also belong, and the more positive view usually taken by anthropologists. Then I discuss the historical analysis of the invention of tradition as presented in the influential collection of essays under that title edited by Eric Hobsbawm and Terence Ranger (1983). Then I look in some detail at the very rich account of tradition presented in Hans-Georg Gadamer's *Truth and Method* (1960). This survey of ideas will put me in a position finally to identify some themes to be discussed in the more detailed individual studies which follow.

A History of the Word "Tradition"

The word "tradition" has a rich and sometimes controversial history. Some meanings of the word which are not directly relevant to literary contexts are nevertheless present to readers as implications or associations. This survey of usage follows Harry Levin's essay "The Tradition of Tradition" (1951), lightly supplemented with observations drawn largely from *The Oxford English Dictionary*, which was probably his major source, as it was for Raymond Williams in his brief account in *Keywords*.[9] The Latin word *traditio* is derived from the verb *tradere*, "to hand over." This means that the two primary meanings of *traditio* in classical Latin are "to surrender" and "to betray." These meanings are not really relevant to our investigation, but one should be aware of them in reading Latin sources.

Our first relevant meaning is based on the same verb *tradere*. "To hand over" can also mean "to teach." Thus, one of the later meanings of *traditio* is "teaching." *Traditio* can be the Latin translation of the Greek *paradosis*: the art of teaching in Plato's *Laws* 803a. This is the meaning of the word "tradition" as used in Francis Bacon's *The Advancement of Learning* (1605), as Levin pointed out.[10]

Second, in the Gospels we come across the word *paradosis* (translated as *traditio*) used as a contrast to the commandments of God. In Matthew 15:2–6 and Mark 7:5–13, the scribes and Pharisees ask Jesus why his disciples transgress the traditions of the ancients. Jesus replies that their traditions transgress the commandments of God, specifically the fifth commandment, to honor thy father and mother. So in this sense tradition means the Jewish history of Biblical interpretation, in this case contrasted with Christ's explication of the true meaning of God's commands.

Third, Saint Augustine in one his letters writes of a strand of Christian teaching which is *non scripta sed tradita*—not written in the Bible but handed down, including the celebration of the anniversary of Easter.[11] Here the idea seems to be that the explicit written Christian doctrine of the Bible is to be supplemented by traditions handed down through the Church. So whereas, in the second meaning from the Gospels, tradition was false and biblical commandment was true, here we have an idea of what is handed down both as different from what is written and as supplementing it rather than being contradicted by it. This is evidently related to the use of the Hebrew word *Mishnah* to denote the teaching which was not written down in the *Torah*, but which was given by God to Moses and handed down orally from generation to generation. In some contexts, "tradition" carries an association of wisdom, history, or memory passed on orally rather than in writing, as in "oral tradition."

The conflict between these second and third uses of "tradition" was revisited and inflamed at the time of the Reformation. Luther and the Protestants rejected accumulated traditions, such as the sale of indulgences, the cult of the saints, and the doctrine of purgatory, and wanted to go back to the scripture itself, the scripture alone. Catholic thinkers, on the other hand, upheld tradition as something passed down legitimately through the successors of Saint Peter. So, as Levin points out, for Milton in *Areopagitica* truth is opposed to tradition, while for the Catholic convert John Dryden in *The Hind and the Panther* scripture and tradition both contribute to true Christian teaching, because tradition is part of truth.[12] These forceful religious connotations may have been one of the reasons why the term "tradition" was not applied to literature earlier than 1858.

Fourth, Enlightenment thinkers generally sought to replace the teachings of tradition, which was now regarded as including all religious teaching, with the light of reason.[13] In his 1999 Reith Lecture on tradition, the British sociologist Anthony Giddens (born 1938) cited the Baron d'Holbach as one of those who called for a turning from tradition to the study of nature.[14] Levin quotes George Eliot's affirmation of the progress achieved by turning from tradition to reason in *The Spanish Gypsy*:

> We had not walked
> But for Tradition; we walk evermore
> To higher paths by brightening Reason's lamp.[15]

This Enlightenment sense is probably the origin for the negative views of tradition which are usual in the sociological literature. For example, in *The Eighteenth Brumaire of Louis Bonaparte* (1852), Marx famously wrote:

> Men make their own history, but they do not make it just as they please; they do not make it under circumstances chosen by themselves, but under circumstances directly encountered, given and transmitted from the past. The tradition of all the dead generations weighs like a nightmare on the brain of the living.[16]

He went on to explain that even the French revolutionaries presented themselves as acting in the spirit of heroes from the past, such as Roman or Greek liberators. For Marx, everything we can think or do is constrained, even malformed, by the weight of past tradition. Even gestures aimed at liberation come to be conducted in clothes borrowed from the past. Marx's task, expressed in words which may owe something to Thomas Paine's ideas, is to liberate his readers from their customary ways of thinking.[17] The sociological antipathy to tradition may also be connected with Max Weber's identification of "traditional authority," in which the right to rule is handed down through heredity, as one of the three types of authority, alongside charismatic authority and legal-rational authority.[18] In *Keywords*, Raymond Williams defines tradition as "a general process of handing down, with a very strong and often predominant sense of this entailing respect and duty" before noting that tradition involves selection and that the words "tradition" and "traditional" are now used dismissively, especially within forms of modernization theory.[19] So we have tradition as opposed to innovation in many book titles, and tradition as opposed to modernity in many cultural histories. Sometimes tradition is distinguished from closely related words like "custom" on the grounds that tradition possesses some quasi-legal force and that traditions may be enforced by their "guardians." Thus, Giddens declares,

> I shall understand "tradition" in the following way. Tradition, I shall say, is bound up with memory, specifically what Maurice Halbwachs terms "collective memory"; involves ritual; is connected with what I shall call a *formulaic notion of truth*; has "guardians"; and, unlike custom, has binding force which has a combined moral and emotional content.[20]

Fifth, the *OED* (sense I.1.d) recognizes a cultural sense of the word in the twentieth and twenty-first centuries: "a literary, artistic or musical method or style, established by a particular person or group and subsequently followed by others." This implies a deliberate choice to imitate or adapt a particular predecessor. Examples cited by the *OED* include academic uses such as "Horace had undertaken to write satire in the tradition of the form established by Lucilius" (1900) and "Writing poetry in the tradition of Donne" (1944). This sense could presumably be extended to include intellectual and philosophical traditions of inquiry, which, according to the Scottish philosopher Alasdair MacIntyre (born 1929), make it possible to understand and evaluate conflicting arguments, both those within that tradition and those involving criticisms from other schools.

> A tradition is an argument extended through time in which certain fundamental agreements are defined and redefined in terms of two kinds of conflict: those with critics and enemies external to the tradition who reject all or at least key parts of those fundamental agreements and those internal, interpretative debates through which the meaning and rationale of the fundamental agreements come to be expressed and by whose progress a tradition is constituted.[21]

Each culture possesses a shared schema by means of which each agent is able to make the actions of others intelligible.[22] For MacIntyre these philosophical traditions are characterized by their ability to be questioned, adapted, and improved. Any tradition may eventually realize its inadequacy, especially in relation to other traditions.[23]

A final, more specialized meaning is hidden somewhere among these: the idea that tradition provides esoteric or secret wisdom. The book titles of Kathleen Raine's *Blake and Tradition* and F.A.C. Wilson's *W. B. Yeats and Tradition* intend to indicate that they will be considering the presence of esoteric wisdom in the works of their chosen poets. Thus, the *OED* records that tradition is sometimes used to translate the Hebrew word *Cabbala*, in addition to its more usual role in translating *Mishnah*.

Meanings and associations of the adjective "traditional" may also be important to our understanding of tradition. In folk music, for example, many songs are simply known as traditional, with the implication that authorship occurred so far back and the song has since been subject to so much adaptation by singers that it is now part of the common repertory of musicians rather than the property of any one writer. Such songs were first passed on from singer to hearer and later transcribed. At both stages, new singers could change words, notes, or sequences, or they could set a given song text to a new tune, whether freshly written or previously "belonging" to an earlier song. Such creative uses of material could in turn be checked or reversed by more scholarly singers who insisted that a particular tune or method of singing belonged to a particular song. Thus, traditional folk music has mechanisms which promote both creativity and limits to free uses of material, but arguably a song becomes a folksong at the moment when singers other than its first author introduce changes to the song.

The word "tradition" is also linked to literature through the concept of a textual tradition—the process by which an older text has been handed down to later generations through the copying of its words. Any manual copying of a manuscript tends to introduce new mistakes, which gradually make the text harder to understand. Scholarly attempts to rectify supposed corruption of a text by making the text better fit later conceptions of grammar and coherence can corrupt the text still further. The modern editors of a text attempt to remove such corruptions by comparing as many copied versions of it as possible. Thus, manuscript copying was both essential to the preservation of a text and instrumental in introducing errors into it.[24] The institutional copying of tablets of text as part of the training of Babylonian scribes is the reason why scholars hope eventually to recover the whole text of *The Epic of Gilgamesh*, of which we currently have around five-sixths.[25]

As the *OED* indicates (senses I.1.a and c), all these meanings of the word "tradition" invoke the idea of a doctrine or custom being handed on from generation to generation and/or of a practice which is generally accepted and has been established for some time within a society. This social element in the meaning of tradition forms part of tradition's coercive power, but it also makes it possible for writers to bounce off or reform shared previous understandings in order to make something new. Some uses of the word imply very different and even contradictory views of the value of tradition. We notice that tradition is often invoked at times of change—to justify conservatism, to give reasons for change, or to suggest that something apparently new which one proposes is in fact a return to previous practice. One attraction of the word to its users may be a certain vagueness and breadth of implication. I know, for example, that I have sometimes used the phrase "Aristotelian tradition" when discussing a doctrine which was taught in medieval or Renaissance schools but was not in Aristotle's own text, and yet was also not presented as an innovation by one of his major followers. It seemed more honest to regard the doctrine as part of a tradition rather than as the distinctive opinion of any philosopher. At the same time the term's inherent breadth enabled me to assert a connection to Aristotle and the teaching of his school which I could not prove in detail. As we shall see in the case of Boccaccio's *Il Filostrato*, critics sometimes assert that a phrase or idea is part of a tradition in order to deny that a writer obtained it from a particular named source (in this case Petrarch).

We need to understand why the term has become so useful and so widely used, but we should also as readers ask why and with what implications the word is used in particular instances. We should be especially careful to ask questions when people speak of "the tradition" or of "tradition" with no further qualification, sometimes implying that there is only one tradition and that it is somehow complete and self-evident. Fortunately, writers at an early stage of a national literature tend to be aware that they are making use of materials from other literatures as well as from what they know of their native folklore. The idea of a literary tradition is most often invoked by writers to support and justify something new, and by readers to propose a new understanding of a particular text through its relationship to past texts. When we examine the implications of both near-synonyms of "tradition" and words which historically preceded it in literary discourse, such as "imitation," "inheritance," "models," and "borrowing," it becomes apparent that these words all imply more selection on the part of the author. Writers sometimes choose to speak of a literary tradition as if to imply that the compelling force of the past absolved them from responsibility for their choices of models.

Sainte-Beuve and Eliot

We turn now to the writers who introduced and developed the concept of literary tradition, Sainte-Beuve and Eliot. In his 1858 lecture "Qu'est-ce-que c'est la tradition littéraire?," the French literary critic Charles Augustin Sainte-Beuve (1804–1869) treats literary tradition as a kind of pantheon. Near the beginning of the lecture, he sets out a three-line outline consisting of three brief sentences.

There is a tradition.

How should it be understood.

How should it be maintained.[26]

For much of the lecture Saint-Beuve outlines the content of this tradition, which is European in origin (Homer, Virgil, Horace, Shakespeare), but then primarily French and based firmly on the authors of the seventeenth century (*le grand siècle*), especially Molière. But the tradition is not only a matter of the works worthy of memory gathered in our libraries; it also includes our laws, our institutions, our customs, and our origin. "It consists in a certain principle of reason and culture which has penetrated deeply into the character of this Gaulish nation."[27] Tradition on this presentation equates very closely with a sort of idealized French nationalism. When it comes to maintaining this literary tradition, Sainte-Beuve's main point is that one must possess it complete, ancient and modern, and that one should not concentrate on a few authors and neglect others.[28] At the same time one should check the tradition, verify it, and rejuvenate it. Sainte-Beuve introduces two key ideas which have added a strong political flavor to discussions of literary tradition: that literary tradition involves establishing a canon of great works, and that literary tradition is an expression of national identity.

In his essay of 24 October 1850, "What Is a Classic?," which is in many ways a first attempt at the topics broached in the lecture on tradition, Sainte-Beuve had taken a more open attitude to the classic. There he explicitly rejects the received opinion that the classic is a universally admired old author and seeks to replace it with a new and wider definition.

A true classic is an author who has enriched the human spirit, who has truly added to its wealth, who has made a further step forward, . . . who has made his thought, his observation or his invention, under any kind of form as long as it is generous and great, delicate and sensitive, healthy and beautiful in itself; who has spoken to everyone in a style which is both his own and also universal, a style which is new without pretentious novelty, new and ancient at the same time, comfortably contemporary with all ages.[29]

At this point, Sainte-Beuve defines the classic according to what the writer does with ideas, emotions, and language, not according to antiquity and wide acceptance. A little earlier in the same essay, he insists that a few scattered writers of talent are not enough to give a nation a solid and imposing foundation of literary wealth. "The idea of the classic implies in itself something which has continuity and consistency, which makes a whole and a tradition, which orders itself, which is transmitted and which lasts."[30] So great work can be new, but the idea of the classic implies a certain continuity and tradition. Later in the essay, he explains that while Montaigne was a kind of premature classic of the family of Horace, capricious as a lost child, the true French classics begin with the seventeenth century, and particularly with Corneille, Molière, and La Fontaine.[31] E. R. Curtius comments on the connections between Sainte-Beuve's ideas here and the mid–second century CE critic Aulus Gellius, who coined the term "classic" in *Noctes Atticae* XIX.8.[32]

In his essay "Tradition and the Individual Talent" (1919), T. S. Eliot (1888–1965) deplores the kind of literary tradition which involves "merely following the ways of the immediate generation," but also wants to insist that real tradition has a positive value for a poet. He argues that the best and most individual parts of a poet's work "may be those in which the dead poets, his ancestors, assert their immortality most vigorously." Tradition cannot be inherited: you must labor for it. To acquire tradition is to develop a historical sense "not only of the pastness of the past but of its presence; the historical sense compels a man to write not merely with his own generation in his bones, but with a feeling that the whole of the literature of Europe from Homer and within it the whole literature of his own country has a simultaneous existence and composes a simultaneous order."[33] Eliot advocates a sort of pantheon of all the writers of the European tradition and the individual national traditions, but he sees the individual possession of this tradition as a prerequisite for writing good poetry. His vision of the pantheon always allows a place for the new; indeed, he sees the pantheon as existing mainly to make possible what is new.

> The existing monuments form an ideal order among themselves, which
> is modified by the introduction of the new (the really new) work of art

among them. The existing order is complete before the new work arrives; for order to persist after the supervention of novelty, the *whole* existing order must be, if ever so slightly, altered; and so the relations, proportions, values of each work of art toward the whole are readjusted; and this is conformity between the old and the new.[34]

So Eliot endorses the idea of tradition as a pantheon but positions it as the cradle as well as the destination of what is truly new. He believes that in order to write something really good, the poet needs an acute possession of what has been written before. The idea that good writing depends on wide and thorough reading of previous writers is also supported in a more open and less ideologically loaded way by contemporary teachers of creative writing. David Morley, for example, teaches students that to be an original creative writer, one must first become an original reader, finding a path of one's own through a mixture of wide and intensive reading.[35]

Like the earlier Sainte-Beuve, Eliot's aim is to rescue literary tradition from meaning merely the continuation of the old and to assert its value in encouraging really significant new writing. At the same time, there is a strong implication that the work that he values conforms to the traditions as well as changing them. He gives pride of place to European traditions (Homer, Dante, Shakespeare) and avoids Sainte-Beuve's implications concerning national identity, yet he is aware that he is also addressing the topic of English literature, and his only quoted example is from the Jacobean dramatist Thomas Middleton.[36] Part of Eliot's intention may be to direct writers away from the reading of their recent predecessors and back to alternative models deeper in the past of European literature.

The influential British literary critic F. R. Leavis (1895–1978), who saw himself as following Eliot, identifies his "great tradition" in 1948 mainly with the special qualities of the major novelists who count, "in the sense that they not only change the possibilities of art for practitioners and readers, but that they are significant in terms of the human awareness they promote; awareness of the possibilities of life."[37] In a way that parallels Eliot's portrayal of the "individual talent" operating in relation to tradition, Leavis sees Jane Austen as in some sense creating the traditions from which she learns.

> If the influences bearing down on her hadn't comprised something fairly
> to be called tradition she couldn't have found herself and her true direc-
> tion; but her relation to tradition is a creative one. She not only makes
> tradition for those coming after, but her achievement has for us a retro-
> active effect: as we look back beyond her we see what goes before, and
> see because of her, potentialities and significances brought out in such
> a way that, for us, she creates the tradition we see leading down to her.[38]

Leavis says that Austen makes a tradition in her present out of writers who happen to be useful to her. Leavis's thoughtful and generous
phrasing here serves to undermine his book's grand contention that
the significant tradition in the English novel can be restricted to
three (or sometimes five) authors. His own restrictive reader's tradition makes space for much more varied and open traditions created
by writers out of materials they find helpful. George Eliot's well-
known familiarity with French, German, and Russian writing ren-
ders Leavis's focus on English-language writers more questionable.[39] At the very least his nationalistic sense of tradition must be
expanded to include writers in other languages and from outside
Europe.

Sociologists, Anthropologists, and Historians

As we have seen, Eliot's generally positive view of tradition acknowledges the negative aspects of merely following the past. Social theorists in particular have tended to take a negative view of tradition
and have emphasized the opposition between tradition and modernity. In his T. S. Eliot Lectures of 1974, the American sociologist
Edward Shils (1910–1995) expresses his surprise that the social sciences have ignored tradition and paints a picture in which progress
and change are widely approved while tradition, linked with super-
stition and dogma, is disparaged.[40] He observes that, while a tradition is likely to change over three generations, its proponents may
regard it as unchanged.[41] Shils sees tradition as opposed both by
rationalizers and by individualists, but he nevertheless sees it as
playing an important role.[42] What tradition provides is widely accepted because it permits life to move along lines set and anticipated
from past experience and thus makes the future more certain and

explicable.[43] The darker side of this kind of reassurance is that it may permit oppressive and prejudicial behaviors to be perceived as normal and acceptable. Anthony Giddens regards late modernity as a "post-traditional society." Whereas in premodern societies tradition provided a relatively fixed horizon of action, supervised by the guardians of tradition, in late modernity people are forced to live in a more open and reflexive way. Where Giddens sees the revival of some traditions in the present as evidence of tradition becoming reflexive in order to survive through reinvention and reinterpretation, his critics respond that traditions have often in the past been reflexive and shown an ability to develop in relation to new circumstances.[44]

For the German Marxist philosopher T. W. Adorno (1903–1969), the category of "tradition" is essentially feudal.

> Tradition is opposed to rationality, even though the one took shape in the other. Its medium is not consciousness but the pregiven, unreflected and binding existence of social forms—the actuality of the past; unintentionally this notion of binding existence was transmitted to the intellectual/spiritual sphere. Tradition in the strict sense is incompatible with bourgeois society.[45]

In opposing tradition to both modernity and rationality, Adorno seems to be drawing on the conventional sociological sense in which tradition is the antonym of modernity. Art has the obligation to respond to the loss of tradition.

> Contemporary art as a whole responds to this loss of tradition. Having lost what tradition guaranteed—the self-evident relation to its object, to its materials and techniques—it must reflect upon them from within. Art now senses the hollow and fictional character of traditional aspects of culture; important artists chip them away like plaster with a hammer.[46]

Even though tradition has lost its former relationship to reality, it remains indispensable.

> Thus tradition today poses an insoluble contradiction. There is no tradition today and none can be conjured, yet when every tradition has been extinguished the march towards barbarism will begin.[47]

The response Adorno tentatively advocates is an uncompromisingly critical rewriting of tradition, taking an appropriate distance, in the full awareness that the meaning that underpins tradition has been "unmasked in the catastrophe." The exemplary figures here seem to be Beckett and Giacometti, who use and mock the resources of tradition while refusing to be assimilated within it. By denying tradition, the artist may be able to retrieve it.[48] While on the one hand Adorno believes that modern life, including both bourgeois society and the catastrophe of Nazism, makes tradition untenable, on the other he also seems to feel the need for older music and poetry and to wish that somehow valid new music and poetry could be made.

Where sociology as a discipline tends toward a negative view of tradition, anthropology and folklore studies are understandably more positive. Anthropologists often aim to recover knowledge about the pre-contact or pre-conquest traditions of indigenous peoples. Much of their research is conducted through collecting oral evidence about the meanings of customary practices and about the histories of villages and peoples. Folklorists, too, work mainly from material originally collected aurally. Tradition may be the memory of a culture. Thus, for anthropologists, tradition may be both a method of study and a goal of knowledge. Some anthropologists have pointed out the difficulty of both strands of this enterprise: the limitations of oral evidence and the risk that the traditions which anthropologists discuss are to some degree their own inventions.[49]

A crucial point which has emerged from historical studies of tradition is that traditions are made and remade in history often for the benefit of the powerful. The case studies in Eric Hobsbawm and Terence Ranger's collection of historical essays, *The Invention of Tradition* (1983), show that many traditions taken to be ancient were in fact invented for political and social purposes relatively recently. The most famous is Hugh Trevor-Roper's demonstration that all the paraphernalia of highland tradition, which was later to become Scottish tradition, the bagpipes, the kilts, the clan tartans, and so on, were in fact an invention—in some instances involving literary forgery—of the later eighteenth and nineteenth centuries. Before that time the highlands and islands of Scotland were essentially Irish, in culture as well as in language. These new traditions were invented in an attempt to rewrite Scottish history to create an indigenous culture for Scotland.[50]

In his introduction to the collection, Eric Hobsbawm emphasizes the connection between invented tradition and nationalism. For him that connection exemplifies a reaction to a new situation which takes the form of reference to an old situation in order to give to a desired change the sanction of precedent—in these cases an invented precedent.[51] Hobsbawm identifies three overlapping types of invented tradition: first, those which establish and symbolize social cohesion and membership of groups (such as invented initiation ceremonies); second, those which establish or legitimize institutions, status, or authority; and third, those whose main aim is socialization and the inculcation of beliefs, value systems, and conventions of behavior.[52] The history of the invention of traditions shows us that traditions are not a historical given. Traditions are detected, promoted, and sometimes even invented by later writers for social and political purposes of their own.

The studies collected by Hobsbawm and Ranger illustrate how tradition, which purports to sum up the wisdom of the past, in fact is deployed, or invented, for purposes in the present.[53] Even though Ranger later came to prefer the term "imagined" over "invented," he insists that, in the colonial period, even genuinely old African traditions were reimagined for new purposes.[54]

The point of invented tradition is not so much that sometimes traditions are invented out of nothing (though that has happened) as that the decisive move is made in the present, when choices are made about which items to use and how to use them. Since the idea of tradition tends to conceal both the present orientation and the real motivation, it is important to focus on the later moments at which tradition is used or invoked rather than the earlier moments in which that tradition is claimed to have originated.

Gadamer

The crucial idea that the moment of tradition (and in his terms, of experience) involves a confrontation between present and past is developed in Hans-Georg Gadamer's intense meditation on reading and deep analysis of tradition in *Truth and Method* (1960).[55]

Gadamer (1900–2002) developed a philosophical hermeneutics on the basis of his studies of Dilthey, Heidegger, and classical philology. He introduces his magnum opus *Truth and Method* as an investigation of the phenomenon of understanding (p. xxi).

> The following investigations . . . are concerned to seek the experience of truth that transcends the domain of scientific method, wherever that experience is to be found, and to inquire into its legitimacy. (p. xxii)

Gadamer foregrounds the truth which is experienced through art.[56] He begins by defending "the experience of truth that comes to us through the work of art" and develops from that "a conception of knowledge and of truth that corresponds to the whole of our hermeneutic experience" (p. xxiii). He wants to recognize in the phenomenon of understanding not only an experience of truth which needs to be justified philosophically but also a way of doing philosophy (p. xxiii). Rather than providing a set of rules for interpretation, he aims to understand what happens in the act of understanding (p. xxviii). He believes that the act of understanding precedes and makes possible scientific knowledge (p. xxix). His book aims to ask a question concerning all human experience of the world and all human living, namely, how is understanding possible (pp. xxix–xxx)? This question gives his work a metaphysical tinge, since he believes that understanding constitutes the basic being in motion of being in the world (*Dasein*; p. xxx).

For Gadamer, tradition is central to the phenomenon of understanding. Even when he seems to focus more on the interpretation of particular texts, the idea that the encounter with tradition shapes understanding underlies his comments.

> Just as in the experience of art we are concerned with truths that go essentially beyond the range of methodical knowledge, so the same thing is true of the whole of the human sciences: in them our historical tradition in all its forms is certainly made the *object* of investigation, but at the same time *truth comes to speech in it*. Fundamentally, the experience of historical tradition reaches far beyond those aspects of it that can be objectively investigated. (p. xxiii)

The encounter with tradition makes possible the experience of something as true. Although our understanding of history tends to overestimate elements of change over things which remain the same, traditions are not weakened by the modern consciousness of history (p. xxiv). Rather "tradition, which consists in part in handing down self-evident traditional material, must have become questionable before it can become explicitly conscious that appropriating tradition is a hermeneutic task" (p. xxxiii). Gadamer believes that "the element of effective history affects all understanding of tradition" (p. xxxiii). His central concept of historically effected consciousness (*wirkungsgeschichtliches Bewusstsein*) is imbued with what he regards as a legitimate ambiguity, since it means both "the consciousness effected in the course of history and determined by history, and the very consciousness of being thus effected and determined" (p. xxxiv).

> It is not only that historical tradition and the natural order of life constitute the unity of the world in which we live as men; the way we experience one another, the way we experience historical traditions, the way we experience the natural givenness of our existence and of our world, constitute a truly hermeneutic universe, in which we are not imprisoned, as if behind insurmountable barriers, but to which we are opened. (p. xxiv)

Being situated within a historical tradition is what opens us up to the possibility of experiencing understanding.

It is not always absolutely clear what Gadamer means by tradition. On occasion he exemplifies tradition through his studies of responses to works of art, verses of the Bible, or injunctions of the law. On page 462, he gives as possible examples a single book or a single historical event (Homer's *Iliad* or Alexander's Indian campaign), but elsewhere he talks of the obligation to confront the whole tradition, which must mean at least very many books and may mean even all the principal expressions of western European culture. In moving between expansive ideas of a whole heritage and particular examples, he follows other writers in exploiting the vagueness which may have helped the word "tradition" become used so widely.

For me, the most attractive and productive part of Gadamer's argument is in the detailed picture he presents of the experience of understanding.[57] Understanding involves a dialogue with tradition.

In opening up an old text or considering a historical event, we begin with prejudices about what it will mean (pp. 277–307).[58] By observing our own prejudices and listening to what the text says to us, by taking it seriously as an interlocutor, we change our earlier views and come to understanding.[59]

> Hermeneutical experience is concerned with *tradition*. This is what is to be experienced. But tradition is not simply a process . . . it is *language*—i.e. it expresses itself like a Thou (p. 358). . . . A person who does not admit that he is dominated by prejudices will fail to see what manifests itself by their light. It is like the relation between I and Thou. (p. 360)

Tradition is made through a kind of conversation between the old text and the new reader. We must acknowledge what we think already before we can learn what tradition or the text has to tell us.

> To be situated within a tradition does not limit the freedom of knowledge but makes it possible. Knowing and recognizing this constitutes the third, and highest, type of hermeneutical experience: the openness to tradition characteristic of historically effected consciousness. It too has a real analogue in the I's experience of the Thou. In human relations the important thing is, as we have seen, to experience the Thou truly as a Thou—i.e. not to overlook his claim but to let him really say something to us. Here is where openness belongs. But ultimately this openness does not exist only for the person who speaks; rather, anyone who listens is fundamentally open. Without such openness to one another there is no genuine human bond. . . . Openness to the other, then, involves recognizing that I myself must accept that there are some things that are against me, even though no one else forces me to do so. This is the parallel to the hermeneutical experience. I must allow tradition's claim to validity, not in the sense of simply acknowledging the past in its otherness but in such a way that it has something to say to me. (p. 361)

As readers in conversation with tradition, we recognize that a tradition may have things to teach us which run counter to our initial prejudices. By acknowledging our prejudices and by listening with an open mind to what tradition tells us, we put ourselves in a position to experience understanding. Historically effected consciousness lets itself "experience tradition and [keeps itself] open to the truth claim encountered in it" (pp. 361–62). In this conversation, which always takes place in language, questions on the part of both questioner and answerer are articulated and their horizons of understanding are merged (pp. 245, 306).[60] "The hermeneutical experience is linguistic in nature; there is a dialogue between tradition and its interpreter" (p. 461).[61] In this experience, something happens which is not fully in the control of the interpreter. The actual occurrence "is made possible only because the word that has come down to us as tradition and to which we are to listen really encounters us and does so as if it addressed us and is concerned with us" (p. 461). The hermeneutical experience involves being addressed by the text and listening to what the text has to tell us.

The historical life of a tradition depends on its being constantly interpreted (p. 397). Whether the tradition is a text or a historical event, it comes into being only when the reader listens to it, interprets it, and applies it in language in relation to the circumstances of the time of interpretation. The linguistic communication between present and tradition is the event that takes place in all understanding (p. 463). That communication takes shape in a series of hypotheses which must be expressed and then amended in order to reach closer to the meaning of the text. The reader starts out from prejudices and reaches toward true understanding.

> A person who is trying to understand a text has to keep something at a distance—namely everything that suggests itself, on the basis of his own prejudices, as the meaning expected—as soon as it is rejected by the sense of the text itself. . . . Explicating the whole of meaning towards which understanding is directed forces us to make interpretive conjectures and to take them back again. The self-cancellation of the interpretation makes it possible for the thing itself—the meaning of the text—to assert itself. (p. 465)

The reader's prejudices and the context of previous interpretations always form part of the hermeneutical experience (p. 472).

> Only because between the text and its interpreter there is no automatic accord can a hermeneutical experience make us share in the text. Only because a text has to be brought out of its alienness and assimilated is there anything for the person trying to understand it to say. Only because the text calls for it does interpretation take place, and only in the

way called for. . . . *Thus the dialectic of question and answer always precedes the dialectic of interpretation. It is what determines understanding as an event.* (p. 472, emphasis in original)

There is no automatic agreement between text and interpreter, but because the text calls for interpretation, readers must make the attempt to give true value to what the text is saying, in the way that the text or the tradition determines. Both the prejudices which readers bring to the text and their capacity to listen to what the text is telling them, and to reject hypotheses of interpretation which do not match what the text says, are essential to the process of understanding.

Gadamer's account of the thinking and dialogue which make up the experience of understanding a text is exceptionally rich and can offer us materials with which to think even if we do not engage with the full philosophical implications of his book. Since neither the critique of Gadamer's position by Habermas nor Ricoeur's attempt to find a middle between the two positions really affects Gadamer's analysis of the interaction between reader and text, I do not discuss them here.[62] At the same time, I would want to give a greater place to the reader's individual choices than Gadamer seems to allow when he says, for example, "it is literally more correct to say that language speaks us rather than that we speak it" (p. 463). When Gadamer writes of the primacy of the game over the players playing it, or of the sense that the players are being played by the game (p. 106), it seems to me that he allows too little space for the individual skills and choices of the players.[63] The game puts compelling restrictions on what the players can do, but nevertheless it is the response of the individual players to those circumstances that makes the game worth watching. While I would accept that the tradition only comes into existence as we interpret it, I would still want to give the individual reader considerable agency within the conversation that is interpretation.

Using Literary Traditions

From Gadamer, and from the studies collected by Hobsbawm and Ranger, we have learned about the importance of the moment at which a later writer chooses to invoke a text or a tradition from the past. Gadamer emphasizes the moment at which a reader confronts a text from the tradition and tries to use her knowledge of tradition to make sense of that text and of her experience of the world through that text. That is what tradition really consists of: a sequence of moments in which individual readers and writers make use of what previous writers and thinkers give them in order to make something new. This moment of individual understanding of a particular text does not contradict the essentially social nature of tradition; rather, it depends on that social assumption, in order both to make a new intervention worthwhile and to communicate with readers. Tradition, seen as a moment of confrontation with an older text or opinion, makes it possible to learn things from the past and to convey them onwards. Where knowledge of such doctrines and texts is shared by writer and audience, the range of ideas conveyed by a new text is enhanced, since the audience has greater awareness of the alternative view which the writer makes meaning by differing from. An audience's awareness that a writer is expanding the reach of an existing genre or working against its grain would be examples.

It would be quite possible to investigate the role of tradition in literature by analyzing the development of one or more particular literary traditions. For example, one might study the development of satire, noting its origin in Near Eastern texts; its correspondence with the deep human need to criticize the condition of the world and attack the faults of other people; the enduring expression given by Horace and Juvenal to different aspects and styles of criticism; Renaissance writers' imitations of Juvenal and Horace in Latin and in vernacular languages; the particular ways in which Cervantes, Pope, and Swift, for example, worked with and developed the forms and conventions of the genre; and finally, the exploitations by Ayi Kwei Armah and Bessie Head of the conventions of satire to find ways of confronting the social realities of Ghana and Botswana. Such a history would show both the changes which writers made to the conventions of satire and the ways in which those conventions enabled and encouraged certain kinds of writing (including in texts which are not entirely or formally satire). It seems to me, however, that the real historical leverage of such a study would remain with the moments in which individual authors used their inheritance (whether from direct reading of individual texts or from the conventions absorbed from magazines and critics) to say something about their own situation (even as they were doubtless also blinded by tradition to other aspects of their situation).

Focusing on the moment of contact rather than the longer development helps us to see that literary tradition is made and developed as it is used in the present moment to interpret old texts and to make new ones. What the reader or writer brings to reading is crucial to what will emerge, as is the willingness to be addressed by, and to listen intently and critically to, the older text. Far from being an obstacle that a writer must set aside in order to write well, knowledge of earlier writing—knowledge of tradition—makes better writing possible. And different readers and writers will use tradition in different ways and will talk about it differently, as we shall see. Because those who create or reinforce tradition in the present do so for the sake of something which they want to do, we must be alert to the motivations of the proponents and users of particular traditions.

In discussing the examples which follow, I shall be concerned with the degree of free choice involved in the process of using and belonging to a literary tradition. Using the word "tradition" implies that this previous body of work is somehow imposingly out there. The earlier word "imitation" made it clearer that a writer was to some extent selecting a model to learn from or to react to. Some models were culturally required—for example, Cicero as a model for writing Latin prose—but one could always choose to imitate other models. Of course, the choice is not entirely free. It would probably be impossible to write a poem or a tragedy if one had no models to work from. Estimating the degree of free choice is a matter of tactful reading of particular instances, but I think it would be misleading to think either that the writer has no choice about the models or that the writer has a completely free choice.

Reading Gadamer, the literary critics, and the social theorists brings up a key problem with the idea of "the tradition." Is the writer or reader required to undertake a whole enormous task of learning, or is tradition also being used when writers and readers have a dialogue with a single work or with a small corpus of works? Individual texts have to be used locally before a more general knowledge of tradition is even conceivable. Or perhaps we should acknowledge that, despite the insistence of authorities on the subject, possessing the whole of any tradition is actually impossible. My proposal to focus on the moment in which an author confronts one earlier text may help us avoid this problem.

It is quite possible that the vagueness of the word "tradition" encourages us to see cultures or eras as a systematic whole in a rather misleading way. We may be better off to acknowledge that we can only ever know a part of our native literary tradition and that we need to be open to learning more about both our own traditions and the traditions of other cultures. Pretending that there is one tradition which a particular writer or critic possesses entire may in fact be a way of closing off attention to potential literary resources. Listening to Ferrante and reacting to Sainte-Beuve and Leavis should lead us to insist on broadening our idea of the traditions to which writers and readers may be open. Our concept of tradition must be international, must include the traditions of women and of marginalized groups within our societies, and, increasingly, must be open to texts and ideas from outside Europe.

At the same time as we observe the positive potential of learning from and using a particular audience's knowledge of traditions, we must also acknowledge that framing a text in relation to a previous text or genre may have the effect of limiting what a writer can say and of blinding the writer to certain problems and prejudices. This problem makes it all the more necessary to investigate a writer's aims in using or invoking a particular text and to be alert to the assumptions or blindnesses that may accompany a given text or genre. As much as tradition meets real psychological needs for belief in continuity, tradition also represents power and proclaims a kind of inevitability. Writers or politicians may invoke tradition as a way of evading responsibility for the consequences of something which they are in fact choosing to do. We shall therefore need to pay attention to the ways in which writers look back at the texts they have written and used as models, and to their suggestions to other writers about how to use past texts. In the examples which follow, both Petrarch and Gaskell seem to be aware that they are helping to make possible future writing, while Chaucer self-consciously and humorously exploits the idea of his dependence on earlier writing to limit possible criticisms of his work. Some writers, consciously or not, have turned out to be very productive for future writing, while others, who absorb as much or more from their reading, seem to be essentially inimitable or imitable only at the level of phrase or episode.

More positively, tradition can also play a psychological role. Knowing the example of previous writers or having their overt support can provide a writer with the courage to pursue a particular line of writing, as Matisse claimed to have been strengthened in all his artistic endeavors by his daily knowledge of Cezanne's *Three Bathers*.[64]

We also need to be alert to the differences between readers' and writers' traditions, and we must investigate the connections between them. Writers select certain texts and organize certain types of tradition in order to write new texts, while readers construct traditions in order to make sense of a particular text, a wider fragment of their reading, or their experience more generally. Writers must always be readers first, but they may choose widely and unexpectedly in searching for material which stimulates them for a particular project. Readers may have a wider range of purposes in view in their constructions of traditions, and the traditions they create may have a stronger implication of denying status to texts they omit. Gadamer's account seems always explicitly to be concerned with reading, but it is easy to see how his idea that a text is only ever realized by being interpreted and applied could be adapted to writing a new text out of one's experience of reading, as Chaucer did in writing *Troilus and Criseyde*, which could be looked on as an interpretation of Boccaccio's *Il Filostrato*.

Within some of these discussions of the value of tradition for thinkers and writers lies the question of how writers learn their craft. Renaissance rhetoric was very clear-sighted about this issue in its focus on imitation, which involved both the choice of model and the ways in which the model would be followed. For Eliot and for Morley, a thorough study of some earlier writers was an essential foundation for anyone writing on their own account. In the studies which follow, we shall see both how authors learned from their predecessors and how they advised their contemporaries about learning to write and using models.

Finally, there are two issues which I want to acknowledge and then park. Discussions of literary tradition since the 1850s have been very closely bound up with, and in fact dominated by, questions of the establishment of a canon of literature and questions of national identity. We need to recognize that these issues arise and that concepts of tradition contribute to our ways of thinking about them, but I would also suggest that people's opinions and motivations in relation to nationalism and canons have too often obstructed their thinking about the ways in which literary tradition operates. I shall write about particular authors' use of their reading in order to analyze the possible effects of working out of reading, out of a tradition, and also because these particular authors interest and appeal to me. I am not arguing or assuming that these authors form the basis for a canon or a national tradition. Evidently they do not, since the authors discussed here neither represent a single national tradition nor include writers who would have to be included in a canon of European or world literature, such as Homer, Dante, Shakespeare, and Tolstoy. But I do recognize that ideas of tradition have implications both for canon formation and for nationalism, and I shall return to these issues in the conclusion.[65]

CHAPTER ONE

Petrarch, Scholarship, and Traditions of Love Poetry

PETRARCH (1304–1374) ENJOYED a very strong relationship, but also a paradoxical one, with traditions which led up to him and those continuing vigorously after him. He has long been regarded as a founder of traditions, but his poetry has also become a victim of the tradition his followers established. Petrarch was one of the first great writers of the Italian language, but he made his poetry largely out of earlier poets in other languages. He took forms and patterns from the troubadours and introduced ideas, motifs, and even translated phrases from classical Latin poetry. Petrarch was immensely influential on later poets. His love poetry gave expression to ideas and expectations about the male lover's adoration of the beloved which can be traced back through around two thousand years of Greek, Latin, and vernacular poetry and philosophy. Petrarch also passed on a repertory of attitudes, ideas, motifs, phrases, and vocabulary to later Italian and European poets, and his vocabulary became the standard poetic dialect of the Italian language. Because his poetry formed a point of departure for so much European love lyric of the following three centuries, it became almost impossible to read Petrarch's own poetry without expectations derived from the work of his sometimes rather slavish and mediocre

followers. One aim of this chapter is to focus on Petrarch's own poetry in order to articulate what he achieved and how he used his
sources. In returning to the source, we shall rediscover how good
Petrarch's poems are and how much their excellence owes to his
subtle and restrained exploitation of the tradition of his poetic
predecessors.

Petrarch also played an important role in European culture more
generally. He served later scholars as an example of what conscious
cultivation of knowledge about the classical world might become.
He was among the first to gather and disseminate hidden Latin
texts, such as letters and orations of Cicero and books of Livy's history of Rome. He inspired later humanists to restore classical levels
of Latin prose composition and to learn Greek. He wrote considerable portions of a Latin epic poem in imitation of his favorite poet
Virgil and collected moral exempla from Roman history and Latin
literature.[1] In his letters, as we shall see, he became a significant
theorist of the art of imitation: how a writer uses material from
reading as a resource from which to write better.[2] In his Italian
poetry, he drew both on the major Augustan poets (Virgil, Ovid,
Horace, and Propertius) and on the vernacular poetry of the troubadours, the *dolce stil novo*, and Dante himself, to create a synthesis
which became a sort of encyclopedia of the images and ideas of love
poetry for Italian, French, English, and German poets of the following three centuries.[3] These poets no longer needed to read Petrarch's
predecessors (though they sometimes did) because Petrarch had
provided them with a heritage of images which they could imitate
and vary. His influence on later European poets was very substantial.[4] We need to understand the term "Petrarchism" as a sort of
shorthand for Petrarch's combination of gathering materials from
earlier traditions and transmitting them to later poets. When we
speak of an image (such as the ship tossed in the storm or the sun
melting the snow) or a phrase as Petrarchan, we often mean not that
Petrarch invented the phrase, but that he gathered it from his reading and transmitted it to later writers.

I shall begin by considering the advice which Petrarch gives
scholars and writers about imitation and the ways of using one's
reading in order to write. He was aware of the role which his own

work might play as a model for other writers, and he advised them on how to use their reading. Drawing on previous scholarship, I shall make some connections between his Italian poems and what he tells us about his life in the collections of letters which he constructed and in his *Secretum*.[5] Then I shall look at some examples of Petrarch's poems, both to substantiate my claim about their excellence and to show how that excellence derives from his creative use of his reading. Finally, I shall consider his attitude to Dante, his immediate and overwhelming forerunner, and discuss the ways in which later writers used Petrarch's work.

Reading and Imitation

Alongside his constantly rewritten portrayal of his struggle with love in the *Canzoniere*, Petrarch also constructed portraits of his life and internal struggles in his *Secretum* and in his collections of letters, notably the *Rerum familiarum liber*, assembled around 1366, and the *Rerum senilium liber*, which collected 128 later letters. In both these collections we see that, as in the *Canzoniere*, Petrarch did not hesitate to rewrite letters or to write new letters supposedly sent earlier in his life. All these collections were self-consciously constructed by Petrarch.[6] The letters tell us many things about Petrarch's life which we are glad to know and which can sometimes be corroborated independently, but the texts, the selection, and the ordering were subject to Petrarch's editorial intervention.

Petrarch in his letters uses his reading to think with and to persuade his correspondents. Scholars have shown that the reading of Saint Augustine so much constructs the experience depicted in his letter on the climbing of Mount Ventoux (*Familiares* IV.1) that we may even doubt whether the climb itself actually took place.[7] When he consoles his correspondents and when he urges them to a course of action, he always backs up his points with quotations from classical literature and Christian authors.[8] In the same way quotations from Virgil and Horace propel the exposition of his internal struggle in the *Secretum*.[9] Reading was intrinsic to everything which Petrarch wrote, and many of the letters concern his attempts to find and obtain copies of books.[10] In the letters he reflects a good deal on his reading and on the relationship between reading and writing, and that is what I shall examine next, beginning with three letters from the *Rerum familiarum liber*.

In *Familiares* VI.4, Petrarch defends himself to Giovanni Colonna against the charge that he uses too many examples. He first explains that he uses examples in his writing because in his own reading he finds that he is most moved and impressed by examples of what outstanding people have done. His experience of the effect of reading prompts his approach to writing. He tells us that when he writes he looks to the greatest writers of the past because they portray for him the magnificent deeds of outstanding men. He uses examples from antiquity in his writing because he knows that these examples have profited him when he read them and he hopes that they will benefit his readers.[11] Later in the same letter, he connects this point to literary imitation. Imitation improved the quality of Latin literature. Virgil and Cicero imitated Homer and Demosthenes; Virgil equaled Homer, while Cicero surpassed Demosthenes. In the same way, the examples of Antonius the Egyptian and Victorinus the rhetorician inspired Augustine to convert to Christianity.[12] Seeing how examples inspire men to emulation and lead them to success and to virtue, and feeling the same result in himself, Petrarch hopes that the examples he cites or retells will inspire his readers.

Familiares XXII.2 addresses Petrarch's friend Giovanni Boccaccio on a range of issues related to copying texts, imitation, and borrowing. The whole letter leads up to two paragraphs in which he admits to two accidental thefts from Virgil and Ovid in his *Bucolicum carmen*, which he asks Boccaccio to rephrase in his copy in order to avoid the copying of words.[13] He begins the letter by explaining that a really slow reading of a text, even by an unskillful reader, helps him see more easily where a phrase needs to be revised. When writing, we sometimes make errors with the material which is most familiar.[14] There are some writers, such as Ennius, Plautus, Martianus Capella, and Apuleius, whom he has read only once and in a hurry. When he happens to use something from writers like these, he is immediately aware of it. But there are other writers, like Virgil, Horace, Boethius and Cicero, whom he has read countless times and whose writings he has so thoroughly absorbed that he no longer knows that a particular phrase is theirs rather than part of his own thinking. In general, where he embellishes his writings with phrases from other authors, he claims that he acknowledges the debt or that he changes the idea in reaching his own expression, in the manner of the bees. Occasionally he borrows without acknowledgment either because of intellectual kinship (with an unfamiliar author) or because of an accident (with a familiar author).[15] Generally, however, he prefers his style to be his own.

> I am a man who delights to follow the path of earlier poets, but not the actual footsteps of these others. I would wish to use other men's writings not stealthily but by begging from time to time, but while I may, I would prefer my own; I am a man pleased by resemblances, but not identity, and the resemblance itself should not be too close, in which the brilliance of the follower's mind should appear, not its blindness or poverty.[16]

He will be inspired by what he reads. He will follow it up to a point, but he will also try to add something of his own. Finally, he mentions Virgil, who consciously borrowed and translated much from Greek literature, not to steal it but rather to compete with it.[17]

Familiares XXIII.19, also to Boccaccio, returns to the topic of the use of reading in discussing the progress of a young writer whom Petrarch is recommending to his friend. Petrarch hopes that this young man will eventually create a personal style from his reading, not necessarily avoiding imitation but concealing it so that what he writes resembles no one else's writing and appears to be new. At the moment, unfortunately, he delights in imitation, is incapable of freeing himself from the writers he tries to follow—Virgil above all— and inserts parts of Virgil's work into his own.[18] This leads to a general statement on imitation: one must try to write something similar but not identical to the original; the resemblance should be more like that of a son to a father than that of a painting to the subject depicted. The imitator may use the coloring and the ideas of the original but should avoid using the same words. This advice can be summarized by using Horace's and Seneca's image of the bee gathering flowers but turning them into something different.[19] One day when Petrarch was admonishing his pupil along these lines, the pupil pointed out to him another phrase from his own *Bucolicum carmen* identical to one in *Aeneid* VI.[20]

Petrarch's construction and preservation of these collections of letters leads us to think that he was consciously advising contemporary and later poets about how they should learn to write and about the right way to use earlier poetry. These comments and his broader practice make it possible to establish Petrarch's position on the use of reading earlier writers in one's own writing. First, it seems that for Petrarch reading is a requirement in order to write. He sometimes remarks that he cannot write a proper reply because he has not got his books with him.[21] Second, he believes that writers should aim to forge their own way of writing out of what they read. They should not imitate other writers too closely or use their same words. They should gather from many sources with the aim of making something new or something similar to, but different from, what they have been reading. Younger writers may find that the authors they imitate dominate them too much. Third, he refers with approval to writers (like Virgil) who have reused and rephrased material from their reading deliberately, with the intention of competing with previous excellent writers. Fourth, he suggests that some apparent similarities between writers may be a consequence of similarities of thought or subject matter rather than of imitation. He first mentioned this idea in a famous letter to Boccaccio about Dante which we shall discuss later. Fifth, he finds that some writers whom he has read continually over his life may be so absorbed into his own thinking, both their ideas and their phrases, that he copies them accidentally, thinking that the phrases and ideas are his own.

There are some tensions between these positions and indeed in Petrarch's practice. Although he would prefer to avoid entirely the use of the same words as an earlier writer, he evidently acknowledges that it can happen, through bad practice, in error, or in order to alert readers to competition. For modern literary critics, verbal identity tends to be what proves a case of suspected imitation or influence, whereas Petrarch wants to suggest such a case would be aberrant. At the same time, he seems to be quite happy with the idea of taking over examples from earlier writers in order to pass their effective teaching on to his readers. He seems to be conscious of how he works, as a writer, between what he has read and thought about and what his readers (who may themselves also be writers) will learn from his works.

Petrarch's Poetry

Although the later letters and the *Secretum* consistently disparage his vernacular writings and his love poetry in particular, manuscript evidence reveals that Petrarch continued to add new poems to his *Canzoniere* and to reorganize the order of poems up to the last year of his life.[22] Both the letter collections and the *Canzoniere* can be regarded as incomplete, in the sense that further changes and additions could have been made, but Petrarch certainly devoted time and attention to reworking the collection of poems until close to his death. The notion he sometimes promoted in his letters that after the age of about forty he had put aside his desire and his love poetry is contradicted by the manuscripts.[23] Probably he privately and in practice came to regard his vernacular poetry as just as important as his Latin letters and his mostly unfinished Latin works. Later readers have regarded the Italian poems as much the greatest part of his legacy.

Sonnet 310 demonstrates a perfect understanding of a form devised by the Sicilian poets in imitation of the troubadours. It shows Petrarch's felicitous use of Ovid and classical mythology.

> Zephiro torna, e 'l bel tempo rimena,
> e i fiori et l'erbe, sua dolce famiglia,
> et garrir Progne et pianger Philomena,
> et primavera candida et vermiglia.
>
> Ridono i prati, e 'l ciel si rasserena;
> Giove s'allegra di mirar sua figlia;
> l'aria et l'acqua et la terra è d'amor piena;
> ogni animal d'amar si riconsiglia.
>
> Ma per me, lasso, tornano i più gravi
> sospiri, che del cor profondo tragge
> quella ch'al ciel se ne portò le chiavi;
>
> et cantar augelletti, et fiorir piagge,
> e 'n belle donne honeste atti soavi
> sono un deserto, et fere aspre et selvagge.
>
> [The west wind returns and leads back the fine weather and the flowers
> and the grass, his sweet family, and Procne who chatters and Philomena

who weeps, and white and vermilion Spring (4). The meadows laugh and the sky grows clear; Jupiter happily looks at his daughter (Venus); air and water and earth are full of love; all animals reconcile themselves to love (8). But for me, alas, the heaviest sighs return, which she has drawn from my deep heart, who has taken its keys to heaven (11); and the birds' song and the meadows' flowering and the delightful actions of beautiful, honorable ladies are a desert and cruel, wild beasts (14).][24]

This poem demonstrates a complete and easy mastery of the form of the sonnet. The language is simple but intense, strongly visual, and at the same time evocative of the poet's feelings. The structure of the poem is based on the simplest and clearest contrast between the beauty of spring and the desolation of the speaker's feelings articulated across the four segments of the poem. In the first quatrain, spring, the fine weather, the birds, and the west wind return. The second associates the flowering of the fields and the serenity of the sky with the growth of love in the world. The first triplet (lines 9–11) provides the *volta*, with the turn from the beauty of spring to the poet's heavy heartfelt sighs, recalling the death of Laura, while the second triplet summarizes and amplifies the contrast of the whole poem. To the poet, the birdsong, the flowering meadows, and the gentle gestures of virtuous ladies have an effect entirely contrary to their blissful description. They are like a desert and the actions of cruel, wild animals. The poem amply illustrates Petrarch's mastery of elegant, visually evocative language and of the logical organization of the sonnet.

This poem also grows out of Petrarch's reading and poetic tradition. As all editors point out, this theme of the contrast between the pleasures of spring and the desolate feeling of the poet is one of the staples of troubadour poetry. Petrarch may have been responding to a poem attributed to Buvalelli, "Pois vei qu'el temps s'aserena," or he may have relied on his general knowledge of troubadour poetry. Reminiscences of Virgil's *Eclogues* and *Georgics* contribute to his evocation of the spring landscape. Petrarch's knowledge of Greek mythology and his reading of Ovid provided him with the references to Zephyrus, Jupiter, Venus, Procne, and Philomena.[25] The last two, with their evocation of the rape of Philomena, introduce a note of mourning (*pianger*), violence, and death to the serenity of the first quatrain, which the sestet will develop further. But the poem wears its learning very lightly. The main impression conveyed by the careful choice of adjectives is of the beauty of the season and the landscape and the desolation of the poet's feelings. The reader feels momentarily unable to imagine how the commonplace feeling of the poem could have been expressed more clearly, briefly, and forcefully.

Sonnet 311 opens with one of 310's subjects, the nightingale's song, this time a male nightingale, with the lament for death as the explicit subject of the song. While the first quatrain elaborates the sweetness and skill of the nightingale's sad song, the second emphasizes the shared mourning of bird and poet, explained by the poet's harsh destiny (*dura sorte*) and his folly in underestimating the power of death.

> Ch'altri che me non ò di ch'i' mi lagne,
> ché 'n dee non credev'io regnasse Morte. (7–8)

> [I have no one to blame but myself, because I did not believe that Death has power over goddesses.]

The first tercet exclaims on the ease with which the poet was deceived and the reasons for his mistake; the second explains that he has now understood what destiny (probably to be understood here as God) was trying to teach him: that everything good in the world will end.

> Or cognosco io che mia fera ventura
> vuol che vivendo et lagrimando impari
> come nulla qua giù diletta et dura. (12–14)

> [Now I know what my harsh destiny wants me to learn through living and weeping, that nothing here below both pleases and endures.]

Where 310 is built on the contrast between spring and the poet's feelings, 311 stresses the commonality between the nightingale's lament and the poet's feelings. The octave ends with the poet's failure to understand the power of death over his beloved, but then the sestet concludes with the poet having learned the more general lesson of the lack of endurance of everything good in the world. The poem is more argumentative and draws more conclusions than its predecessor, but much of its force rests on two strong images: the

elaboration of the nightingale's mournful song and the shock of seeing Laura's two eyes, conventionally brighter than the sun, now
turned to clay.

> Que' duo bei lumi, assai più che 'l sol chiari
> chi pensò mai veder far terra oscura? (10–11)

> [Who would ever think to see those two beautiful lights, brighter than
> the sun, made into dark earth?]

Where 310 seems to be perfect in itself, 311 gains from its connection
with the earlier poem and argues that the feeling of desolation, however strong and justified, needs to be incorporated into a better understanding of the nature of the world. The destiny which seems
cruel also serves the function of developing the poet's understanding, in ways that chime perfectly with Petrarch's evocation of Boethius's teachings in his letters and elsewhere.[26] Petrarch takes the
formal idea of pairs (or larger groups of sonnets) from earlier Italian poets, rethinks, deepens, and intensifies it, and transmits it to
his European successors.

Sonnets 132 to 134 belong to the troubadour genre of *devinalh*,
in which, according to Marco Santagata, puzzles or paradoxes are
created through the accumulation of contraries.[27] All three poems
develop and transmit the idea of the paradoxical and bittersweet
quality of love which is so strong in the Western tradition, including
poets like Sappho and Catullus, whose works Petrarch did not know
directly.[28] In sonnet 132, these paradoxes are developed for the first
nine lines.

> S'amor non è, che dunque è quel ch'io sento?
> Ma s'egli è amor, perdio, che cosa et quale?
> Se bona, onde l'effecto aspro mortale?
> Se ria, onde sì dolce ogni tormento?

> S'a mia voglia ardo, onde 'l pianto e lamento?
> S'a mal mio grado, il lamentar che vale?
> O viva morte, o dilectoso male,
> come puoi tanto in me, s'io nol consento?

> Et s'io 'l consento, a gran torto mi doglio.
> Fra sì contrari vènti in frale barca
> mi trovo in alto mar senza governo,

sì lieve di saver, d'error sì carca
ch'i' medesmo non so quel ch'io mi voglio,
et tremo a mezza state, ardendo il verno.

[If love does not exist, what is it that I feel? But if it is love, by God, what
and how is it? If it is good, where does the bitter killing effect come
from? If it is evil, how is every torment so sweet (4)? If I burn volun-
tarily, why the weeping and torment? If against my will, what is the
profit in lamenting? O living death, o pleasing harm, how can you have
so much power over me if I do not consent (8)? And if I consent to it, I
am wrong to complain. Among such contrary winds in a frail boat, I
find myself in the high seas with no rudder (11), so short on wisdom, so
loaded with error, that I myself do not know what I want, and I shiver
in midsummer, burning in winter (14).]

The main explicit verbal contrariety is normally placed in the first
half of each line ("S'amor non è / Ma s'egli è amor; Se bona / Se ria"),
but Petrarch's aim seems to be not to express the pure perplexity of
the troubadours but to attempt to see through psychological confusion to a sort of definition of love. In spite of the paradoxes, the
argument does seem to move forward. Probably what he is feeling
is love (1–2). The effect of love is painful, but the torment is also
pleasing (3–4). Almost certainly his love is outside his control (5–6).
This leads to a definition of love ("viva morte . . . dilectoso male," 7)
and another dilemma ("s'io nol consento / Et s'io 'l consento," 8–9)
in which he confronts his pain and the lack of justification for a
complaint. Love as he has defined it and his psychological state are
then illustrated with the image of the ship tossed by contrary winds
in a storm—so lacking in wisdom and so full of error, the poet does
not know what he truly wants—and he suffers from a fever diametri-
cally opposed to the season, as in sonnet 310, shivering with cold in
summer and burning with heat in winter. The balanced expression
of the opposing statements produces an image of love as a sweet
pain and a powerlessness which is painful and enjoyable. The paradoxical nature of love and the confusion of the lover are expressed
delicately and clearly. Both the storm-tossed boat and the lover out
of harmony with the seasons represent ideas taken from his reading
of earlier love poetry, but Petrarch expresses both forcefully in the
final five lines, the boat through amplification and the temperature
through brevity.[29] In this case, then, Petrarch takes the formula of

paradox from his reading, extends it into a (still familiar) definition of love, and wraps that definition in powerful but still borrowed images. He makes something new by rewriting and combining elements from his reading.

Sonnet 133 is based around four recurring images taken from Petrarch's reading: arrows directed at a target (1, 5, 9, 11), the sun melting snow (2, 8, 9, 11), fire melting wax (2, 8, 10, 11), and the wind dispersing clouds (3, 8, 12–14). The arrows and the sun come from earlier vernacular love poetry, including Petrarch's own.[30] The wind (Job 21:18, Isaiah 17:13) and the fire (Psalms 68:2) are taken from the Bible. In the first quatrain, Love has attacked the poet in the way expressed by the four images, and he has called on the lady for mercy but in vain. In the second quatrain, each of the four aggressive agents is said to emerge from the lady. The first tercet summarizes the assertions made about the first three images.

> I pensier' son saette, e 'l viso un sole,
> e 'l desir foco; e 'nseme con quest'arme
> mi punge Amor, m'abbaglia et mi distrugge. (9–11)

> [Thoughts are arrows and the face is a sun and desire is a fire; and with these weapons together Love wounds me, blinds me, and destroys me.]

Love's three weapons against the poet are linked to the lady's face and the poet's thoughts about her and desire for her. Love uses these to harm the poet with a wittily aligned string of verbs suited to each image (*punge, abbaglia, distrugge,* 11). The final tercet develops the image of the wind and presents the pun between breeze ("l'aura") and Laura.

> Et l'angelico canto et le parole,
> col dolce spirto ond'io non posso aitarme,
> son l'aura inanzi a cui mia vita fugge. (12–14)

> [And the angelic singing and the words, together with the sweet breath from which I cannot defend myself are the breeze before which my life flees.]

Where previously the image of the wind has seemed a little unexpected and enigmatic, here it is linked to Laura's singing, speech, breath, and name, as well as to the poet's inability to defend himself and to the danger to his life. The poem keeps all four images elegantly in play before developing the fourth in a way which is both witty and emotional. For later poets, at least three of these images and the attitude of doomed powerlessness would become staples, but here the way in which all four are managed and the combination of wit and emotion are very effective.

Sonnet 134 presents a series of paradoxes intended to display the confusion which the lover feels. They lead up to the accusation in the final line that this whole state of confusion in the poet" is the responsibility of the lady: "In questo stato son, donna, per voi" (I am in this state, lady, because of you). Petrarch manages to combine an astonishing range of balanced contraries with a clear and effective line through the poem. The control, clarity, range, and balance are very impressive, though perhaps one responds more to the skill than to the emotion. For later poets, this sonnet would offer a catalog of images in which to express the contradictory and bittersweet nature of love.

> Pace non trovo, et non ò da far guerra;
> e temo, et spero; et ardo, et son un ghiaccio;
> et volo sopra 'l cielo, et giaccio in terra;
> et nulla stringo, et tutto 'l mondo abbraccio. (1–4)

> [I find no peace and have no means to make war; I both fear and hope; and I burn and am ice; and I fly above the heaven and lie on the earth; and I hold nothing and embrace the whole world.]

All three poems draw on, and indeed follow, the tradition of expressing perplexity through the combination of opposites; all three present a definition of love as a state of confusion. They draw on classical Latin poetry, the *dolce stil novo*, the troubadours, and the Bible, and they transmit a group of fertile ideas and rich images to Petrarch's followers. In each case, the angle of approach and the tone of the concluding claim is different. All three demonstrate a complete mastery of the form of the sonnet, and all three depend on Petrarch's deep knowledge of poetic tradition.

Canzone 126 is simply one of the loveliest poems in the world. It evokes the landscape of the valley of the Sorgue, made sacred for the poet by the presence of Laura's lovingly described body. The poem manages to evoke recollections of an Ovidian outdoor bathing scene and the poet's feelings about both the landscape and the lady without quite specifying that such a scene could have been witnessed by the poet.

> Chiare, fresche et dolci acque,
> ove le belle membra
> pose colei che sola a me par donna;
> gentil ramo ove piacque
> (con sospir' mi rimembra)
> a lei di fare al bel fiancho colonna;
> herba et fior' che la gonna
> leggiadra ricoverse
> co l'angelico seno;
> aere sacro, sereno,
> ove Amor co' begli occhi il cor m'aperse:
> date udïenza insieme
> a le dolenti mie parole extreme. (1–13)

[Clear, fresh, and sweet waters, where she who alone to me seems a woman placed her beautiful limbs; noble tree where it pleased her (with sighs I remember) to make a column with her beautiful side; grass and flowers that covered her beautiful dress and angelic breast; sacred calm air, where Love opened my heart with her beautiful eyes, listen all together to my final sorrowful words.]

Difficult rhymes are placed with astonishing sweetness. Some of the imagery seems to be developed from Virgilian and Horatian evocations of a delightful landscape (*locus amoenus*).[31] The adjectives infuse Laura's lovingly depicted body with respect, holiness, and spiritual power. The poem is addressed to the landscape sanctified by this apparition, and Petrarch closes the introductory stanza by asking the landscape to listen to his sorrowful last words. Nancy Vickers has shown how Petrarch uses the earthly paradise sections of Dante's *Purgatorio* (especially cantos 30 and 31) here.[32]

In the second stanza, Petrarch develops the idea of his death for love, wishing to be buried in this restful spot, and in the third stanza he imagines that Laura might one day visit this place and that her pity at his death might win him an easier passage to heaven. We shall see how Ariosto, Tasso, and Spenser develop this idea in the next chapter.

> Già terra in fra le pietre
> vedendo, Amor l'inspiri
> in guisa che sospiri
> sì dolcemente che mercé m'impetre,
> et faccia forza al cielo,
> asciugandosi gli occhi col bel velo. (34–39)

> [Seeing me already earth among the stones, Love will inspire her to sigh
> so sweetly that she will win grace for me, and exert her force on heaven,
> drying her eyes with her beautiful veil.]

Love here eludes his normally hostile and aggressive persona. The dead poet may inspire a sigh from Laura which will function on his behalf like a devout prayer, inspiring pity from heaven, even as Laura wipes her tears with her married woman's veil. Inspired by this posthumous visitation, the fourth and fifth stanzas present a vision of an apotheosis of Laura in the landscape.

> Da' be' rami scendea
> (dolce ne la memoria)
> una pioggia di fior' sovra 'l suo grembo;
> et ella si sedea
> humile in tanta gloria,
> coverta già de l'amoroso nembo.
> Qual fior cadea sul lembo,
> qual su le treccie bionde,
> ch'oro forbito et perle
> eran quel dì a vederle;
> qual si posava in terra, et qual su l'onde;
> qual, con un vago errore
> girando, parea dir:—Qui regna Amore.—

> Quante volte diss'io
> allor pien di spavento:
> Costei per fermo nacque in paradiso.
> Così carco d'oblio
> il divin portamento

e 'l volto e le parole e 'l dolce riso
m'aveano, et sì diviso
da l'imagine vera,
ch'i' dicea sospirando:
Qui come venn'io, o quando?;
credendo esser in ciel, non là dov'era.
Da indi in qua mi piace
questa herba sì, ch'altrove non ò pace. (40–65)

[From the lovely branches descended (sweet in the memory) a rain of flowers over her lap; and she sat, humble among so much glory, already covered with the amorous cloud (45). One flower fell on the hem of her dress, another on her blond braids, which seemed like burnished gold and pearls that day; one fell on the ground; one on the water and another with a lovely wandering seemed to say, as she turned, "Here Love reigns" (52). How many times I said, then full of fear, "For certain she was born in Paradise." Her divine posture and her face and words and sweet smile had so filled me with forgetfulness and so separated me from the true image, that I said, sighing (61): "How did I come here and when?"; thinking that I was in heaven, not there where I was. From that time onwards this grass has pleased me so much that I have no peace anywhere else.]

The rain of flowers in the fourth stanza is fairly evidently inspired by Dante's description of the appearance of Beatrice in the earthly paradise of *Purgatorio* 30 (lines 28–32):

Cosí dentro una nuvola di fiori
che da le mani angeliche saliva
e ricadeva in giú dentro e di fori,
sovra candido vel cinta d'uliva
donna m'apparve.

[Thus within a cloud of flowers which rose up from the angelic hands and fell down outside and within the chariot, a woman appeared to me, above a white veil and crowned with olive leaves.]

Petrarch develops the scene, makes it more delightful still, and gives us more of the poet-viewer's response. Love covers her with flowers, and yet she is humble amid such glory. At the same time, the poet is transported by her words, her laughter, and her deportment. In retrospect, the poet understands that the scene was deceptive ("sì diviso / da l'imagine vera," 59–60), but within the scene he wonders at how he came there, believing himself to have arrived in heaven. Truly or falsely, he remembers being there, and from that time on the place is so sanctified that it becomes a sort of earthly paradise, like its original in Dante.[33] From the time of that vision no other place on earth can give him rest. The real place somehow links memory, desire, and imagination to provide repose for his normally conflicting emotions. One could make a case that this is Petrarch's greatest poem, but it was not imitated by later poets in the way that other poems were, perhaps because it would have been so hard to equal. Later poets could best work with fragments from the poem, just as Petrarch had incorporated and developed fragments from Virgil, Horace, and Dante.

Canzone 264 introduces the second half of the *Canzoniere*, though it may have been written before Petrarch conceived the notion of such a second part consisting of poems supposed to have been written after the death of Laura. The notional prompting for the poem is the poet's sense of his own mortality and his perplexity over harboring both a desire for love and fame and a wish to leave earthly things behind him and concentrate on saving his soul. Petrarch presents a psychological conflict within the poet which adds to the sorrow of his unrequited love.

Once again Petrarch represents himself as tearful, but this time from a different kind of sadness and a different kind of self-pity. Finding himself nearer to death, he hopes that God, in a Christian-Platonist image, will provide him with the wings to lift his soul to heaven from the prison of the earth. It is his own fault that he cannot be raised. He sees the open arms of God's mercy before him, but he is too fearful and too committed to other goals to reach them (1–8). The poem develops as a dialogue between a self-accusing voice and the counterweight of his other motivations.

> L'un penser parla co la mente, et dice:
> —Che pur agogni? onde soccorso attendi?
> Misera, non intendi
> con quanto tuo disnore il tempo passa?
> Prendi partito accortamente, prendi;
> e del cor tuo divelli ogni radice

del piacer che felice

nol pò mai fare, et respirar nol lassa.

Se già è gran tempo fastidita et lassa

sè di quel falso dolce fugitivo

che 'l mondo traditor può dare altrui,

a che ripon' più la speranza in lui,

che d'ogni pace et di fermezza è privo? (19–31)

[One thought speaks to my mind and says: "What do you want? From where do you expect help? Wretched one, do you not understand with how much dishonor to you the time passes? Decide wisely, decide and pull from your heart every root of the pleasure which can never make you happy and will not let you breathe (26). If for a long time you have been disgusted and wearied by that false fleeting sweetness which the treacherous world can give, why do you place more hope in what lacks all peace and endurance?"]

The voice urges him to leave behind the unsatisfactory, indeed suffocating, pleasures of the world and use his will to choose peace and stability while there is still time. The language of the voice is extremely forceful in denouncing both the poet's delay and the emptiness of the fugitive pleasures of the world. Critics have linked this poem to the dialogue with Saint Augustine which Petrarch stages in his *Secretum*, in which Augustine urges him to give up all thoughts of love, earthly happiness, and fame and Petrarch finds himself not quite able to agree.[34] In canzone 264, too, the focus seems to be on the need to turn away from all earthly commitment of which love for a woman stands only as a particularly alluring example. The opposing view is narrated rather than being given direct speech. Petrarch uses conflicts in the vocabulary (for example, "dolce et agro," "faticosa et dilectevol," 55–56) to express his inner confusion. He knows that thoughts of love and fame are ultimately destructive, but he feels their strong sweetness just the same. The idea of fame sustains him through the sufferings of love, and even when he tries to obliterate it, it returns stronger than before. He fears that his desire for fame will end only with his death. At the same time, he recognizes that even if he does achieve posthumous fame, it will be nothing but a wind. Afraid of wasting his life on something worthless, he wishes to leave shadows behind and embrace the truth, but even then he must recognize the other desire (his love of Laura) which takes away all care for the fate of his soul and sweetly destroys and imprisons him. The shifts in decision between the different half-stanzas give the reader a vivid idea of Petrarch's mind in motion and of the conflicting desires, thoughts, and recollections to which he is subject.

Quel ch'i' fo veggio, et non m'inganna il vero
mal conosciuto, anzi mi sforza Amore,
che la strada d'onore
mai nol lassa seguir, chi troppo il crede;
et sento ad ora ad or venirmi al core
un leggiadro disdegno aspro et severo
ch'ogni occulto pensero
tira in mezzo la fronte, ov'altri 'l vede:
ché mortal cosa amar con tanta fede
quanta a Dio sol per debito convensi,
più si disdice a chi più pregio brama.
Et questo ad alta voce ancho richiama
la ragione sviata dietro ai sensi;
ma perch'ell'oda, et pensi
tornare, il mal costume oltre la spigne,
et agli occhi depigne
quella che sol per farmi morir nacque,
perch'a me troppo, et a se stessa, piacque. (91–108)

[I see what I am doing and ignorance of the truth does not trick me; instead I am forced by Love, who never lets anyone who believes in him too much follow the path of honor. And I often feel arise in my heart a noble and severe disdain which makes every secret thought visible to all through my blushes; for to love mortal things with the faith one owes to God alone, is more disgraceful the more one prizes honor (101). And this disdain with a loud voice calls back my reason drawn away by the senses. But although reason hears and thinks of turning back, bad habit draws it further and pictures for my eyes her who was born only to make me die since she pleased me and herself too much.]

The first two lines of this sixth stanza are an almost direct translation of two lines of Medea's speech from Ovid's *Metamorphoses*

("Quid faciam video: nec me ignorantia veri / decipiet, sed amor": I see what I am doing and it is not ignorance of the truth which deceives me, but love, 7.92–93), in which she wonders at the power which love has over her will and reason. Yet they seem to be absorbed perfectly into Petrarch's account of the confusion which overcomes him. He can see the truth clearly but is nevertheless compelled by love. These are perfect lines to express the confusion which the onset of love has brought about in Medea's mind and in Petrarch's. Perhaps Petrarch also intends the translated quotation to evoke a deep memory of the eventual deceptiveness of Medea's love, when Jason deserts her and she takes revenge on their children. Honor here stands for personal integrity and the need to fulfill God's commands, whereas love, as in medieval romance, delights in its power to overcome the lover's idea of honor. Yet although he can see very clearly what he should do, the ambivalent power of love and the image of the woman who was born to make him die are too powerful for his will. The repetition of the motif increases the reader's sense of the poet's inner confusion and powerlessness.

> Et da l'un lato punge
> vergogna et duol che 'ndietro mi rivolve;
> dall'altro non m'assolve
> un piacer per usanza in me sì forte
> ch'a patteggiar n'ardisce co la morte.
>
> Canzon, qui sono, ed ò 'l cor via più freddo
> de la paura che gelata neve,
> sentendomi perir senz'alcun dubbio:
> ché pur deliberando ò vòlto al subbio
> gran parte omai de la mia tela breve;
> né mai peso fu greve
> quanto quel ch'i' sostengo in tale stato:
> ché co la morte a lato
> cerco del viver mio novo consiglio,
> et veggio 'l meglio, et al peggior m'appiglio. (122–36)

[And from one side shame and regret strike me and try to turn me back, while on the other a pleasure which custom has made so strong in me does not leave me free so that it dares to negotiate with death (126).

Song, here I am, and I have a heart much colder from fear than frozen snow, feeling myself undoubtedly perish: for while I deliberate I have turned on the spool a great part of my now short thread; nor have I ever felt any weight so heavy as what I now carry in this state. With death at my side I seek new advice about my life and I see the better and hold on to the worse.]

The conclusion to the seventh stanza sums up the contraries which Petrarch has been exploring throughout the poem, but it places the emphasis firmly on the strength of his attachment to love and to the world. Now that he is near to death he knows that he ought to turn away from the world, but the strong pleasure to which he is accustomed makes him ready to confront death without change. The *envoi* instead dramatizes the closeness of death and the strength of his fear and his consciousness of the time he has wasted in deliberation. The poem ends with another direct translation from Medea's speech which perfectly summarizes the battle between intellect and feeling: "video meliora proboque, / deteriora sequor": I see and approve the better, but I follow the worse (*Metamorphoses* 7.20–21). A similar idea is expressed in Romans 7.19: "For the good that I would I do not: but the evil which I would not, that I do." Petrarch uses his translations of Ovid to reinforce and generalize the reader's sense of the power of love to overcome wisdom and prudence. This poem forcefully dramatizes Petrarch's dilemma, giving a vivid idea both of his understanding that the world is transitory in comparison with eternity and of his powerful commitment to the love of Laura and the pursuit of earthly fame.

Canzone 359 describes a dream-vision in which Laura returns from heaven to comfort the ailing poet at his bedside. Petrarch seems to want the reader to have in mind both Boethius's Lady Philosophy and Beatrice's care for Dante from her place in heaven. Quite soon her concern for the poet's sadness moves into a reproach. The poet's continual laments disturb her peace in heaven, and she struggles to understand how he can be sorrowful for her when she has gone to a better place. Someone who loves her as much as he claims to should be glad of her departure from the misery of earthly life and her arrival in heaven (12–22). This apparently cruel inversion of Christian arguments of consolation for grief underlines the difference between earthly and spiritual understandings of the world.

Their dispute becomes more tense as her offered solution prompts a new perplexity in Petrarch (58–71). The woman beside his bed embodies the eyes and the hair which tied him to earthly love. Laura rejects the foolish mistake of this response, pointing out that she has taken on her former shape only to help him and that in fact her body rots in her grave. Then she gives a strong physical emphasis to her persuasion and promise by asserting that once they meet in heaven (and after the resurrection of both their bodies) she will be much more beautiful and also more loving to him than she ever was on earth. At the same time, she points out (as both the *Secretum* and some other poems placed late in the sequence also do) that her lack of response to him was in the deeper sense a kindness, since it avoided the damage to his soul of an excessive (and extramarital) physical love. Petrarch has here contrived a disturbing mixture of intellectual and spiritual understanding of the rottenness of the world with the same kind of wish-fulfilling physical promise that seemed to underlie canzone 126. The way in which Laura is portrayed in this poetic vision confirms that his desire for her body is still strong. This confusion of motifs presents in a different manner the struggle between wanting the better and choosing the worse which we saw in canzone 264. Fittingly, the poem ends with more tears and with a combination of pity and anger on the part of Laura. It is as frustrating for her as it is for him that he cannot simply choose the salvation which Christ offers him but longs for a kind of succor from her which she is only partly (and only later) willing to give.

Sonnet 363 represents this dilemma within the tighter framework required by the sonnet form.

> Morte à spento quel sol ch'abagliar suolmi,
> e 'n tenebre son li occhi interi et saldi;
> terra è quella ond'io ebbi et freddi et caldi;
> spenti son i miei lauri, or querce et olmi:
>
> di ch'io veggio 'l mio ben, et parte duolmi.
> Non è chi faccia et paventosi et baldi
> i miei penser', né chi li agghiacci et scaldi,
> né chi li empia di speme, et di duol colmi.

Fuor di man di colui che punge et molce,
che già fece di me sì lungo stratio,
mi trovo in libertate, amara et dolce;

et al Signor ch'i' adoro et ch'i' ringratio,
che pur col ciglio il ciel governa et folce,
torno stanco di viver, nonché satio.

[Death has destroyed that sun which used to blind me, and my healthy
eyes are in darkness; she is dust from whom I had cold and heat; my
laurels have faded and have now become oaks and elms (4), in which I
see my advantage but I still lament. No one makes my thoughts fearful
and bold; no one freezes and scorches them or fills them with hope or
sorrow (8). Out of the hands of one who wounds and cures and who
formerly tormented me for so long, I find myself in bitter and sweet
liberty (11); and to the Lord whom I adore and thank and who governs
and supports the world with his eyebrow, I turn back, weary of life
rather than satiated (14).]

The first quatrain focuses on the transformation which death has
wrought on Laura. The old poetic symbols of his love (the brightness, the sunlike eyes, the laurels; the poet's chills and fevers) are
gone. In the second quatrain, he understands the advantage of the
departure of his obsession, but he remains pained by the loss, again
expressed in terms of the paradoxes of love ("paventosi / baldi; ag-
ghiacci / scaldi; speme / duol"). In the first tercet, he finds himself
freed from the dominance of Love, but both that dominance and his
freedom are expressed in terms of contraries ("punge et molce,"
"amara et dolce"). In these first three sections, the explication of
change has been conducted through paradoxes that remain oddly
the same as they were in his earlier love poems. The second tercet
explains that this time, as a result of Laura's death, the poet has been
able to turn to the Lord, whom he thanks and adores and who—with
an allusion to Horace, *Odes* III.1—controls the heavens with his eyebrow. A slight qualification remains in the enigmatic final phrase
("stanco . . . nonché satio"), but the main meaning here seems to be
that while remaining discontented with living in the world, he is
now overwhelmingly tired of life. This poem therefore represents a
more decisive turning against the world and against love—which is

repeated in the next three poems—without the ambiguous and contradictory consolation of the wish that Laura would comfort him in heaven.

Petrarch constructs his descriptions out of plain vivid language. He finds the words to extend a comparison or an allegory over as much as two quatrains. He can combine the logical clarity which the sonnet form requires with a strong sense of contrast and mystery, using powerful images or references to earlier poems to bring to life confusion of feelings. In different sonnets, he can employ different balances between imagery and logical argument. He finds images with the right degree of shock to take advantage of the lightness of the sonnet. He knows how to express paradox and internal conflict within the clarity and brevity the form demands. He uses pairs or trios of sonnets to explore different facets of the same emotion or the powerful attractions of competing approaches to a problem. In the canzoni, he finds space for more evocatively sensual descriptions of landscape and event and for dialogues between opposing positions which can be developed at greater logical length. These longer poems show off his mastery of difficult rhymes and the musical effects of contrasting line lengths. They enable him to go further both in emotion and in self-interrogation. He gives a strong sense of the struggle between what he knows he should do and what he feels actually motivates him. The canzone enables him to present a greater sense of the impact of the world and the people outside on his inner struggles. He gives full value to his inner confusion and his sense of powerlessness, at the mercy of often conflicting emotions. He depicts a mind in motion between physical desire, poetic ambition, and religious truth. Through understanding what he has already lost, he is enabled, belatedly, to move toward change. As a whole, the sequence presents both the depth of Petrarch's frustration and confusion and, eventually in the final poems, a movement out of confusion to fuller understanding.

His deep knowledge of Augustan poetry, of the troubadours, of the poets of the *dolce stil novo*, and of Dante is reflected in the images and phrases employed in his poems. His visual imagination is often stimulated by his reading of Dante or the Bible. The linking of sonnets, too, is a technique he developed from his reading of the troubadours. Many of the ideas and images of the poems are drawn from and follow his reading. Petrarch absorbs his inherited material within a convincing portrayal of his own psychological struggle between his understanding of what Christians should believe about the world and his desire for earthly fulfillment, imaged in particular in his love of Laura, and for fame among his contemporaries and his successors.

Traditions: Dante, Petrarch, and Petrarch's Afterlife

One can understand more about the implications of Petrarch's theory and practice by comparing him with Dante, who also used the writings of his predecessors, who was much admired as soon as his works became available, and whose own writing was troublingly present to Petrarch. Like Petrarch, Dante was formidably learned. He knew fewer Latin poets and historians than Petrarch, but he was very well read in troubadour and Italian poetry, in Aristotelian philosophy and science, and in theology. Unlike Petrarch, who left many projects unfinished, Dante brought all his knowledge to bear on the completion of a great masterpiece which sums up his entire achievement. Dante was both knowledgeable about science and theology and original in some of the positions he took. He seemed to know everything, but he could also make surprising mistakes. The extraordinary quality of his achievement was obvious from the first publication of the *Inferno* around 1315 (though he would be one of the major Italian poets even without the crowning achievement of the *Divina Commedia*). Many of the earliest manuscripts have been lost; according to Marcella Roddewig, 827 manuscripts exist. The earliest we have is probably Ashburnham 828, in the Laurentian Library in Florence, written before 1335. One Florentine bookseller, Ser Nardo, is said to have organized the production of over 100 manuscripts, so high was the demand for copies in Florence in the 1340s and after.[35] Commentaries in Italian and Latin began to be produced even in Dante's lifetime, and from 1374 the city of Florence financed lecture series on his work. It was immediately obvious that Dante had written the greatest poem since antiquity, and this view was not only sustained throughout the fifteenth and sixteenth centuries but continues up to the present.

Dante's poem as a complete synthesis is essentially beyond imitation. There is no school of Dantean poets. A later poet can retell one of his incidents, rephrase some of his ideas, or echo his words for another purpose. Still, the example of Dante's use of his predecessors to create something new and exceptional may be an inspiration to later poets.

One of the principal early promoters of Dante's work was Petrarch's friend Giovanni Boccaccio, who wrote a life of Dante, copied at least three manuscripts of the *Commedia*, and began an extensive Italian commentary. Seeing that Petrarch appeared to have no copy of the *Commedia*, Boccaccio copied one for him and sent it to him in Avignon in 1351.[36] Petrarch responds to a later letter about Dante from Boccaccio in 1359 by defending himself against the implication that he is envious of Dante and against the supposedly widespread belief that he hates or despises him. Petrarch assures Boccaccio that he does not dislike Dante, provides several reasons why he should not be hostile to him, and even claims to admire his work, but he nevertheless writes enough by way of self-exculpation to reveal his anxiety.[37]

> Yet what appearance of truth does it have that I should envy the man who devoted his whole life to this kind of poetry to which I barely granted the flower of my youth, so that what was to him, if not his only skill then surely his finest, was to me just play, consolation and an exercise of intellect?[38]

> This is something I don't conceal, since if anything I said in that language resembled his words or those of any other poet, or if something even identical with someone else's work was perhaps found in mine, this was not surreptitious or with the intention of imitating, two very common offenses which I always shunned like the reefs—especially in vernacular writing, but had occurred either by accident or from similarity of intellect, as Cicero suggests, and my following in the same footsteps was unwitting. Believe this is true if you will ever believe me in anything; nothing is more true.[39]

Modern scholars cannot accept Petrarch's belittling of Dante's achievement or his claims in the same letter that he himself had abandoned the youthful folly of writing in the vernacular.[40] His attack on the vulgar crowd's ignorant appreciation of Dante looks like the worst kind of blind, elitist self-deception.[41] Marco Santagata and other critics have argued that in fact Petrarch knew the *Divina*

Commedia almost by heart, and they have shown that he echoes and draws on many different parts of Dante's work in the *Canzoniere*. Nancy Vickers has argued at length for the dependence of the great canzone 126 on the earthly paradise sections of the *Purgatorio*.[42] Although he never lived in Florence, Petrarch must have been aware of the extraordinary impact of Dante's work, and he himself claims to appreciate the quality of Dante's Italian poetry as few others could.

Peter Hainsworth has argued that Petrarch had felt compelled to reorganize the previous generation's understanding of the development of Italian poetry in order to make room for his own work. "Before Petrarch Italian lyric poetry found its terminus in the *Divina Commedia*. After him the *Commedia* was excluded: lyric poetry led to Petrarch himself."[43] In his reading of sonnet 133, Hainsworth shows how Petrarch combined elements from a number of previous Italian and Provençal poets, including Dante, and yet created something which was integrated and distinctive.[44] He further points to the selectiveness of Petrarch's reorganization of the history of poetry. Canzone 73 ("Lasso me") suggests that the high points of the development are the troubadour Arnaut Daniel, Cavalcanti, the lyric poetry of Dante, Cino da Pistoia, and Petrarch himself.[45] In Hainsworth's view, Petrarch dealt with Dante by removing from vernacular poetry the intellectual topics which had been prominent in the *Commedia*, such as politics, religion, and philosophy, and restricting it to the love-lyric.[46] He allows the *Commedia* to emerge in his poetry only in fragmentary form, but his frequent reminiscences are well integrated into his own work.[47]

Just as Petrarch created and used a genealogy of previous poets in order to make space for his own work, so later poets chose to follow his example for reasons that made sense to them. Fifteenth-century poets like Giusto de' Conti (d. 1449) and Gasparo Visconti (1461–99) borrowed the idea of writing collections of lyric poems, as well as some of the sufferings and images which Petrarch had transmitted, but the really strong impetus to imitate Petrarch belonged to the sixteenth century, with Pietro Bembo's (1470–1547) promotion of Petrarch as the linguistic model for Italian poetry in his *Prose della volgar lingua* (1525). Bembo wrote poetry of his own in a manner which combined Petrarchan images and Platonic themes, but he also edited Petrarch's *Canzoniere* and wrote a commentary on it. Bembo's designated successor, Giovanni della Casa (1503–56), also wrote Petrarchan sonnets and canzoni. Male and female Italian poets of the later sixteenth century, such as Celio Magno (1536–1602), Vittoria Colonna (1490–1547), and Gaspara Stampa (1523–54), found their own ways to use Petrarch's legacy, in religious verse or in laments on the sporadic absences and final departure of a male lover. Petrarch provided them with collections of words and images and with forms which they could exploit in religious and amatory poetry.[48]

In England, too, after the pioneering, near-contemporary translation by Chaucer, which will be discussed in the next chapter, interest in Petrarch was revived by Sir Thomas Wyatt (1503–1542), who found Petrarch's imagery and vocabulary a helpful way of thinking about the sometimes treacherous amatory and political world of Henry VIII's court. Wyatt's translations of Petrarch helpfully instructed him in the construction of sonnets and in the amount of material which a well-controlled sonnet could contain. Later English poets, like Sir Philip Sidney and Michael Drayton, followed Wyatt, Bembo, and French poets in using Petrarchan images and vocabulary to express extravagant compliments and quasi-Platonic ideas about the progress from the love of physical beauty to the love of virtue. Spenser used the imagery of the notably anti-marriage and sometimes misogynistic Petrarch to describe his courtship of, and planned marriage to, his second wife.[49] Shakespeare mocked Petrarchan commonplaces, either for comic effect in *As You Like It*, III.5 or to sustain and amplify the very different claims he wanted to make about his mistress in Sonnet 130. Donne took Petrarchan ideas as the basis for his amplification of his experience of love, which he also explored through a decidedly anti-Petrarchan choice of imagery and vocabulary.[50] Even when their reaction was critical, Petrarch continued to provide poets with an unfailing resource of poetic structures (such as the sonnet-sequence), models, ideas, and images which they could turn to their own purposes.

Petrarch took from other writers elements that he could use in his own poetry. He borrowed forms and contents from the Sicilian poets and the troubadours and motifs, ideas, and phrases from Latin poetry and from Dante. Grateful successors used Petrarch's work as a treasure-house of phrases and images for talking about love and other subjects, but in their obsessive quarrying of a range of amatory images and, in some cases, their deliberate posing of their experiences as different from his, their work has had the effect of obscuring and reducing Petrarch's true achievement. So Petrarch counts as historically perhaps the most important contributor to the European tradition of love poetry—in his gathering of material from previous poets and transmission of images and ideas to his successors—but the sometimes rather slavish and predictable ways in which later writers were able to make use of him may have harmed his subsequent reputation. His successors often missed the art with which he made new while following his reading. Today we can respond to his poetic skill and to his forceful depiction of his internal struggles without wishing to adopt him as a model or being misled by his gifts to his successors, at the same time as we can appreciate Dante's overwhelming and almost inimitable greatness.

CHAPTER TWO

Chaucer and Boccaccio's
Il Filostrato

WHERE PETRARCH'S ITALIAN POEMS draw on the forms and preoccupations established by troubadour poetry and the phrases and ideas of a range of Latin poets, Chaucer's relationship to literary tradition can be explored through his study, translation, and adaptation of one Italian poem. In the introduction, I argued that literary tradition is best exemplified by the way in which a later writer chooses to use a predecessor. That is what we shall observe in Chaucer's reading of Boccaccio's *Il Filostrato*.

Once the Trojan parliament has decided that Chaucer's Criseyde will be sent to the Greek camp in exchange for the ransom of Antenor, several Trojan women come to her house to tell her the news, to congratulate her on being reunited with her father, and to commiserate with her for leaving Troy. When she bursts into tears at the thought of leaving Troilus, they assume that she is sad to leave them, since they are unaware of her love affair.

> And thilke fooles sittynge hire a-boute
> Wenden that she wepte and siked sore
> By-cause that she sholde out of that route
> Deperte and neuere pleye with hem more.
> And they that hadde y-knowen hire of ʒore

Seigh hire so wepe and thoughte it kyndenesse,
And ech of hem wepte ek for hire destresse.

And bisyly they gonnen hire comforten
Of thyng, god woot, on which she litel thoughte,
And with hire tales wenden hire disporten,
And to be glad they often hire bysoughte.
But swiche an ese therwith they hire wroughte
Right as a man is esed forto feele,
ffor ache of hed to clawen hym on his heele.[1]

Readers are apt to think of this moment of comedy in the middle of tragedy as typically Chaucerian: the attention to the thoughts and gestures of unnecessary figures in the story, their openhearted but comically misplaced sympathy for Criseyde, and the striking image in which the futility of their pity is revealed. It can be quite a shock then to read Boccaccio's *Il Filostrato* and to find that all the elements of this passage were already present in a single stanza of the source.[2]

E ciascuna voleva confortarla
pur sopra quello ch'a lei non dolea;
parole assai dicean da consolarla
per la partenza la qual far dovea
da lor, né erano altro che grattarla
nelle calcagne, ove il capo prudea;
ché ella di lor niente si curava,
ma di Troiolo solo il qual lasciava. (IV.85)

[And each of them wanted to comfort her for something which she did not mourn for; they said enough words to console her for leaving them, which was no different from scratching the heel to cure a headache; she did not care about them at all, but only about Troiolo whom she was leaving.]

Chaucer has evidently amplified Boccaccio's stanza as he has the whole episode (eight stanzas as opposed to Boccaccio's six). Perhaps he has given more attention both to the sincere sympathy of the women and to the conventionality of the visits and the sentiments, but the fact remains that the idea of the episode, its comic treatment, the contrast of sentiments, and the image of scratching the heel to cure a pain in the head were all devised by Boccaccio, though Branca suggests that the image is proverbial and is found elsewhere in the cantari.[3] David Wallace has written of finding elements in Boccaccio which seem typically Chaucerian.[4] I want to unpack his perception a little by looking at moments in *Il Filostrato* which seem to have appealed to Chaucer or to have provided him with things to learn from, to adapt, and to make his own.

Today Chaucer is best known as the author of *The Canterbury Tales*, unfinished at his death but including tales first drafted in the 1380s. He is celebrated for his intense interest in the relations between narrators, stories, and audiences, which he dramatizes in *The Canterbury Tales* but which feature in his other works as well. His interest in the role of the audience and their reception of texts makes him particularly wary and inventive at the moment of closing a text, as if he wishes to guard against appearing to deliver a definitive final message. He favors tight plots in which he often invites us to understand and sympathize, at least temporarily, with lively, highly developed characters we would ordinarily condemn. Many of his characters are constructed out of contrasting elements and are animated with an extraordinary zest for life. Chaucer, who had an intense imagination, often directs us to surprising elements of a scene. He mixes comedy and tragedy and plays mock-heroic games with style, mixing the high and low styles to sometimes bewildering effect. These seem to me the main characteristics of his best work.

Chaucer was in the generation of the first major writers in English, along with Langland, Gower, and the Gawain poet. His greatest stimuli were his knowledge of classical Latin poetry and the recent French and Italian writers, whose work he sought out and imitated. This chapter considers the role of reading, and especially of reading Boccaccio's *Il Filostrato*, in Chaucer's unique literary achievement. I argue that many of Chaucer's most distinctive and successful literary strategies were copied from or prompted by his reading of Boccaccio.

Chaucer (1343–1400) seems to have known some classical Latin literature well. He frequently refers to Virgil and Ovid and uses passages from their works. He knew Cicero's *Dream of Scipio* and Macrobius's commentary on it. His knowledge of Seneca and Horace may have come from medieval compilations rather than from direct reading of the text.[5] He mentions Statius and Lucan as poets to whom he would like *Troilus and Criseyde* to be compared (V.1792). He translated Boethius's late antique *Consolation of Philosophy* into English, and he probably used the late antique, purported Latin translations of the supposedly firsthand accounts of Troy attributed to Dares and Dictys. He certainly knew Geoffrey de Vinsauf's twelfth-century *Poetria nova*.[6] He translated part of the thirteenth-century *Roman de la Rose* from French into English and used it extensively in his works.[7] But his real speciality was recent French and Italian literature, notably Guillaume de Machaut (c.1300–1377), Jean Froissart (c.1337–1405), Dante (c.1265–1321), Petrarch (1304–1374), and Boccaccio (1313–1375).[8] Chaucer was the first English writer to translate and use passages from these authors in his own work. On his travels in France and Italy, and through his contacts with merchants in London, Chaucer seems to have sought out recent and contemporary French and Italian poetry as aids to writing something new in English. Chaucer was an original, successful, and innovative poet before he worked on Boccaccio, but translating and adapting Boccaccio helped him make great advances in style, approach, and characterization. A better-informed Chaucer specialist could probably find earlier examples of some of the features I identify as Chaucer's learning from Boccaccio, but even in that case the concentration of things to be learned or reinforced from his study of Boccaccio would be very telling.

Chaucer used Boccaccio's youthful experiment *Il Filostrato* (1335) to create *Troilus and Criseyde* (1385), an enduring masterpiece and unquestionably his greatest completed work. Maria Gozzi has shown that Boccaccio blends six French, Latin, and Italian narrative sources in order to create the prequel to the story of Briseida from Benoît de Sainte-Maure's *Roman de Troie*.[9] Benoît's story opens at the moment when Briseida leaves Troy and begins to consider transferring her affections from Troilus to Diomede. Boccaccio creates a love story which goes wrong, presenting first the anguish of the male lover, then the ecstasy of the fulfillment of love, and finally the suffering, first of parting and then of the recognition of betrayal. Wallace, adapting George Kane's words, calls it "a beautiful, amoral fantasy of love."[10] Boccaccio introduces a certain amount of soft-focus sexual wish fulfillment, as when Criseida asks Troiolo if he would like her to remove her undershirt (III.31–32). Boccaccio tells readers that his aim in writing the poem is to portray his sorrow at Filomena's absence.[11] The narrative arc suggests, however, that he may also, within his fictional frame, have wished to entice his imagined addressee with poetry of fulfillment and to warn her of disgrace such as that which befalls Criseida after her betrayal.

Boccaccio wrote his poem by combining learned traditions of romance and Trojan history with the popular Italian form of the *cantari*. His poem has a strong narrative drive but also includes important lyric moments, some of them drawn from Cino da Pistoia and from Dante. Some of the versification has seemed a bit clumsy to readers and critics.[12] The poem portrays a sophisticated and self-assured woman, a naive lover, and an overengaged and helping friend. It reflects the chivalric atmosphere of the Neapolitan court where Boccaccio lived at the time, without perhaps fully understanding the nuances of courtly behavior. The general critical view is that this is definitely apprentice work and far from Boccaccio's most impressive poetry or narrative.

Chaucer's Copying from Boccaccio

In the next two sections, I examine twelve aspects of *Il Filostrato* which prompt Chaucer at times to straightforward imitation, at times to considerable amplification of an idea, and at times to a corrective reaction. We shall see that many of these aspects—which represent Chaucer in different ways learning from and being stimulated by Boccaccio—also came to seem like key characteristics of Chaucer's mature work. Chaucer became the poet he was partly through intense reflection on Boccaccio's ideas and techniques. The first six aspects discussed here are predominantly stylistic. They derive from the task of translating Boccaccio, but in each case Chaucer also uses the same technique in places other than those where he simply translates. Translation teaches him a device he can use elsewhere.

Several times in *Il Filostrato,* Boccaccio uses a comparison or a simile to introduce a change of mood or a new thought. In part II, when Pandaro returns to Troiolo after first telling Criseida of Troiolo's love, his news of success is mirrored by a simile comparing Troiolo to flowers closed for the night which open when the sun's light reaches them (80). Similarly, in part III, when Pandaro brings back the news that Criseida will see Troiolo privately, his reaction is portrayed in a simile of the revival of the trees, flowers, and meadows in spring (12). When he returns to his room after the parliament has decided to send Criseida to the Greek camp, he is compared to a bull swaying around after he has received a mortal blow (IV.27). Chaucer reuses all these similes (II.967–71, III.351–57, IV.239–42), but he also uses the same technique on his own account. When he wishes to present a change in the sexual dominance of Criseyde over Troilus in the middle of the consummation scene, he introduces the change with a comparison.

> What myghte or may the sely larke seye,
> Whan that the sperhauk hath it in his foot? (III.1191–92)

Suddenly Criseyde is the lark in the claws of the merciless sparrowhawk Troilus. This movement toward being dominated is then repeated in a second proverbial image of her quaking like an aspen leaf, before she reasserts her own agency in her response to his demands.

> Ne hadde I er now, my swete herte deere,
> Ben 3olde, i-wis, I were now nought heere. (III.1210–11)

At the moment when he wants to change the balance of their relationship, Chaucer announces and reinforces that change using comparisons, in a technique he seems to have learned from Boccaccio.[13] Similarly, in book I, when he describes Criseyde modestly standing at the back of the temple, he adds the comparison with a star under a black cloud.

> Nas neuere 3et seyn thyng to ben preysed derre,
> Nor vnder cloude blak so bright a sterre,

As was Criseyde, as folk seyde euerichone,
That hir behelden in hir blake wede. (174–78)

Formally the comparison is with her beautiful person in her modest widow's dress, but the simile implies both her exceptional brightness and prominence in the story to come and the cloud hanging over her, which presages a doom for her and for Troy, briefly illuminated by her beauty and her love. Chaucer provides one of the strikingly foreboding moments of the beginning of the poem by reusing a technique he learned from translating Boccaccio.

A second borrowed technique follows Boccaccio's use of *come* ("as," "like") to introduce ambiguities in describing Criseida's reactions. Thus, Chaucer introduces her reply to Diomede's speech about the futility of loving anyone in Troy with a sort of ambiguous comparison.

And thus to hym she seyde as ȝe may here,

As she that hadde hire herte on Troilus
So faste that ther may it non arace;
And strangely she spak and seyde thus. (V.952–55)

In saying that she spoke like someone who had her heart firmly devoted to Troilus, Chaucer is not quite asserting that she actually was so devoted. His introduction of the phrase with the particle "as" significantly weakens the statement in comparison with Boccaccio here, who writes:

A traverso mirandol dispettosa,
tanto poteva ancor Troiolo in essa. (VI.26)

[She looked at him askance and angrily—Troiolo still had so much power over her.]

Boccaccio uses the particle *come* to introduce a certain distance and ambiguity elsewhere. For example, when she first hears that she will be sent back to her father, Criseida reacts

come a colei ch'avea volto il disio
a Troiolo il quale più ch'altro amava. (IV.79)

[like one who had turned her desire towards Troiolo, whom she loved more than anyone else.]

Chaucer translates this in a way which strongly parallels his later usage.

> As she that hadde hire herte and al hire mynde
> On Troilus i-set so wonder faste,
> That al this world ne myghte hire loue vnbynde,
> Ne Troilus out of hire herte caste. (IV.673–76)

To say that she reacts like one who has her heart and mind fixed on Troilus falls short of stating that that is how she feels. Here and in other places in the poem, Chaucer suggests that the reader should not be entirely certain of Criseyde's actual feelings. There is plenty of room for us to be surprised by her responses. One of Chaucer's ways of introducing changes in readers' perception of Criseyde's character is learned from Boccaccio.

Third, Boccaccio sometimes uses the rhetorical figure of apostrophe to generalize and moralize but also to introduce a certain element of comic contrast between the personal and petty activities of an individual and the larger processes of fate. When Troiolo leads his band of young men in mocking lovers and love, Boccaccio comments:

> O ciechità delle mondane menti,
> come ne seguon sovente gli effetti
> tutti contrarii a' nostri intendimenti! (I.25)

> [O Blindness of earthly minds, how often the effects follow entirely contrary to our intentions!]

Chaucer translates this and amplifies it before inserting a long sequence of authorial comments, mocking Troilus and half-humorously insisting on the power of love and instructing young people to give way before it.

> O blynde world, O blynde entencioun!
> How often falleth al the effect contraire
> Of surquidrie and foul presumpcioun!
> ffor kaught is proud, and kauȝt is debonaire:
> This Troilus is clomben on the staire
> And litel weneth that he moot descenden—
> But alday faileth thing that fooles wenden.

As proude Bayard gynneth forto skippe
Out of the weye, so pryketh him his corn,
Til he a lasshe haue of the longe whippe,
Than thynketh he, "though I praunce al byforn
ffirst in the trays, ful fat and newe shorn,
ȝet am I but an hors, and horses lawe
I moot endure, and with my feres drawe." (I.211–24)

Chaucer's amplification of the apostrophe certainly increases the mismatch between event and language which alerts us to irony and self-mockery, but the suggestion for the apostrophe and the way of using it to underscore the moment of Troilus's fall into love comes from Boccaccio. As we have seen on other occasions, Chaucer prepares for the change in Troilus with a simile, rendered comic on this occasion through the introduction of the talking horse. This introduces a seven-stanza insertion into Boccaccio's text which seems to modern readers especially Chaucerian because of its overamplified comic finger-wagging and because of the way Chaucer uses it to cover over the moment of Troilus falling in love. The idea for this insertion and for some of the techniques which it employs came to Chaucer from reading Boccaccio.

Right at the end of the poem Chaucer takes over and repeats another rhetorical figure from Boccaccio, and this is my fourth category. Two of the last six stanzas of the poem are marked by a use of anaphora which is so heavy as almost to undermine the high sentiments expressed.

Swich fyn hath, lo, this Troilus for loue,
Swich fyn hath al his grete worthynesse;
Swich fyn hath his estat real aboue,
Swich fyn his lust, swich fyn hath his noblesse;
Swich fyn hath false worldes brotelnesse:
And thus bigan his louyng of Criseyde,
As I haue told, and in this wise he deyde. (V.1828–34)

Lo here, of payens corsed olde rites,
Lo here, what alle hire goddes may auaille;
Lo here, thise wrecched worldes appetites;
Lo here, the fyn and guerdoun for trauaille

Of Ioue, Appollo, of Mars, of swich rascaille;
Lo here, the forme of olde clerkis speche
In poetrie, if ʒe hire bokes seche. (V.1849–55)

Undoubtedly Chaucer wants to remind us of everything that Troilus has achieved and lost, of the sorrow of his death and the uncertainty of the world, but he also clearly underlines the idea that all this loss was unnecessary and was founded on the error of loving something as unstable as another human being, as well as on the falsehood of the pagan gods. The repetition overstates and thus undermines the moralizing point. Only the first of these stanzas was prompted by Boccaccio, but the imitation is so clear that we must assume that Chaucer was encouraged by Boccaccio's example to repeat the effect.

Cotal fine ebbe il mal concetto amore
di Troiolo in Criseida, e cotale
fine ebbe il miserabile dolore
di lui al qual non fu mai altro eguale;
cotal fine ebbe il lucido splendore
che lui servava al solio reale;
cotal fine ebbe la speranza vana
di Troiolo in Criseida villana. (VIII.28)

[Such end had the ill-conceived love of Troiolo for Criseida, and such end had his wretched sorrow which was never equaled; such end had the bright splendor which he observed at the royal court; such end had the vain hopes of Troiolo in the ignoble Criseida.]

Boccaccio is much stronger in his condemnation of Criseida ("villana") in this stanza than Chaucer. Like him, Boccaccio condemns Troiolo and Criseida's earthly love (and will go on to advise young people to avoid it, as Chaucer also does: VIII.29; V.1835–48). But where Boccaccio seems to remain within the narrative's pagan historical period, Chaucer adds a condemnation of the pagan gods and the command to focus love on Christ. The mockery of pagan love and belief can become another motive for his turn to Christ at the end of the poem.

Fifth, several critics have noted that Boccaccio inserts lyrical episodes, such as songs and poetic letters, into *Il Filostrato*. One particularly clear example is his insertion of four stanzas from the most famous canzone of Cino da Pistoia ("La dolce vista e 'l bel guardo") in part VI, stanzas 62–65, but there are many other examples.[14] Chaucer undoubtedly followed Boccaccio in including lyrics within his narrative.[15] Robert O. Payne has identified ten "examples of lyric elaboration" in *Troilus and Criseyde*.[16] Several of the Chaucerian examples are translations of lyrics from Boccaccio, but Chaucer also takes the opportunity to write new lyrics and to incorporate the first English translation of a sonnet by Petrarch as Troilus's first song of love.

> If no loue is, O god, what fele I so?
> And if loue is, what thing and which is he?
> If loue be good, from whennes cometh my woo?
> If it be wikke, a wonder thynketh me,
> Whenne euery torment and aduersite
> That cometh of hym may to me sauory thinke,
> ffor ay thurst I the more that ich it drynke.
>
> And if that at myn owen lust I brenne,
> ffrom whennes cometh my waillynge and my pleynte?
> If harme a-gree me, wherto pleyne I thenne?
> I noot, ne whi vn-wery that I feynte.
> O quike deth, O swete harm so queynte,
> How may of the in me swich quantite,
> But if that I consente that it be?
>
> And if that I consente, I wrongfully
> Compleyne, i-wis; thus possed to and fro,
> Al sterelees with-inne a boot am I
> Amydde the see, bitwixen wyndes two,
> That inne contrarie stonden euere mo.
> Allas, what is this wondre maladie?
> ffor hete of cold, for cold of hete, I dye. (I.400–420)

Chaucer translates each of the three sections (two quatrains and a sestet) of Petrarch's sonnet 132, discussed in the previous chapter, into a single rhyme royal stanza.[17] In general, he follows Petrarch very closely but allows himself some elaboration and explanation of

Petrarch's "sweet torment" in the last four lines of the first stanza. His translation captures both the confusion of mind which Troilus and Petrarch's speaker experience and the poem's anthology of Petrarchan images ("sauory torment," "quike death," "swete harm," "sterelees amydde the see," "bitwixen wyndes two," "maladie," "cold hete").[18] Boccaccio himself had included some of these images (III.83–84, V.54–55), and critics used to assume that he too was thinking of Petrarch, though the modern consensus is that they were well established images in the tradition.[19] In the spirit of adding lyrical impulses to his narrative, Boccaccio frequently adapted phrases from other poets, especially Dante, into his poem. This may well have encouraged Chaucer's similar appropriation of phrases from Dante at key points of the poem, but Dante was an important inspiration for Chaucer's poetry over a long period.

Sixth, Boccaccio introduces into his narrative comments on the theme of Fortune and the uncertainty of fate. Chaucer hugely increases this aspect of the poem. Encouraged by Boccaccio, Chaucer uses Boethius for many of his examples and phrases. Boccaccio raises the issue of Fortune at the end of part III in a stanza which Chaucer chooses as the inspiration for the first two stanzas of book IV.

> Ma poco tempo durò cotal bene,
> mercé della Fortuna invidiosa,
> che 'n questo mondo nulla fermo tene:
> ella gli volse la faccia crucciosa
> per nuovo caso, sì com'egli avviene
> e sottosopra volgendo ogni cosa
> Criseida gli tolse e' dolci frutti,
> e' lieti amor rivolse in tristi lutti. (III.94)

[But such good lasted only a short time, thanks to envious Fortune, which holds nothing firm in this world: she turned her vexatious face towards him, by a new chance, as it happens, and turning everything upside down, took Criseida from him and turned sweet fruits and joyous love to sad mourning.]

Envious Fortune ensures that good cannot last long. She turns her vexatious side to Troiolo and, turning everything upside down, takes away the sweet fruits and turns joyous love to sad mourning.

Chaucer's expansion of the passage draws on Boethius's *Consolation of Philosophy* II, prosa 1, and metrum 1.

> But al to litel, weylaway the whyle,
> Lasteth swich ioie, y-thonked be fortune,
> That semeth trewest whan she wol bygyle,
> And kan to fooles so hire song entune,
> That she hem hent and blent, traitour comune;
> And whan a wight is from hire whiel y-throwe,
> Than laugheth she and maketh hym the mowe.
>
> ffrom Troilus she gan hire brighte face
> Awey to writhe and tok of hym non heede,
> But caste hym clene out of his lady grace,
> And on hire whiel she sette vp Diomede;
> ffor which right now myn herte gynneth blede. (IV.1–12)

At the end of part IV, Criseida urges Troiolo to defy Fortune and overcome her with noble courage.

> Dunque prendi conforto, e la Fortuna
> col dare il dosso vinci e rendi stanca;
> non soggiacette a lei giammai nessuna
> persona in cui trovasse anima franca. (IV.154)
>
> [Therefore take comfort and conquer Fortune by turning your back on
> her and tiring her out. No person in whom a noble soul might be found
> should ever be subject to her.]

Chaucer amplifies this passage by adding a proverb and emphasizing the reference to Fortune.

> Thus maketh vertue of necessite
> By pacience, and thynk that lord is he
> Of fortune ay that naught wole of hire recche;
> And she ne daunteth no wight but a wrecche. (IV.1586–89)

Earlier in part IV, Troiolo had used an argument from Boethius II, prosa 4, which Dante had also used (*Inferno* V. 121–23) to reject Pandaro's suggestion that he get over his sorrow and find another lover.

> Ch'ogni dolor trapassa quell che ria
> fortuna adduce a chi stato è felice. (IV.56)

[The sorrow which fortune brings to the person who has been happy is greater than any other.]

When Chaucer translates this in book IV, he makes it an even stronger denunciation because he had given the same idea to Pandarus earlier, in book III, when he had been warning Troilus to be careful of his newly won success.

> ffor of fortunes sharpe aduersitee
> The worste kynde of infortune is this,
> A man to han ben in prosperitee,
> And it remembren whan it passed is. (III.1625–28)

> Whi gabbestow, that seydest vn-to me,
> That hym is wors that is fro wele ythrowe,
> Than he hadde erst noon of that wele y-knowe? (IV.481–83)

Presumably Chaucer's first use of this maxim was partly prompted by his reading of part IV of *Il Filostrato*. Perhaps he wanted to give it additional emphasis by mentioning it twice, or perhaps he decided in translating part IV to take advantage of the addition he had already made to book III. In either case, Chaucer expanded and further emphasized something which Boccaccio had already included in his story. Chaucer had opened his book III with a hymn to love translated from a hymn to love, based on Boethius, *On the Consolation of Philosophy*, II, metrum 8, which Boccaccio had written for Troiolo when speaking to Pandaro after his first night of love with Criseida (III.74–77). At the equivalent point in his narrative, Chaucer writes Troilus a hymn to love based on the same section of Boethius (III.1744–71), so again Chaucer's use of Boethian words to praise love was suggested by Boccaccio and then redoubled by Chaucer.[20] Chaucer goes on to make many further comments on Fortune and the changeability of the world, with frequent references to the text of Boethius, which he knew extremely well.[21]

Chaucer's Development and Adaptation of Boccaccio

In the seventh type of change, Chaucer took much further the process of generalizing the love affair of Troiolo and Criseida that Boccaccio began. We have already seen, at the end of part III, that Boccaccio says that Fortune kept nothing in the world stable and turned everything upside down.

> che 'n questo mondo nulla fermo tene:
> . . . e sottosopra volgendo ogni cosa . . . (94).

> [which holds nothing firm in this world . . . and turning everything upside down . . .]

In part VIII, Boccaccio starts to think further about the implications of this narrative for our view of human nature. He has Troiolo lament his fate and decry the injustice of the world. If Criseida is untrue, how can any oath ever be trusted?

> Chi crederà omai a nessun giuro,
> chi ad amor, chi a femmina omai,
> ben riguardando il tuo falso spergiuro? (13)

> [Who will again believe in any oath, in love, or in any woman when he thinks of your false lies?]

Finally, Boccaccio draws lessons from the story for young men, which Chaucer will draw on.

> O giovinetti, ne' quai con l'etate
> surgendo vien l'amoroso disio,
> per Dio vi priego che voi raffreniate
> i pronti passi all'appetito rio. (VIII.29)

> [O young men, in whom the desire for love rises with your age, by God I pray you to restrain the easy steps to evil appetites.]

Where Boccaccio's lesson here is directed to young men and advises them to avoid the fickleness of some young women, Chaucer generalizes the teaching further to address young women as well.

> O ȝonge, fresshe folkes, he or she,
> In which that loue vp groweth with ȝoure age,
> Repeyreth hom fro worldly vanyte,
> And of ȝoure herte vp casteth the visage
> To thilke god that after his ymage
> ȝow made, and thynketh al nys but a faire
> This world that passeth soone as floures faire.

And loueth hym the which that right for loue
Upon a Crois oure soules forto beye,
ffirst starf and roos and sit in heuene aboue;
ffor he nyl falsen no wight, dar I seye. (V.1835–45)

Where Boccaccio had urged young men to avoid love and lecherous appetites, Chaucer calls them back from all worldly vanity. Rather than urging them to choose a lover wisely, he commands them to devote their love to Christ, who will never betray anyone. Chaucer adds a strong reference to the central Bible narrative of the crucifixion. His decision to add a turning to divine love to the end of Boccaccio's long poem about human love might have been inspired by his reading of Boccaccio's friend Petrarch, and in particular by the last four poems of the *Canzoniere*.[22] Chaucer's greater appetite for generalizing the story from these particular lovers to any form of human happiness had also been evident in one of Criseyde's speeches in book IV.

Endeth thanne loue in wo? ȝe, or men lieth,
And alle worldly blisse as thynketh me:
The ende of blisse ay sorwe it occupieth.
And who-so troweth nat that it so be,
Lat hym vp-on me, woful wrecche, ysee. (IV.834–38)

At different key moments of the poem, Chaucer suggests to his readers that this story of love and its failure is one extreme example of the general limitation or even futility of all human happiness. In so doing, he goes much further in generalizing the import of his poem than Boccaccio did, but once again he is developing a line of thought which Boccaccio had already introduced.

Eighth, Boccaccio introduces the question of the reasons why, and the methods by which, stories are told, which becomes a central preoccupation for Chaucer, both in *Troilus and Criseyde* and in *The Canterbury Tales*. It is now clear that Boccaccio's elaborate preface addressing this poem to the Filomena who has left Naples, like his later addresses to the figure of Fiammetta, is an elaborate literary game.[23] This game foregrounds the purposes which writers have in telling stories—in this case, overtly to encourage Filomena to return to Naples and, possibly, to respond to his advances. Nor can we discount revenge as a possible motivation here since, as we have just seen, the end of the poem proposes the lesson that young men should choose their lovers carefully and that young women should be less flighty and self-satisfied. As well as raising the question of why people tell stories, Boccaccio also makes some interventions in the telling of the story. For example, in part VI, after a soliloquy in which Criseida explains the difficulties she faces but expresses her resolve nonetheless to return to Troy, Boccaccio points out that it will not be long before she changes her mind.

> Ma da sì alto e grande intendimento
> tosto la volse novella amadore.
> Or prova Diomede ogni argomento
> che el potea per entrarle nel core,
> né gli falli al suo tempo lo 'ntento,
> e 'n brieve spazio ne cacciò di fore
> Troiolo e Troia, ed ogni altro pensiero
> che 'n lei fosse di lui o falso o vero. (VI.8)

> [But a new lover soon turned her from this noble intention. Now Diomede tries every argument that he knows to enter her heart, and he does not fail in his aim this time. In a short time he chases from her Troiolo and Troy and every other thought she had of him, true or false.]

A little earlier in the same section, Boccaccio had observed that anyone seeing Criseida's bitter regret at having left Troy would have had pity on her.

> Né saria stato alcun sì dispietato
> ch 'udendo lei rammaricar dolente,
> con lei di pianger si fosse temprato. (VI.3)

> [Nor would anyone be so heartless as, on hearing her sorrowful lament, to refrain from crying with her.]

Chaucer translates both these passages:

> In al this world ther nys so cruel herte
> That hire hadde herd compleynen in hire sorwe,
> That nolde han wepen for hire peynes smerte. (V.722–24)

> But god it wot, er fully monthes two
> She was ful fer fro that entencioun;

ffor bothe Troilus and Troie town
Shal knotteles thorugh-out hire herte slide,
ffor she wol take a purpos for tabide. (V.766–70)

In general, Chaucer intrudes his own voice into the narration much more than Boccaccio did, and he quite frequently adds a verb in the first person to emphasize this, as Wallace has shown:[24]

Men seyn—I not—that she ʒaf hym hire herte. (V.1050)

Chaucer sometimes introduces a contrast between what the story or his sources tell him and what he knows or wants to tell us about the story—for example, in book I when he claims to have translated every word of Troilus's song (which turns out to be the Petrarch sonnet) rather than the general meaning ("sentence") of it, which his author Lollius has done (I.393–99). Chaucer introduces his work by telling us that he hopes to gain favor with successful lovers by telling the story of Troilus's double sorrow (I.15–52). A little later in the story, he uses the example of Troilus to advise everyone to give way to love, since love is so powerful that he can overcome any resistance (I.232–59). At the end, as we have seen, he explains that the story shows that young people should turn away from earthly vanity and concentrate on the love of God (V.1835–48). These instances are enough to show the complex games which Chaucer plays with the means of telling the story and in thinking about the purposes for which stories are told. In this aspect of his rewriting, he develops ideas which will be very important to him throughout his work, but again he does so by taking much further ideas which were already present in *Il Filostrato*.

Ninth, as is well known, Chaucer greatly expands and complicates the ending of the poem, but here again the example of Boccaccio's approach is an important prompt to Chaucer, both positively and negatively. Achilles kills Troiolo (VIII.27) fourteen stanzas before the end of poem. Boccaccio uses the remaining stanzas to moralize the story of Troiolo's love, suffering, and vain hope (in the *Cotal fine* stanza quoted earlier, VIII.28) and to warn young men against desire, lust, and the flightiness of young women (VIII.29–31). He advises readers to choose a lover wisely, to have compassion on Troiolo, and to pray that he may rest in peace and that they may love wisely and avoid being betrayed (VIII.32–33). In part IX, he addresses his poem, gives thanks for finishing it, and sends it to address his beloved in the hope that she will have compassion on him. The poem will need the support of Apollo and Love in order to achieve a good result (IX.1–8).

Chaucer's ending, which has been so well studied by E. T. Donaldson, is evidently very strongly developed from Boccaccio's.[25] It sets off, however, from moralizing the story (in words adapted from Boccaccio, as we have seen), from sending the poem into the world, and from thinking about the effect it will have on readers.[26] Where Boccaccio was content to attack the sincerity of young women, Chaucer is very keen to resist any interpretation on those lines, and instead asks pardon from his female readers, offers to write stories about virtuous women (which will become *The Legend of Good Women*, prompted by Boccaccio's *De mulieribus claris*), and points out that men are far more likely to be treacherous in love than women are (V.1772–85). He also wants to present a rather different ending for Troilus himself. First, he discreetly alters Troilus's recognition of Criseyde's betrayal (VIII.15 compared to V.1695–1701), adding the willed determination to continue loving her in spite of her betrayal, whereas Troiolo's continuing love was against his will.

> Thorugh which I se that clene out of ȝoure mynde
> Ȝe han me cast, and I ne kan nor may,
> ffor al this world, with-inne myn herte fynde
> To vnlouen ȝow a quarter of a day.
> In corsed tyme I born was, weilaway,
> That ȝow that doon me al this wo endure
> Ȝet loue I best of any creature. (V.1695–1701)

This idea sets up the very radical move of sending Troilus's spirit after his death up to the eighth sphere, from where he looks down on human follies and sees their vanity and insignificance in comparison to the full happiness in heaven (V.1807–20). This radical addition to Boccaccio's poem is itself taken from Chaucer's reading of the ending of Boccaccio's *Teseida* (XI.1–3), which in turn is based on Cicero, Dante, and Lucan. In this instance, then, Chaucer's radical and carefully planned rewriting of Boccaccio's *Il Filostrato* is itself based on Boccaccio and the Latin and Italian literary traditions on which he draws.

Tenth, while all accounts of Chaucer's rewriting of Boccaccio emphasize his great expansion of the character of Pandaro, nevertheless some of these changes seem to develop on lines suggested by Boccaccio. Chaucer loads Pandarus's speeches with proverbs, anecdotes, and generalizations, but already in Boccaccio, Pandaro was inclined to tell stories and repeat proverbs. Chaucer builds this up to overwhelming comic effect more than he invents this side of Pandarus. Chaucer's Pandarus is notable for his excessive involvement in the love affair and for taking the side of Troilus rather than his niece Criseyde. Both these characteristics would also be true of Pandaro, though not nearly to the degree to which Chaucer amplifies them. There is nothing in Boccaccio to correspond to the scene in which Pandarus helps Troilus into bed (III.1093–1125) or to his questionable embrace of Criseyde on the morning after (III.1555–82). Chaucer gives Pandarus a self-consciousness about the excessive part he has played in the love affair, and he makes Pandarus use this fact to extract a promise of good behavior from Troilus.

> And wostow whi? for shame it is to seye:
> ffor þe haue I bigonne a gamen pleye
> Which that I neuere do shal eft for other,
> Al-though he were a thousand fold my brother.
>
> That is to seye, for the am I bicomen,
> Bitwixen game and ernest, swich a meene
> As maken wommen vn-to men to comen. (III.249–55)

This passage is a direct translation from Boccaccio.

> Io son per te divenuto mezzano,
> per te gittato ho 'n terra il mio onore,
> per to ho io corrotto il petto sano
> di mia sorella. (III.6)
>
> [For you I have become a go-between, for you I have thrown my honor
> to the ground, for you I have corrupted the pure breast of my sister.]

Chaucer makes essentially the same points as Boccaccio here, though he develops the ideas at much greater length and with much stronger comic effect.

Chaucer certainly increases the comic element in the whole love affair and creates new comic scenes, but here again—and this is the eleventh aspect of *Il Filostrato* imitated by Chaucer—some of the comic action seems to be suggested by reading Boccaccio. Part of the comedy is created through character and in particular through the extreme passivity of Troilus, caused partly perhaps by his sensitivity and partly by the extremity of his fall into love. This naïveté in Troilus is already present in Boccaccio, though Chaucer certainly increases it, removing some of Troiolo's confidence and increasing his dependence on Pandarus. The development of the character of Pandarus, with his endless fund of stories and proverbs and his propensity to interfere at all points of the love affair, contributes to the comedy of character. There is also a physical aspect to the comedy, most notably when Troilus, embarrassed by having lied about being jealous in order to gain access to Criseyde's bedroom, faints. This whole episode, together with Pandarus's machinations to bring about the consummation, is added by Chaucer, but the idea of the fainting may have been suggested by reading Boccaccio. Later in part IV, when Troiolo and Criseida meet, Criseida, desperate about having to part, faints and Troiolo prepares to commit suicide, but his death speech is comically interrupted by her sigh of recovery. Chaucer's decision to double the fainting makes this second occurrence even more effective; a rich comedy is drawn from the contrast between Pandarus's and Criseyde's energetic efforts to revive him and Troilus's pose of the Stoic suicide in relation to Criseyde's supposed death. There is also a strong element of intrigue in the comedy of the poem, particularly in the elaborate interior geography that Pandarus exploits to ensure that both in Deiphebus's house (with Deiphebus and Helen in the garden beyond the bedroom, II.1695–1708) and in his own house (with the trapdoor bypassing the women in the outer room, III.741–42), anyone outside the room would assume that Criseyde had various chaperones instead of being alone with Pandarus and Troilus.

Finally, Chaucer aims to build a very different portrayal of Criseyde, but he does so largely by retaining most of the words and actions Boccaccio provided, adding to them in places and using his narrator figure to create uncertainty about how Criseyde should be viewed. Boccaccio's Criseida seems by comparison much more straightforward and easier to understand. A young woman who makes rational choices in difficult circumstances, she would prefer not to have a lover, but sees Troiolo's attractions and advantages. She feels pressured by Pandaro, but accepting that she will need to sleep with Troiolo, she makes the arrangements for their secret meetings. Criseida enjoys Troiolo's love and is devastated that they will have to part. Rejecting Troiolo's suggestion that they elope, she puts forward a plan for returning but then is very upset to realize how difficult it will be to return. By the end of part VI, however, it is very clear that she has decided to abandon Troiolo and is attracted to Diomede.

> Egli era grande e bel della persona
> giovane fresco e piacevole assai,
> e forte e fier, sì come si ragiona,
> e parlante quant'altro greco mai,
> e ad amor la natura avea prona;
> le quai cose Criseida ne' suoi guai,
> partito lui, seco venne pensando,
> d'accostarsi o fuggirsi dubitando.
>
> Questo la fer raffredar nel pensiero
> caldo ch'avea pur di voler reddire;
> queste piegaro il suo animo intero
> che 'n ver Troiolo aveva, ed il disire
> torsono indietro, e 'l tormento severo
> nuova speranza alquanto fé fuggire;
> e da queste cagion sommossa, avvenne
> che la promessa a Troiol non attenne. (VI.33–34)

[He was big and beautiful, young, fresh, and pleasing enough, and strong and proud, as men say. He spoke as well as any Greek and nature had disposed him toward love. When he had gone Criseida thought these things over in her sorrow, wondering whether to approach him or to flee from him (33). This made her cool in her thoughts the heat of her desire to return. These things turned her whole heart which was intent on Troiolo and turned back her desire, and new hope made her severe torment flee somewhat, and overcome by this cause, it happened that she did not keep her promise to Troiolo (34).]

Criseida thinks over Diomede's personal attractiveness and fine speech. This first weakens her determination to return and then provides her with a new hope, which was the reason for her failure to keep her promise. Boccaccio acknowledges Criseida's sorrow about leaving Troiolo and the future destruction of Troy, but the emphasis in this passage is on her rational choice of a more attractive alternative.

Chaucer approaches this problematic change of loyalty very differently. In his translation of the first of these stanzas, Chaucer puts more emphasis on Criseyde's loneliness and fear ("And that she was allone and hadde nede / Of frendes help," V.1026–27). He replaces the second with another visit by Diomede.

> The morwen com and, gostly forto speke,
>
> This Diomede is come vnto Criseyde;
>
> And shortly lest that ȝe my tale breke,
>
> So wel he for hym seluen spak and seyde,
>
> That alle hire sikes soore adown he leyde;
>
> And finaly, the sothe forto seyne,
>
> He refte hire of the grete of alle hire peyne. (V.1030–36)

In place of the direct access to Criseida's reasoning, Chaucer gives us euphemisms, an uncertain but longer period of time, and a more passive role for her. This stanza is followed by a long inserted passage insisting on her regret, putting the blame on the story told to him, sowing doubt about how long it all took, and asking the reader not to blame her too much (V. 1037–99). Earlier in the poem, too, Chaucer had placed on Pandarus all the responsibility for the practical arrangements for meeting, which Criseida conducts in Boccaccio. Although, as we have seen, she claims that she chose to be alone with Troilus (III.1210–11), in the inserted buildup it seems as if she has to be forced each step of the way by Pandarus. This has the effect of diminishing her responsibility for the love affair and making her more innocent and more passive, though there are other moments when she seems to consider her options rationally and to choose Troilus (II. 695–931) in a section greatly expanded from Boccaccio (II. 69–78). Many of the narrator's comments are also devoted to making it more difficult to be sure what Criseyde is thinking or deciding or how the reader should evaluate it. My suggestion is that the creation of a more complex view of Criseyde is largely a matter of adding conflicting and complicating material to what Boccaccio gives. But Chaucer does reassign one very telling speech. At the end of part IV, Troiolo praises the moral and noble qualities in Criseida that made him love her (IV.164–66). In the light of what follows, this praise can seem like irony on Boccaccio's part, or like an indication of Troiolo's poor judgment. Chaucer alters and expands this speech and transfers it to Criseyde, providing her with a moment of immense generosity and dignity just as everything is about to be taken away from her.

> ffor trusteth wel that ȝoure estat roiale,
> Ne veyn delit nor only worthinesse
> Of ȝow in werre or torney marciale,
> Ne pompe, array, nobleye or ek richesse,
> Ne made me to rewe on ȝoure destresse;
> But moral vertue grounded vp-on trouthe,
> That was the cause I first hadde on ȝow routhe.
>
> Eke gentil herte and manhod that ȝe hadde,
> And that ȝe hadde, as me thoughte, in despit
> Euery thyng that souned in-to badde,
> As rudenesse and poeplissh appetit,
> And that ȝoure resoun bridlede ȝoure delit;
> This made, abouen euery creature,
> That I was ȝoure and shal while I may dure.
>
> And this may lengthe of ȝeres naught fordo,
> Ne remuable fortune deface. (IV.1667–82)

Chaucer here gives Criseyde greater insight into the world than Troilus possesses and a sense of the idealism which he, partly through circumstances, is able to live up to while she cannot. It is an example of the sympathetic understanding of characters of all types which we often think of as typical of Chaucer, but here it derives from reassigning a speech invented by Boccaccio.

So far I have argued that many of the changes which Chaucer made to *Il Filostrato* were derived from what he learned about writing from reading Boccaccio or from features of Boccaccio's text which appealed to him or stimulated him. By translating and adapting Boccaccio, Chaucer learned how to become a great writer. In an important essay on the relationship of Chaucer to the English and European traditions, Derek Brewer acknowledges the role of Chaucer's reading in French and Italian literature, but argues that this reading was grafted on to a narrative style founded on a reading of the Middle English romances. His main evidence is a passage from *The Book of the Duchess* in which Chaucer adds to the text of Froissart, which he is translating, phrases also found in earlier English romances.[27] David Wallace extends this analysis by showing that *Troilus and Criseyde* also has oral features of Middle English romances. He provides many parallels in order to argue that "the *Filostrato* and the *Troilus* are . . . deeply innested within medieval traditions of oral performance."[28] While I would accept that Chaucer learned part of his narrative technique from English romances (and probably also from saints' lives and sermons), what interests me here is these critics' invocation of "tradition." For Brewer, "the English tradition" in this context means something like "the habits of a group of romance writers," though he also uses the word to apply to individual French and Italian works which Chaucer chose to translate. The English case here seems to be vaguer and perhaps more unconscious on Chaucer's part. For Wallace, the "traditions" shared by *Filostrato* and *Troilus* are rooted in the conditions of a social practice, the oral narration of stories, though again the vagueness of the word "tradition" seems to be useful in invoking a generalized group of fictions which are somehow present in Chaucer's (and perhaps also in his audience's) memory rather than the specific works he has chosen to imitate.

Both of these uses of the word "tradition" seem to me different from the most famous instance of the phrase in relation to Chaucer, Charles Muscatine's *Chaucer and the French Tradition* of 1957, arguably the best book on Chaucer of the mid-twentieth century.[29] Muscatine in fact describes two French traditions: one noble tradition, which he associates with romance and with the first part of *Le Roman de la Rose*, and another popular tradition, which he links with *fabliaux* (short comic tales in verse) and with Jean de Meun's continuation of the *Roman*. Muscatine's point is to discuss a good deal of Old French literature and to argue, convincingly, that Chaucer works between, and combines, these high and low styles. It seems to me that these two "traditions" are names which Muscatine has given to particular poems and sections of poems which Chaucer chose to read and imitate in his works. We cannot know if Chaucer himself regarded these two traditions as internally coherent or even distinct from each other. Some scholars have argued, for example, that the *fabliau* was an elite rather than a popular form.[30] To my mind, Muscatine's "French tradition" is a reader's tradition designed to help readers make sense of parts of Chaucer's work by connecting them to a group of French texts, some of which Chaucer had certainly read. Muscatine finds an internal coherence in these two groups of French texts which encourages Chaucerians to read them and helps them to understand differently those texts and perhaps Chaucer as well. This is a worthwhile form of criticism, but the difference in meaning also illustrates the mobility of the term "tradition," which can be applied to a wide range of possible claims about similarity and influence.

Chaucer's Adaptation to The Canterbury Tales *of What He Learned from Boccaccio*

In this section, I want to look at the longer-term effect of Chaucer's use of Boccaccio and to ask how much the great qualities of *The Canterbury Tales* can be linked to what Chaucer learned from translating and adapting *Il Filostrato*. In the first place, there is the issue of the purpose of stories and the motives and techniques of storytellers. In *Troilus and Criseyde*, this emerges through the many interventions and reflections on the nature of storytelling by the narrator, who even at times takes account of the role of the reader in rewriting any story.

> But sooth is, though I kan nat tellen al,
> As kan myn auctour of his excellence,
> ʒet haue I seyd, and god to-forn, and shal
> In euery thyng al holly his sentence;
> And if that ich, at loues reuerence,
> Haue eny word in-eched for the beste,
> Doth therwith-al right as ʒoure seluen leste.
>
> ffor myne wordes, heere and euery parte,
> I speke hem alle vnder correccioun
> Of ʒow that felyng han in loues arte,

And putte it al in ȝoure discrecioun
To encresse or maken dymynucioun
Of my langage, and that I ȝow biseche. (III.1324–36)

Chaucer here presents himself as doing his best to tell the story which he only has at second hand. He admits, however, that he may have added a word here and there to his source, out of reverence for love, and he asks his readers to amplify or abbreviate his text as seems best to them out of their superior understanding of love. In part this is one of Chaucer's elaborate denials of responsibility for the story he is telling. In another way, however, he is setting up an idea of four levels governing the relationship between his story, reality, and his audience. In the first place are the events, which are told, in the second place, by his *auctour*, who has told the story very well. In the third place, Chaucer is totally reliant on his *auctour*, whose meaning he has relayed with the addition of some words of his own. In the fourth place, the audience is asked to in effect rewrite the story as they read it, amplifying and abbreviating according to their better knowledge of love.

In *The Canterbury Tales*, this meditation on the nature of storytelling is foregrounded through the pilgrims. We see them tell stories which sometimes reflect their own character but are sometimes motivated by a desire for revenge on one of the other pilgrims. We see how certain pilgrims interpret tales they hear according to their own knowledge of the teller and understanding of the world. The reaction of the pilgrims invites the reader to understand the tales differently and also to judge the pilgrims by the tales they tell and the ways they react. At the same time, the frame story presents us with the competitive and collaborative nature of the game they are playing. Each of the pilgrims aims to win the competition, but by competing they collaborate in making the pilgrimage more enjoyable. And their motives for undertaking the pilgrimage are also divided between the religious, the sensuous, and the personal. Boccaccio's explanation of his (fictional) reasons for writing *Il Filostrato* may have contributed to Chaucer's thinking about the reasons for telling stories and the motives behind reactions to them, as may Chaucer's certain reading of *Il Filocolo* and possible reading of *The Decameron*.

Second, Chaucer's method of creating character continues to owe something to what he has learned in rewriting *Il Filostrato*. In *Troilus and Criseyde*, Chaucer had worked with the main elements of each character from Boccaccio but rethought them, adding new ideas, increasing uncertainty about judgments, and showing sympathy for characters who could expect to be reviled. He applies the same approach to his creation of character descriptions in the *General Prologue*. From estates satire, which was the major source for the *General Prologue*, one would expect the rich and worldly monk to be reviled, but Chaucer seems to appreciate him in his own terms and projects the idea that he is a likable person in the wrong job.[31]

> Ful many a deyntee hors hadde he in stable,
> And whan he rood, men myghte his brydel heere
> Gynglen in a whistlynge wynd als cleere
> And eek as loude as dooth the chapel belle
> Ther as this lord was kepere of the celle.
> The reule of Seint Maure or of Seint Beneit—
> By cause that it was old and somdel streit
> This ilke Monk leet olde thynges pace,
> And heeld after the newe world the space.
> He yaf nat of that text a pulled hen,
> That seith that hunters ben nat hooly men,
> Ne that a monk, whan he is recchelees,
> Is likned til a fissh that is waterlees—
> This is to seyn, a monk out of his cloystre.
> But thilke text heeld he nat worth an oystre;
> And I seyde his opinion was good.
> What sholde he studie and make hymselven wood,
> Upon a book in cloystre alwey to poure,
> Or swynken with his handes, and laboure,
> As Austyn bit? How shal the world be served?
> Lat Austyn have his swynk to hym reserved! (General Prologue,
>   I.168–88)[32]

Chaucer provides us with plenty of evidence for a damning view of the monk, who ignores his vows and devotes himself to a life of hunting and pleasure, but the tone of the passage is wondering and appreciative, like the sound of the jingling bell on the bridle which reminds us of the bells regulating a life of work and prayer in the monastery. The question that Chaucer asks about the point of this man devoting himself to books and study is unanswerable. Even more striking is the example of the Wife of Bath. We know that almost everything that Alison says about herself in her Prologue is taken from antifemale satire and yet the picture that emerges is of someone who turns that satire on its head and who makes her own way in the world in spite of the prejudices she faces.[33] Chaucer absorbs the intention of the source material and transforms it through the Wife of Bath's defiance and will for life.

> Thou liknest eek wommenes love to helle,
> To bareyne lond, ther water may nat dwelle.
> Thou liknest it also to wilde fyr;
> The moore it brenneth, the moore it hath desir
> To consume every thyng that brent wole be.
> Thou seyest, right as wormes shende a tree,
> Right so a wyf destroyeth hire housbonde;
> This knowe they that been to wyves bonde.
>
>   Lordynges, right thus, as ye have understonde,
> Baar I stifly myne olde housbondes on honde
> That thus they seyden in hir dronkenesse;
> And al was fals, but that I took witnesse
> On Janekyn, and on my nece also.
> O Lord! The peyne I dide hem and the wo,
> Ful giltelees, by Goddes sweete pyne!
> For as an hors I koude byte and whyne.
> I koude pleyne, and yit was in the gilt,
> Or elles often tyme hadde I been spilt. (Wife of Bath's Prologue,
>   III.371–88)

Alison records the accusations which have been made against her and then reports the measures which she took to have her revenge. Both the accusations against women and the confessions that she makes about her own behavior come from the same antifemale sources, but the situations in which she is placed and the things which men say about women justify her response. Most of her reported comments are taken from Saint Jerome's *Adversus Jovinianum*, which often refers back to sources in Proverbs, including in two cases here (lines 371 and 373).[34] The liveliness with which the Wife of Bath upholds her position makes readers admire her, even when she admits to lying and violence, which in other situations they might condemn. Chaucer encourages us to reinterpret Alison's enthusiasm in the light of her understanding of herself and her position in life.

> But—Lord Crist!—whan that it remembreth me
> Upon my yowthe, and on my jolitee,
> It tikleth me aboute myn herte roote.
> Unto this day it dooth myn herte boote
> That I have had my world as in my tyme.
> But age, allas, that al wole envenyme,
> Hath me biraft my beautee and my pith.
> Lat go. Farewel! The devel go therwith!
> The flour is goon; ther is namoore to telle;
> The bren, as I best kan, now moste I selle;
> But yet to be right myrie wol I fonde.
> Now wol I tellen of my fourthe housbonde.
>   I seye, I hadde in herte greet despit
> That he of any oother had delit.
> But he was quit, by God and by Seint Joce!
> I made hym of the same wode a croce;
> Nat of my body, in no foul manere,
> But certeinly, I made folk swich cheere
> That in his owene grece I made hym frye
> For angre, and for verray jalousye. (III.469–88)

Adapting and developing part of the speech of the Old Woman (La Vieille) from *The Romance of the Rose* (12,936–48) at the start of this passage, the Wife of Bath develops an attitude to aging which is clear-eyed and admirable.[35] The memory of her enjoyment of the world and her body when she was young fills her with joy and partly reconciles her to growing old. At the same time, she recognizes that nothing in the present or the future will be as good. More tragically, she speaks of having to make her way in the world, and specifically in the marriage market, by bargaining away her aging body now that her beauty and strength have gone. And yet, in spite of the realization that only dross remains, she will do her best to find as much enjoyment as she can. This is a joyfully worldly view of aging, indeed almost a rejection of the turn from the world to religion that we find in Petrarch for example, and it seems to transform the confession of revenge that follows.

Shortly before this extract opens, Alison has informed us that her fourth husband was a party-lover who had a mistress. Although in theory she expects that a husband should be willing to share her favors provided that he has enough sex with her (III.323–36) and we might therefore expect that the same principle would apply to her husband, in fact she is shocked and offended by her fourth husband's behavior. In response, she takes pleasure in confronting him with his own medicine. She will make him jealous (while stopping short of actually cuckolding him) as a repayment for the feeling of jealousy which he has aroused in her. Her portrayal at this point involves a comprehensive turning of tables. The double standard which men in general and her husbands in particular apply to the behavior of women will now be turned back on them. They will be required to acquiesce in their own sexual humiliation. The liveliness and forcefulness of the Wife's responses impress readers as much as their consciously unfair justice.

Chaucer's originality and insight here is driven by his use and inversion of inherited materials and traditional attitudes. Being aware of his use of these materials helps readers better understand the kind of work he has been doing. It is a good example of a way in which a discovered reader's tradition improves our understanding of Chaucer's art and its effect. At the same time, Chaucer could not have worked against cultural expectations in this way without having become critically aware of the problematic beliefs implicit in the texts he was reading. He needed to have read those texts and pondered them in order to decide how best to write against them.[36]

A third great feature of the tales is the combination of a tight comic plot with interestingly developed characters. This is also what happens in *Troilus and Criseyde*. A story which could be told in five or six sentences is enlivened by Chaucer's expansion and adaptation of the main character roles, which Boccaccio himself had already developed significantly. The best examples from *The Canterbury Tales* are furnished by the fabliau-tales, and especially by *The Miller's Tale*. We know of no other fourteenth-century English writer who composed fabliaux.[37] It was entirely Chaucer's own choice to read and use this type of material. Most fabliaux are rather low-level, plot-driven "funny stories" which play to prejudices against women, priests, and the aspirant classes. Stories about, for example, priests making love with widows on their husband's grave have a fairly limited appeal. Chaucer redeems the form by combining stories to provide satisfyingly complicated plot machines and by introducing characters who make the stories more meaningful and more affecting.[38] At the same time, his fabliaux cannot escape the problematic assumptions of the genre. It is not easy for modern readers to accept the Reeve's assurance that Malyne enjoyed John's surprising incursion into her bed seeking revenge for his humiliation by her father (Reeve's Tale, I.4236–48); it would not stretch the evidence far to call it a rape. The genre of fabliau depends on presenting quite negative stereotypes about people—for example, that everyone is only interested in sex—as norms of human behavior.

So how does Chaucer make us want to regard *The Miller's Tale* more favorably? He devotes the majority of the tale to the description of four reasonably complex and appealing characters: John, the carpenter who proves to be kind and gullible and who also makes the stereotypical fabliau mistake of marrying a wife too young for him; Alison, who is lively and inventive, though stereotypically easily seduced by the nearby young student; Nicholas, the student, who collects books and instruments and devises exceptionally complicated and fantastical schemes for committing adultery; and the rejected second suitor, Absolon, who improves himself by acquiring skills open to town boys but who is overromantic for his class and somewhat squeamish.

> A myrie child he was, so God me save.
> Wel koude he laten blood, and clippe and shave,
> And maken a chartre of lond or acquitaunce.
> In twenty manere koude he trippe and daunce
> After the scole of Oxenforde tho,
> And with his legges casten to and fro,
> And pleyen songes on a smal rubible;
> Therto he song som tyme a loud quynyble;
> And as wel koude he pleye on a giterne.

In al the toun nas brewhous ne taverne
That he ne visited with his solas,
Ther any gaylard tappestere was.
But sooth to seyn, he was somdeel squaymous
Of fartyng, and of speche daungerous . . .
This parissh clerk, this joly Absolon,
Hath in his herte swich a love-longynge
That of no wyf took he noon offrynge;
For curteisie, he seyde, he wolde noon. (I.3325–38, 3348–51)

Absolon makes himself ridiculous by aping the amatory behavior of courtiers and troubadours toward a town girl who not only is already married but already has a student, and therefore higher-class, lover, who has adopted a more direct approach. Readers enjoy getting to know these characters and exploring the wonderfully realized world they inhabit, down to the hole in the wall the cat uses to enter Nicholas's room. They also enjoy the strange imaginativeness of Nicholas's plan and the way he uses his understanding of John's character and slender biblical knowledge to persuade him to prepare for the second flood. The catastrophe of the story is very well managed as the foolish overconfidence of the successful lover is painfully branded by the vengefulness of his rival, setting in motion John's fall from the kneading trough and discovery of his humiliation. Furthermore, the characterization gives the tale a stronger system of justice than that provided by *The Knight's Tale*, to which it replies by parody of plot structure. John is humiliated for marrying a younger wife and for thinking himself so much better than his neighbors that he is willing to let them be drowned in the second flood; Nicholas is brought down to earth by the red-hot plowshare for his overconfidence in assuming that Absolon could be tricked the same way twice. Absolon is punished for his squeamishness and for aspiring to be a courtly lover by accidentally kissing the delighted Alison's arse. Alison is left happy because she acted just as fabliau conventions would expect her to—taking sex and amusement when they are offered to her.

Chaucer uses the conventions of the fabliau as he finds them, but he builds up the characters from the stereotypical roles assigned to them by the fabliau plot. His additions encourage readers to sympathize with characters, like the wronged husband and the fastidious town boy, whom the plot would normally encourage them to despise. Both are placed firmly within the communities of town and church life. Nicholas is given enough guile and Alison enough sense of fun to make them sufficiently appealing to balance readers' responses. To enjoy *The Miller's Tale* we need to accept the general logic of fabliaux (even if we have never met one before), but we are also enabled to think and sympathize in a much more inclusive way than other fabliaux permit. In comparison with the high conventions presented by *The Knight's Tale*, readers can feel that *The Miller's Tale* offers a complementary view of human nature which recognizes its physicality and the demands of surviving in a small-town economy and society. The model stories chosen and combined by Chaucer endorsed forms of humor and views of the world which he wanted to be heard, but he added to them to broaden their import and sympathy. In *Troilus and Criseyde*, too, he inherited a basic plot but developed the characters—for example, by adding material which both complicated our view of Criseyde and made her position and actions more sympathetic to us.

A fourth strong feature of *The Canterbury Tales* is Chaucer's use of a creative mismatch between language and event, which he developed from Boccaccio's use of anaphora and apostrophe in *Il Filostrato*. *The Nun's Priest's Tale* creates an immense running joke with the heroic description of the cockerel and the elaborate medical and philosophical debate on the significance of dreams between the cock and the hen, brought down to earth from time to time by reminders of their farmyard activities. The narrator joins in the fun by deliberately mistranslating Latin tags (VII.3163–66) and by combining his over-the-top apostrophe to the newly arrived fox with the opening of a philosophical discussion on predestination, which he promptly closes down.

> A col-fox, ful of sly iniquitee,
> That in the grove hadde woned yeres three,
> By heigh ymaginacioun forncast,
> The same nyght thurghout the hegges brast
> Into the yerd ther Chauntecleer the faire
> Was wont, and eek his wyves, to repaire;

And in a bed of wortes stille he lay,
Til it was passed undren of the day,
Waitynge his tyme on Chauntecleer to falle,
As gladly doon thise homycides alle
That in await liggen to mordre men.
O false mordrour, lurkynge in thy den!
O newe Scariot, newe Genylon,
False dissymulour, O Greek Synon,
That broghtest Troye al outrely to sorwe!
O Chauntecleer, acursed be that morwe
That thou into that yerd flaugh fro the bemes!
Thou were ful wel ywarned by thy dremes
That thilke day was perilous to thee;
But what that God forwoot moot nedes bee. (VII.3215–34)

Chaucer employs the same comic technique of overuse of apostrophe in *The Nun's Priest's Tale*, which he learned from adapting Boccaccio's *Il Filostrato* into *Troilus and Criseyde*. The jokes depend, first, on an enjoyment of deploying literary and scientific knowledge so inappropriately and unnecessarily as to be laughable, and second, on the gulf between the low-life activities of the farmyard—food, sex, and dung—and the over-the-top heroic language in which it is proclaimed to the audience. To compare the fox to Judas Iscariot, Ganelon (from *The Song of Roland*), and Sinon (from *Aeneid* 2) is an amusingly excessive way of denouncing his villainy. Later the Nun's Priest compares the capture of Chauntecleer to the death of Richard I and the fall of Troy (VII.3338–65). At times he lays on his trite morals so heavily that the reader imagines that the idea of moralizing a beast-fable—which is, after all, the fundamental point of the genre—is itself being mocked. Here the fox completes a long oration to Chauntecleer.

This Chauntecleer his wynges gan to bete,
As man that koude his traysoun nat espie,
So was he ravysshed with his flaterie.
    Allas, ye lordes, many a fals flatour
Is in youre courtes, and many a losengeour,
That plesen yow wel moore, by my feith,
Than he that soothfastnesse unto yow seith.

Redeth Ecclesiaste of flaterye;

Beth war, ye lordes, of hir trecherye. (VII.3322–30)

As he turns his moralizing advice to the readers ("ye lordes"),the Nun's Priest reminds them of the dangers of flattery, which the tale illustrates, and of the biblical texts where they can seek further instruction on this theme. The reader is expected to enjoy the mixing of styles and to accept a courtly and learned version of Chauntecleer and Pertelote alongside the farmyard animals. As the fox runs off with Chauntecleer in his mouth, the extravagant rhetorical lament leads into a return to the everyday world with a chase of all the people and animals of the village, which is compared to the peasants' revolt. Chauntecleer finds the words to trick the fox into opening his mouth, and after both animals give their moralization of their mistakes, the Nun's Priest draws his conclusions, which turn out to be remarkably similar to the ones he has apparently mocked (VII.3436–43).

In *The Merchant's Tale*, Chaucer presents May as a person who might have good reason to take a lover, even beyond the fabliau expectation that any young woman married to an older man will do so. Chaucer makes very clear to the reader both the entirely superficial way in which Januarie sets about choosing his wife and the extraordinary self-deception with which he endows her with the idealized qualities of a romance heroine (IV.1577–1604). But Chaucer also takes considerable trouble to make May's lover Damyan seem contemptible (going as low to Januarie as a dog for a bone, for example, IV.2009–14) and to dress her adultery up in the language of romance.

"Certeyn," thoghte she, "whom that this thyng displese

I rekke noght, for heere I hym assure

To love hym best of any creature,

Though he namoore hadde than his sherte."

Lo, pitee renneth soone in gentil herte!

    Heere may ye se how excellent franchise

In wommen is, whan they hem narwe avyse.

Som tyrant is, as ther be many oon,

That hath an herte as hard as any stoon,

Which wolde han lat hym sterven in the place

Wel rather than han graunted hym hire grace;
And hem rejoysen in hire crueel pryde,
And rekke nat to been an homycide.
    This gentil May, fulfilled of pitee,
Right of hire hand a lettre made she,
In which she graunteth hym hire verray grace.
Ther lakketh noght, oonly but day and place,
Wher that she myghte unto his lust suffise,
For it shal be right as he wole devyse. (IV.1982–2000)

The vast gulf between May's actions and the inappropriate romance language ("gentil," "franchise," "pitee," and so on) in which they are couched serves as a bitter satire on the language of romance. But this gap also has the effect of making May's actions seem more hypocritical than they would in a pure fabliau. This is further emphasized later in the tale when May berates Januarie for not trusting her while motioning Damyan up into the pear tree, where they will shortly copulate (IV.2185–2216). Chaucer keeps the audience at an ironic distance from both Januarie and May, allowing us to sympathize a little with Januarie when he is the blind victim of the young people, and again with May when the blind distrustful Januarie insists on keeping her within touching distance all the time. There is something pitiable as well as contemptible about the image of the blind Januarie helping May up into the tree, supposedly because of her pregnant woman's obsessive desire for fruit, but in fact in order to join her lover and become pregnant. But the way the language of romance is applied so inappropriately to May's actions has the effect of damning her character and of questioning the assumptions lying behind that use of language, wherever we find it, even in *The Knight's Tale*.

A fifth characteristic of *The Canterbury Tales* which reflects lessons Chaucer learned from adapting *Il Filostrato* is the mixture of comedy and epic in *The Knight's Tale*, which is adapted and greatly shortened from Boccaccio's epic *Il Teseida*.[39] Chaucer distances the reader from all three main human characters of the poem, partly by identifying each of them with one of the pagan gods who seems to control the poem, and partly through characterization: he provides an empty role for Emily and emphasizes the pettiness of the dispute between Palamon and Arcite. At the same time, Chaucer develops a view of human existence which is both comic and tragic. Near the end of part I, readers are invited to laugh at the overamplified way in which each of the heroes sees only the disadvantages of his own position and the advantages of his cousin-rival's. Yet by the end of the poem, Palamon's words, which seemed comically overstated when he spoke them, will look like a fair summary of Arcite's experience.

> Thanne seyde he, "O crueel goddes that governe
> This world with byndyng of youre word eterne,
> And writen in the table of atthamaunt
> Youre parlement and youre eterne graunt,
> What is mankynde moore unto you holde
> Than is the sheep that rouketh in the folde?
> For slayn is man right as another beest,
> And dwelleth eek in prison and arreest,
> And hath siknesse and greet adversitee,
> And ofte tymes giltelees, pardee.
> What governance is in this prescience,
> That giltelees tormenteth innocence?" (Knight's Tale, I.1303–14)

Such a comic initial treatment of issues which come to seem very serious is also at the heart of *Troilus and Criseyde*, where we laugh at how love debilitates Troilus in the first half of the poem before realizing, in the second half, the overwhelming importance of what he has lost. Arcite puts Palamon's question in a different way at the beginning of his speech to Palamon and Emily, in which he employs anaphora to lament his sudden loss.

> Allas, the deeth! Allas, myn Emelye!
> Allas, departynge of oure compaignye!
> Allas, myn hertes queene! Allas, my wyf,
> Myn hertes lady, endere of my lyf!
> What is this world? What asketh men to have?
> Now with his love, now in his colde grave
> Allone, withouten any compaignye. (I.2773–79)

Formally, Palamon's deep question about the role of the gods in the world will be answered by Theseus at the end of the poem in the

long speech which he makes about Jupiter's foresight and his be-
nevolent and farsighted control over the limitations of human life.
Since all human life is limited, he explains, rather than being down-
cast by Arcite's early death, we should be glad that he died at the
height of his fame and should make the best of what is left by fur-
thering Emily's marriage with Palamon (I.2987–3089). But Chaucer
has also undermined this speech by placing self-contradictions
within it and by adapting the story so that the control of divine intervention belongs to the malevolent figure of Saturn.

> Why grucchen we, why have we hevynesse,
> That goode Arcite, of chivalrie flour,
> Departed is with duetee and honour
> Out of this foule prisoun of this lyf?
> Why grucchen heere his cosyn and his wyf
> Of his welfare, that loved hem so weel?
> Kan he hem thank? Nay, God woot, never a deel,
> That both his soule and eek hemself offende,
> And yet they mowe hir lustes nat amende.
>   What may I conclude of this longe serye,
> But after wo I rede us to be merye,
> And thanken Juppiter of al his grace?
> And er that we departen from this place
> I rede that we make of sorwes two
> O parfit joye, lastynge everemo. (I.3058–72)

There can hardly be one perfect joy lasting evermore in a world
which is defined by limitation and which can also be described, in
an almost Christian way, as a foul prison (3061). Readers recognize
that Theseus is making the best of a bad job, amplifying both the
relief to Arcite of leaving the world when he did and the possible joy
which Emily and Palamon might find in their marriage. Theseus's
speech is highlighted by its position at the climax of the poem, but
there have also been enough reminders of Arcite's suffering for us
to feel the justice of Palamon's earlier comments. Arcite was crushed
by his horse just as he won the tournament and lived his few remaining days in great pain, thanks to a fury sent by Saturn to ensure
that both Venus and Mars could have their promises fulfilled. There
is no evidence in the poem of the goodwill of the gods toward hu-

mans which Theseus asserts. Thus, between Theseus's kindly meant but evidently flawed explanation and Palamon's comically excessive overreaction to his circumstances in part 1, which comes to seem more justified by part 4, the end of *The Knight's Tale* leaves the reader with open questions about the nature of human life and the role of divine intervention in the world. This open ending, which could also be extended to the prospects of marriage, is highly suitable for the opening story of a collection, which the Miller will immediately answer ("quite," 3127).

We have seen that Chaucer uses some of the same literary techniques he learned from Boccaccio in *The Canterbury Tales*, most notably in his use of apostrophe for comic purposes in *The Merchant's Tale* and *The Nun's Priest's Tale* and in his more seriously emphatic use of anaphora in *The Knight's Tale* (see also I.2456–70 and 2919–62). The Pardoner uses apostrophe seriously (VI.498–504, 512, 534–40, 895–903), though such a strong emphasis on a figure which has already been rendered comic may draw attention to the artificiality of the figure. The technique Chaucer developed of repeating a motif from Boccaccio for comic effect may be replicated in his repetition of two key lines from *The Knight's Tale* ("For pitee renneth soone in gentil herte," I.1761, and *The Merchant's Tale*, IV.1986; and "Allone, withouten any compaignye," I.2779, and *The Miller's Tale*, I.3204).

In this chapter, I have tried to show that Chaucer became a great poet because of what he learned from working on Boccaccio's *Il Filostrato* and by adapting and rewriting French and Italian sources. He was heavily dependent on what he took from his reading, but he learned to adapt that reading in highly original ways. I have argued that some of the greatest achievements of *The Canterbury Tales* can be related to the techniques he learned both directly from Boccaccio and from adapting his texts. For the most part, Chaucer chose his own basic material. Like his contemporaries, he owed something to medieval philosophy and science and was impressed by French romance and the *Roman de la Rose* in particular. But he made a personal choice to investigate contemporary French and Italian literature—and in particular the work of Boccaccio, from whom he learned so much—not least as a way of absorbing aspects of Dante's overwhelming achievement into his own writings. Chaucer's choices seem freer than Petrarch's, perhaps because the significance and achievement of English poetry prior to Chaucer was less imposing. Petrarch could choose among possible models for love poetry, but he must have felt pressure to take up a position in relation to the troubadours, the *dolce stil novo*, and Dante. A thorough investigation of Chaucer's earlier work might well show that some of what Chaucer learned from Boccaccio was earlier present in his borrowing from Machaut, but an argument of this kind could not account for the extraordinary leap in Chaucer's achievement from *Troilus and Criseyde* onwards. Chaucer became a great writer because of what he learned from Boccaccio and from the process of applying and extending those lessons in *The Canterbury Tales*.

CHAPTER THREE

Renaissance Epics: Ariosto, Tasso, and Spenser

ORLANDO FURIOSO (1516, 1532), *Gerusalemme Liberata* (1581), and *The Faerie Queene* (1596) are the recognized epic masterpieces of their eras. They draw in succession on each other and on a wide range of classical and romance texts, many of them known to the first audiences of these three poems. In this chapter, I investigate the ways in which Ariosto, Tasso, and Spenser used their predecessors and the different effects they achieved from this shared heritage. Whereas in the previous chapter I focused on Chaucer's use of Boccaccio, here I examine the ways in which a series of authors used both their immediate predecessors and their sense of a long tradition of epic writing to create something new. Awareness of a shared tradition turns out to be an encouragement to do things differently. I argue that Ariosto aimed to shock and surprise his audience, drawing on their preexisting knowledge, which he assumed, of Virgil and Boiardo. Tasso reacted to Ariosto by combining a more serious and unified epic on the lines of the *Iliad* with a more emotional treatment of ancillary episodes drawn from Ariosto and Virgil. Spenser's idea of devoting each book to a hero and a virtue presents a structure which is easier to comprehend than Ariosto's, yet looser and more open to surprises than Tasso's. Reading and rewriting episodes from Ariosto and Tasso helped him present his own conflicted and complicated vision of the world. To show how Tasso and Spenser changed what they borrowed from Ariosto, I begin with an account of *Orlando Furioso*, and to avoid a very lengthy regression, I shall say less about Ariosto's use of his many sources. Instead, my discussion focuses on the approaches and the material to which Tasso and Spenser will respond: Ariosto's narrative style and his handling of the figures of Angelica, Ruggiero, and Bradamante.

Ariosto's Orlando Furioso

Ludovico Ariosto (1474–1533) wrote *Orlando Furioso* initially for his patrons in the Este court in Ferrara, where Count Matteo Boiardo (1441–1494) had also written his unfinished *Orlando Innamorato*.[1] Ariosto's work proved extraordinarily successful and popular throughout the sixteenth century: over 144 Italian editions were published before 1580, and translations into all the major European vernaculars had appeared by the end of the century. Daniel Javitch has shown that even the criticism to which the poem was subjected by Aristotelian critics later in the sixteenth century can be seen as evidence of its early classic status.[2]

The poem has an amazingly varied and complex plot, full of bizarre situations, dreadful threats, and surprising last-minute escapes. Ariosto makes inventive use of magical objects and mythical beasts. Thanks to the hippogriff, knights, magicians, and ladies travel far and wide across the globe and even to the moon. Although it takes place within a context of war, which from time to time calls the knights to their duties, love is the main motivation in all the plots, often interrupted by errands of mercy and other chivalric duties. In addition to twenty important relationships, many of the inset stories told by peasants, innkeepers, and messengers are related to love.[3] Several of the plotlines are driven by rivalries between the knights over honor, perceived insults, equipment, or jealousy. Ariosto deploys an immense cast of beautiful ladies and handsome warriors, subject to a fascinating array of conflicting motivations. It is easy to understand why readers and listeners were captivated by the stories. At the same time, as the great Italian novelist Italo Calvino (1923–1985) argues, the detached and ironic mode of narration inspired *Don Quixote* and the comic European novels which follow from it.[4]

As Pio Rajna and others have shown, Ariosto borrowed almost every story, character, and detail in his poem from his reading. He took most of all from his immediate predecessor Boiardo, who had introduced the idea of Orlando falling in love; Ariosto took it one stage further and made him mad with love. Both Ariosto and Boiardo drew on the romances on the subject of the battles of Charlemagne and his knights against the Moors, which had come to Italy from France and been taken up by the popular singers, the *cantastorie*, or *cantarini*.[5] Boiardo established three main lines of plot which Ariosto continued: the war between Charlemagne and various Moorish commanders, including the rout of the Christians and their retreat to Paris; the rivalry between the cousins Rinaldo and Orlando over the pagan princess Angelica; and the romance between the moor Ruggiero and Bradamante (Rinaldo's sister), which will lead to the founding of the Este dynasty, who are glorified in both poems. According to Brand, because of Boiardo's technique of maintaining multiple plotlines simultaneously, he had left ten or twelve actions incomplete when he abandoned the poem. Although he took up the matter of Boiardo's story rather than commencing at the point where he left off, Ariosto nevertheless completed all these actions, within his own complex narrative.[6] Following Rajna, scholars have analyzed Ariosto's use of episodes and motifs from classical and Italian literature, especially from Virgil, Ovid, Statius, Dante, Petrarch, and Boccaccio.[7] Albert Ascoli and Sergio Zatti have recently argued for an even stronger form of Ariosto's reliance on knowledge of earlier literature shared between author and audience. In their intertextual readings, Orlando, for example, is driven mad when he sees the Petrarchan writings of Angelica and Medoro in canto XXIII because he realizes that he is not in fact living in the Boiardan universe he thought he inhabited.[8] The reading I propose gives more emphasis to the changeability, shock, and surprise which Ariosto cultivates in his poem and in his readers.

Orlando Furioso exhibits immense narrative energy. The poem thrives on surprise and unexpected escapes from apparently impossible situations, but also on being made to see things which we think we already know in new and different ways. *Orlando Furioso* gives its readers (who may well have been listeners in its first diffusion) the pleasure of many lively, compelling, and surprising narratives, but also the pleasure of unexpected thought, of being asked to see an event or a person in several different ways, some of which may be opposed to their usual ways of thinking, as we shall see. In general, the poem upholds the traditional values of the warrior elite, such as bravery, loyalty, honor, self-sacrifice, and concern for the weak, but it also shows us their violence, their selfishness, and the cynicism of the powerful in promoting their own interests. Over and over again the poem does something utterly surprising with a plotline or an episode taken from its sources. Because the poem depends so much on surprise, irony, and inversion of expectations, we should not expect it to be fully consistent.

Orlando is portrayed as one of the great heroes of the Christian side, capable of extraordinary feats in battle, who is driven mad by jealousy when he realizes that the beautiful Angelica has given herself fully and finally to Medoro, in spite of what Orlando sees as his own deserts (XXIII.101–23). In the central cantos of the poem, we are presented with an Orlando who is naked, filthy, irrational, at times incapable of speech, and terrifyingly violent. The poet provides graphic descriptions of Orlando maiming or killing many men and women, animals, and trees (XXIII.129–36, XXIV.4–14, XXIX.50–73, XXX.4–15).[9] He is depicted as subhuman and as possessing superhuman strength. There is plenty here to put readers off Orlando. He seems to be the opposite of a hero; indeed, he seems scarcely human at all. The reasons for his descent into madness seem entirely inadequate to the rage of anger and destruction he unleashes. And when he emerges from madness, it is through the almost comic device of Astolfo's journey to the valley of the moon, where all the things which have been mislaid on earth come to rest, among them portions of the brains of many people who apparently continue to flourish. Astolfo is permitted to recover the portion of his own brain which lies there, together with the much larger vial containing Orlando's brain, which he transports back to earth (XXXIV.69–87). A few cantos later (XXXIX.44–58), Oliver succeeds in binding and fastening the mad Orlando. Once he has been washed to clean the filth from his naked body, and once Astolfo has used herbs to seal his mouth and force him to breathe through his nose, Orlando sniffs his brain back into his skull and immediately becomes serene, graceful, lucid, and regretful. And he goes on to win many battles for the Christians. Before we can decide how to understand this, Saint John provides Astolfo with an explanation: God punished Orlando with the loss of his wits because he misused the gifts of strength and invulnerability which God gave him. Instead of using his strength to fight the Muslim armies, he gave himself over to rivalry with Rinaldo over their love for Angelica.

The two explanations offered (jealousy and divine punishment) are not incompatible, but neither are they strongly consistent. In that they resemble the near-comic reversal of the narrator's views between cantos XXIX and XXX.[10] At the end of canto XXIX, he shocks the reader by praising Orlando's violence and wishing that the ring had not been there to preserve Angelica and even that Orlando had had the opportunity to take violent vengeance on the whole female sex (XXIX.73–74). Immediately he curses himself for what he has just said, offering it as an example of what goes wrong when someone allows anger to overcome reason. His apology to women for the outburst is then undone by his decision to blame his mistress, who has driven him mad with desire and (we assume) mistreated him (XXX.1–4). The portrayal of Orlando's madness mixes comedy and violence in ways which surprise and shock the reader. Astolfo's recovery of Orlando's brain is amusing and delightful, but the return to the naked and murderous Orlando confronts us with the violence of both the illness and its cure. Ariosto seems to want readers to experience these different sensations and to use the narrator's words to intensify different possible reactions to the story and its teller. Although he offers us the narrative resolution of Orlando recovering his wits and returning to significant action, the confusion which we have experienced as he has told us the story is only partially resolved. Through its artistic construction, the poem gives the reader a sense of the alienness and uncontrollability of some events, before moving on and leaving us only partly reassured.

Men desire and pursue Angelica. In the first few stanzas of the poem, we learn that, as in Boiardo's *Orlando Innamorato*, Orlando and Rinaldo are fighting over her, that Charlemagne has offered her

as a prize to whichever of the two kills more Saracens, and that Ferraù and Sacripante are also pursuing her. Since she is faced with this
ocean of infatuation matched by disregard for her own wishes, we
should not be surprised that Angelica's calculations lead her to take
a path of survival which employs her only power over these men,
though we may note the narrator's hostile tone.

> Ma dura e fredda più d'una colonna,
> ad averne pietà non però scende,
> come colei c'ha tutto il mondo a sdegno,
> e non le par ch'alcun sia di lei degno.
>
> Pur tra quei boschi il ritrovarsi sola
> le fa pensar di tor costui per guida;
> che chi ne l'acqua sta fin alla gola
> ben è ostinato se mercé non grida.
> Se questa occasione or se l'invola,
> non troverà mai più scorta sì fida;
> ch'a lunga prova conosciuto inante
> s'avea quel re fedel sopra ogni amante.
>
> Ma non però disegna de l'affanno
> che lo distrugge alleggierir chi l'ama,
> e ristorar d'ogni passato danno
> con quel piacer ch'ogni amator più brama:
> ma alcuna finzione, alcuno inganno
> di tenerlo in speranza ordisce e trama;
> tanto ch'a quel bisogno se ne serva,
> poi torni all'uso suo dura e proterva. (I.49–51)

[Hard, though, and cold as a stone pillar, she would not stoop to pity:
it would seem she disdained all human kind and believed that no man
was worthy of her (49). And yet, seeing herself alone in the woods, she
thought of taking him as a guide—for when the water is up to your neck
you must be very stubborn not to cry for help. If she let this opportunity
slip, she would never again find so trustworthy an escort: she already
had long experience of the king's fidelity above every lover (50). But she
had no intention of alleviating the misery which destroyed him because
of love or of healing his previous suffering with the pleasure which all
lovers desire more. But she would spin a tale, devise a trick to keep him

in hope for as long as she needed him, and then she would return to her customary hardness and arrogance (51).][11]

The narrator emphasizes her coldness and her lack of pity, but he also shows us the desperate nature of Angelica's situation. Faced with all these men pursuing her, her best chance may be a temporary and conditional alliance with Sacripante, whom she thinks she can trust. When we enter his mind a few stanzas later (I.57–58), we realize that she has miscalculated and that he plans to deprive her of the rose he so much values (I.42–44) in the immediate situation of opportunity. Luckily another knight, who soon turns out to be a woman, approaches and unhorses him. Then Rinaldo begins a fight with Sacripante and Angelica takes the opportunity to escape. Rinaldo's approach enables the narrator to inform the audience of Angelica's former hopeless love for Rinaldo and of the two fountains in the Ardennes which had subsequently made him love her and her hate him (or remind them of it, since these fountains are also in Boiardo). Although the narrator takes the male viewpoint on Angelica's coldness and cunning, he also shows us the powerful forces, social, human, and magical, arrayed against her and thereby illustrates the narrow margins in which she must exercise her wit to survive. In canto VIII, alone on a beach, she accuses Fortune of conspiring against her, unjustly depriving her of home and reputation.

> Ma che mi possi nuocere non veggio,
> più di quel che sin qui nociuto m'hai.
> Per te cacciata son del real seggio,
> dove più ritornar non spero mai:
> ho perduto l'onor, ch'è stato peggio;
> che, se ben con effetto io non peccai,
> io do però materia ch'ognun dica,
> ch'essendo vagabonda io sia impudica.
>
> Ch'aver può donna al mondo più di buono,
> a cui la castità levata sia?
> Mi nuoce, ahimè! ch'io son giovane, e sono
> tenuta bella, o sia vero o bugia.
> Già non ringrazio il ciel di questo dono;

che di qui nasce ogni ruina mia:
morto per questo fu Argalia mio frate,
che poco gli giovar l'arme incantate. (VIII.41–42)

[But I cannot see how you (Fortune) can hurt me more than you have done already. Through you I have been banished from my royal throne, where I have no hope of ever returning. I have lost my honor which is worse, because although I have committed no sin, yet I give everyone the excuse to say that because I am a wanderer, I must be a shameless woman (41). Deprive a woman of her virtue and what other benefit can she enjoy in the world? I suffer for being young and for being regarded, rightly or wrongly, as beautiful. I cannot thank heaven for this gift since it is the source of all my sorrows. It was for this reason that my brother Argalia died; his enchanted weapons did him little good (42).][12]

That she is young and considered beautiful has been a curse to her rather than a blessing because it has caused the death of her brother, the conquest of her father's kingdom, and the loss of all her possessions. Death would be a comfort to her at this point. Instead, she meets a hermit, who drugs her but is luckily too impotent to rape her, and is carried off by sailors, who need a victim to offer to the monstrous sea-serpent, the Orca (VIII.45–50, 61–67). Although Angelica stimulates the desire which motivates several of the poem's leading knights, she sees herself as essentially a victim of fortune and men's eyes, and the audience is made to understand that viewpoint.

Later in the poem, Medoro is often regarded, especially by Angelica's disappointed lovers, as a rather debased character, a pretty boy of low birth, but our first introduction to him is in a heroic role. In a passage which Ariosto imitates from the Virgilian episode of Nisus and Euryalus, the Muslim warriors Medoro and Cloridano try to recover the body of their lord Dardinello, through a night raid against the victorious Christians outside Paris (XVIII.164–XIX.16). Medoro is characterized by the purity and loyalty of his motivation: he risks death in order to fulfill the feudal duty of burying his dead lord. Unlike Virgil in *Aeneid* IX or Homer in *Iliad* 10, Ariosto frames this episode to praise the valor of the enemy fighters, the Moors. Cloridano is killed while trying to save or at least avenge his friend Medoro. Medoro is severely wounded but is still alive when Angelica comes upon him. The extent of his wounds and his persistence in wanting to bury Dardinello elicit her unaccustomed pity.

Quando Angelica vide il giovinetto
languir ferito, assai vicino a morte,
che del suo re che giacea senza tetto,
più che del proprio mal si dolea forte;
insolita pietade in mezzo al petto
si sentì entrar per disusate porte,
che le fe' il duro cor tenero e molle,
e più, quando il suo caso egli narrolle. (XIX.20)

[When Angelica saw the wounded boy languishing, near to death, grieving more for his unburied king than for his own hurt, an unaccustomed pity stole into her heart by some unused door, which made her hard heart tender and soft, the more so when he related his story to her.][13]

She fetches herbs and applies them. As she nurses him back to health, she begins to notice a deep wound in her own heart. As Medoro returns to health, she languishes in a fever described in vocabulary and images which recall Petrarch's poems.

La sua piaga più s'apre e più incrudisce,
quanto più l'altra si ristringe e salda.
Il giovine si sana: ella languisce
di nuova febbre, or agghiacciata, or calda.
Di giorno in giorno in lui beltà fiorisce:
la misera si strugge, come falda
strugger di nieve intempestiva suole,
ch'in loco aprico abbia scoperta il sole. (XIX.29)

[Her wound enlarged and festered just as his dwindled and healed. The boy grew better; she languished with a strange fever, now icy, now hot. From day to day beauty flowered in him, while the unhappy lady wasted away, just as an untimely flake of snow is usually destroyed when the sun finds it in an open place.][14]

The narrator has pre-explained this to us as Cupid's revenge for her haughtiness and disdain (XIX.18–19, 28), but what we see is a flowering of tenderness and concern. The image of the melting snow borrowed from Petrarch's sonnet 133 is especially telling. Aware of her longing and of the need to help herself, she puts aside all shame and, ardent in eye and tongue, asks him for pity, which he readily grants (XIX.30). Immediately the narrator imagines what a bitter blow it would be to those other men, Orlando, Sacripante, Agricane, and Ferraù, whose nobility, valor, and great deeds have made no impression on her, to see her in this boy's arms (XIX.31–32), but we see rather a short idyll of secluded love before they decide to return to Cathay and reclaim her kingdom. In that interval, they hang on each other's limbs and decorate the tree trunks, wells, and caves with the inscriptions and the Petrarchan song which will drive Orlando mad (XIX.35–36, XXIII.103–10). The narrator speaks of them clothing their actions in the appearance of virtue by marrying under the herdsman's roof (XIX.33–34). Although criticisms of her decision to marry a common soldier and a pagan recur, especially in relation to Rinaldo's continuing obsession with her (XLII.38–39), the story presents us with a woman who feels pity, makes her choice, acts positively and sincerely, and sees her decision through. Rather disdainfully, Ariosto leaves the remainder of her story to another poet (XXX.16–17), but readers are encouraged in different interpretations of her actions, which are reckless by contemporary social standards, but in our terms are independent and determined.

The principal hero of *Orlando Furioso* is Ruggiero, the pagan who is destined to convert to Christianity, marry Bradamante, found the Este dynasty, and die violently through treachery (III.24). Early in the poem his curiosity leads him to mount the hippogriff, who, under Atlante's command, carries him to the magic island of the enchantress Alcina. Atlante had been hoping to save his pupil Ruggiero from early death by keeping him away from Bradamante, choosing for him a long life without honor and renown (VII.43–44). In spite of the warnings of Astolfo (here transformed in Virgilian imitation into a tree, VI.29–53), Ruggiero allows himself to be imprisoned in Alcina's love and in her palace of sensual delights. The wise and good enchantress Melissa, who helps Bradamante, determines to rescue Ruggiero (VII.38–39, 42, 45–47).[15] So we are invited to see this episode both as a personal fall into sensuality for Ruggiero and as a struggle between the conflicting wills of two (or perhaps three) magicians. Ruggiero is both responsible and not responsible for his fall. By pretending to be Atlante and by allowing him to put on the ring which dispels magic and reveals truth, Melissa convinces Ruggiero that his life of pleasure with Alcina is in fact a disgusting and corrupt fraud (VII.51–80). Although readers' trust in Melissa and support of the heroic values she upholds encourages them to endorse Ruggiero's rejection of Alcina, they still have the sense of Ruggiero's relative passivity in relation to these competing magicians.

When Ruggiero returns to heroic action, he rescues Angelica by using the power of his enchanted shield to stun the Orca (X.92–110). Riding the hippogriff, he transports her to the mainland and to a shady wood of oaks where, in another echo of Ovid and Petrarch (X.113), the cry of Philomena seems to resound continually. He resolves to take advantage of her nakedness, but while he fumbles with his clothes she remembers the magic power of the ring he had given her to protect her from the effects of his shield, places it in her mouth, and disappears (X.107–9, 114–15, XI.2–7).[16] This episode is disturbing for many different reasons: first, that Ruggiero, who has been rescued from Alcina's sensual world in order to win renown and marry Bradamante, should be overcome with criminal desire so soon; second, that the narrator appears to find Ruggiero's behavior normal (XI.1–3); third, that the presentation of the episode employs comedy both in the narrator's puns on riding and steeds and in Ruggiero's problems with laces that seem to keep retying themselves (X.114–15); and fourth, that once Angelica has disappeared, Ruggiero upbraids her for ingratitude in taking the ring and failing to reward him for saving her life by allowing herself to be raped (XI.7–9). It may well be that Ariosto intends this episode to undermine all those claims which knights make about the obligation of women to reward them sexually for their chivalric services (a lesson which we could then apply to Orlando and Angelica's other admirers), but it is equally likely that he intends a sequence of surprises and shocks which reverse each other. He wants us to be shocked at Ruggiero's behavior, to be surprised at the narrator's jokes and explanations, to be relieved at Angelica's escape from danger, and to be entertained by Ruggiero's futile attempt to recover the ring. These shocks and reversals elicit the kind of pleasure in narrative which Ariosto aims at. The immediate repetition of this episode in

Orlando's killing of the Orca and saving of Olympia (XI.28–68) at least points up the wrongness of Ruggiero's behavior. Nevertheless, Ruggiero's intended rape, the apparent complicity of the narrator, and Ruggiero's neglect of his obligations to Bradamante show the hero and potentially the epic itself in a bad light.

Ariosto is interested in Ruggiero's internal conflicts, especially in balancing his chivalric obligations as a prominent Muslim warrior and vassal of Agramante against his personal promise to convert to Christianity in order to marry Bradamante (XXII.31–36). When he is summoned back by Agramante at the end of canto XXV, he reflects that, if he were to convert at that moment, he might seem to be acting out of cowardice and that the difficulties facing the Muslims increase his obligation to go to the aid of his feudal lord. He writes to Bradamante to explain that deserting Agramante now would damage his reputation so badly as to make him unworthy to become her husband, and he renews his promise of future conversion (XXV.80–91). When he is compelled to fight Rinaldo, he is so anxious not to harm Bradamante's brother that he fights feebly and has to be rescued by Melissa's trick, which Ariosto develops from the behavior in *Aeneid* 12, 222–43, of Turnus's sister, the nymph Juturna: Melissa pretends to be the pagan general Rodomonte and urges Agramante to break the truce because Ruggiero is fighting so badly (XXXIX.1–11). Dilemmas like Ruggiero's provided opportunities for complications and surprise resolutions of plotting which must also have been attractive to Ariosto.

Ruggiero's long delay in returning also allows Ariosto to write tormented soliloquies for Bradamante, who fears that Ruggiero may have betrayed her with Marfisa but knows that she will never be able to leave him (XXXII.36–44). This prepares for a series of anguished confrontations in canto XXXVI, where the disguised Bradamante challenges Ruggiero to fight. While he hesitates, fearing that it might be her and anxious not to kill his beloved, Marfisa intervenes and draws on herself Bradamante's vengeful fury (XXXVI.11–32). When Bradamante jousts against Ruggiero in a broader melee between Christians and Muslims, neither can fight effectively, he because he feels too guilty about his delay and she because she feels too sorry for her lover (XXXVI.31–39). Moved by his request to be heard, she leads him to a secluded valley, but Marfisa follows, seeking revenge for being unhorsed by Bradamante. This intrusion on their privacy makes Bradamante even more angry and even more sure that Marfisa has stolen Ruggiero's affections. Ruggiero fails in his verbal and physical attempts to separate the two ferociously fighting women, but when Marfisa attacks Ruggiero, who tries to defend himself without harming her, a voice from the tomb declares that Ruggiero and Marfisa must not fight because they are long separated siblings (XXXVI.41–59). This semidivine intervention in the quarrel eliminates Bradamante's fears (since Marfisa can no longer be her sexual rival) and enables the two heroines to become friends. Ariosto has used the absence of Ruggiero from Bradamante and the prowess of Marfisa to create a sequence of confrontations between internally divided fighters. Audiences experience unusual types of anxiety from the uncertain feelings of the participants in each situation and from the rapid sequence of different conflicts, which culminates in granting them the relief of a restoration of affection between the three knights. The effects of such narrative contortions on an audience seem more interesting to Ariosto here than exploring the psychologies of the participants or drawing lessons from their behavior, which would have been more important to other writers of epic or romance.

Ariosto's mastery of his many-threaded sequence of plots is astonishingly impressive. Anyone who reads *Orlando Furioso* experiences a feast of storytelling, enlivened with beautiful descriptions, unusual events, and an ironic narrative tone. Many of the most memorable stories are told by servants or innkeepers, sometimes as background for the exploit they must undertake or as explanation of a character's behavior, but other times simply for (often misleading) instruction or entertainment. Some of these stories introduce antifemale material of a fabliau or *Decameron* type, which effectively broadens the already hybrid form of the popular epic-romance.[17] Elsewhere Marfisa or Rinaldo or an old man makes speeches asserting the rights of women and decrying the ways in which men have wronged them (IV.63–67, XXVI.78–81, XXVIII.76–84). The narrator's introductory comments to each canto, which so often contradict each other and draw attention to the fictional nature of the whole work, could be regarded, along with these other examples, as entertainment posing as teaching.[18] Or perhaps the point is to maintain both positions together. Ariosto is a su-premely well-informed craftsman whose stories always provoke thought, but he also resists expectation and solemnity and promotes narrative and intellectual surprise. The materials and the expecta-tions which he uses are almost always traditional, but he exploits their possibilities in new and surprising ways.

Tasso's Gerusalemme Liberata

Torquato Tasso (1544–1595) entered the service of Cardinal Luigi d'Este in 1565 and moved permanently in 1567 to Ferrara, where he wrote for the Este court with, from 1575, the official title of court historiographer. He was strongly aware of, and impressed by, the popularity and success of the writings of Boiardo and Ariosto, but as he composed *Gerusalemme Liberata,* he resolved to write an epic with greater seriousness, stronger unity, and a tragic tone. He rec-ognized the usefulness of wonders and marvels, but the atmosphere of the Counter-Reformation and his own temperament inclined him toward a stronger religious emphasis. Although he adapted many incidents from Ariosto, he also intensified the emotional impact of his poem, particularly through a focus on the divided loyalties of strongly developed female characters.[19] My discussion of the poem focuses on how, by choosing to read Homer and Aristotle and adapt-ing episodes from Ariosto and Virgil—which were almost required to be his sources—Tasso achieves greater unity and seriousness in his presentation of the emotional conflicts of Erminia, Tancredi and Clorinda, and Rinaldo and Armida.

Tasso seems to have written *Gerusalemme Liberata* mainly be-tween 1565 and 1575, when he read portions of the poem (at that time named *Goffredo*) to Alfonso II d'Este, Duke of Ferrara, and his sister Lucrezia, Duchess of Urbino. Plagued by uncertainty, he cir-culated the poem to critics in Rome and was dismayed by some of their responses. Following a series of breakdowns after 1576, he was confined in an asylum from 1579. Portions of the poem appeared in print, without his authorization, from Genoa in 1579 and from Ven-ice in 1580. Faced with the publication of a complete pirated edition from Parma in 1581, Tasso was consulted on but did not proofread or authorize two editions which appeared from Ferrara in 1581.

These are the basis of the poem as we normally read it today. Freed from his imprisonment, Tasso later returned to work on the poem and produced in effect a different poem, the *Gerusalemme Conquistata*, which met many of the objections of his first critics and was published in 1593.[20]

As a young man, Tasso followed a series of lectures on Aristotle's *Poetics* delivered by Carlo Sigonio in Padua in 1561–62, which led him to write his *Discorsi dell'arte poetica* in 1562. This work, which had probably been revised in the interim, was first published in 1587.[21] Because it was first composed before Tasso embarked on the *Gerusalemme Liberata* and probably revised around the time he was composing the poem, the *Discorsi dell'arte poetica* provides us with ideas which may be helpful in reading the poem. Tasso requires that an epic poem have completeness and unity, but he also draws from Ariosto's example the need for the marvelous, for license for the imagination, and for episodes which provide variety.[22] An epic poem should combine unity with variety. It is like a little world: it can contain orders, battles, exodus from cities, duels, fires, hunger, and thirst.[23] An epic poem needs to present the excellence of warlike chivalry and deeds of courtesy, generosity, piety, and religion. It must include changes of fortune, recognition, and dolorous action.[24] An epic should mainly be written in the grand style because this style elicits wonder and admiration, which is part of the aim of the epic, but the style must also be varied according to decorum and may become lyrical when it touches lyric subjects, as in Ariosto.[25] We can see that Tasso learned how to write an epic by thinking about both the reasons for Ariosto's success and the traditional requirements of the classical epic.

Following his own precepts, Tasso chose a subject from Christian history, remote enough from his own time to allow him opportunities for invention. He based many details of his account of the capture of Jerusalem (1099) from the Muslims in the First Crusade on the *Chronicle* (1184) by William of Tyre (1130–1186). This subject maintains a link to contemporary politics and the sixteenth-century wars against the Turks that is similar to Boiardo's and Ariosto's choice of Charlemagne's battles.[26] At the same time, the choice of the siege of a city for his narrative aligns him with Homer's *Iliad*. Right from the opening stanzas, Tasso places a strong emphasis on

Goffredo as a good leader who is strongly focused on the aim of liberating Jerusalem from Muslim control and who is directly supported and chosen by God (I.7–12). At important moments in the poem, angels and saints fight alongside the Christian knights (VII.80, IX.58–65, XVIII.92–96); God provides weather which relieves or assists the Christians (XIII.75–80, XVIII.86); an angel heals Goffredo's wound (XI.72–73); Goffredo prays to God (XI.3–11, XIII.70–72, XVIII.62); and Goffredo is transfigured by God (VIII.78, 84, XX.20; compare Matthew 17:2, Mark 9:3, and Luke 9:29). The supernatural battle between good and evil surrounding the narrative is emphasized in the council in hell in canto IV and in the way in which devils and furies motivate the soldiers and magicians fighting against the Christians (IV.19–20, V.18, VIII.1–4, IX.1–3, 8, XIII.1–11). In keeping with his greater religious emphasis, Tasso generally presents Muslim knights and their religious beliefs much more negatively than Ariosto had. In canto XI, he states that the Muslim women pray to hell but that no one hears them there (29–30).

Goffredo's task is to harness the differing talents and sometimes conflicting aspirations of the Christian knights to achieve their common goal. Goffredo is consistently helped by Piero the hermit, who preached in favor of the crusade and who was in the renaissance believed to have inspired it. Tasso marks his strong emphasis on Goffredo by rewriting the conflict between Agamemnon and Achilles from Homer's *Iliad*, which was one of the main motivating factors of that plot. In canto V, Tasso provides a partial justification for Rinaldo's desertion of the army—he was insulted by Gernando and refused to be punished for killing him—whereas Achilles's refusal to fight until the Trojans reach the ships can be seen as merely petulant. Much more significant is the way in which Tasso improves Goffredo's position compared with Agamemnon's. Although Goffredo understands the importance of Rinaldo to the Christian side, his breach of army discipline in killing a fellow soldier in the course of a private quarrel about honor demands that Goffredo act against him. Where Agamemnon seems to demand Achilles's prize girl for the sake of his own offended dignity, Goffredo clearly acts with the greater good of the Christian army in mind. Later in the poem, he is willing to forgive Rinaldo and recall him to the army (XIV.12–26,

XVIII.1–3) in order to achieve success. Here, as in many of the decisions Goffredo has to take, the audience is shown his internal conflict (V.32, 36–39, 89–92, VIII.79–81, XIII.50, 70) and is generally invited to admire the resolution he makes. Even when Raimondo counsels him not to take part in the assault on the town in the dress of an ordinary soldier, the audience may at first be disposed to respect his fulfillment of his vow, even though the wound he receives shows that his decision here was wrong (XI.20–25, 54–60).

The whole poem is made to lead up to the climactic scenes of the battles for the walls of Jerusalem (XVIII–XIX) and against the Egyptian army (XX). Tasso choreographs a very *Iliad*-like sequence of individual aristeiai and fights between heroes which gives a realistic sense of the ebb and flow of battle, but he also portrays very vividly the cost of the Christian victory in suffering and horror (XVIII.105, XIX.29–31, 38, XX.50–52). This focus on the main task and its climax is strong and effective, yet nevertheless the most memorable and appealing sections of the poem concern the internal conflicts of the leading knights and especially the women. Tasso adapts motifs from Ariosto (and Virgil) to enrich the main plot, for which he has chosen Homer rather than Ariosto as the model.

We first meet the Muslim princess Erminia in canto III, where she takes on the role of Helen (*Iliad* 3) in identifying the Christian heroes for Aladino, the king of Jerusalem. Even there we are made aware of her conflict of loyalties: she longs for Tancredi to be captured so as to take revenge on him, but then reveals her true and potentially treacherous motive with the sigh which she cannot quite hold back (III.20). In canto VI, Erminia watches the duel between Tancredi and Argante. She is dismayed by the wounds Tancredi receives and longs to use her royal healing arts (an echo of Angelica in *Orlando Furioso* XIX) to cure him. She is not afraid to go over to the Christian side, but she is concerned for her reputation.

Né già d'andar fra la nemica gente
temenza avria, ché peregrina era ita,
e viste guerre e stragi avea sovente,
e scorsa dubbia e faticosa vita,
sì che per l'uso la feminea mente
sovra la sua natura è fatta ardita,

e di leggier non si conturba e pave
ad ogni imagin di terror men grave.

Ma più ch'altra cagion, dal molle seno
sgombra Amor temerario ogni paura,
e crederia fra l'ugne e fra 'l veneno
de l'africane belve andar secura;
pur se non de la vita, avere almeno
de la sua fama dée temenza e cura,
e fan dubbia contesa entro al suo core
duo potenti nemici, Onore e Amore. (VI.69–70)

[Fear had she none to go amid a race / of enemies, since she was a fugitive, / inured to seeing war's and slaughter's face, / forced in uncertainty and pain to live. / Hard use had taught her female soul to embrace / daring beyond its kind, nor did she give / easy access to fear or to dismay / when lesser shapes of terror came her way (69). But what drives, more than any other cause, / fear from her breast is dauntless Love; when he / commands she trusts among the envenomed claws / and fangs of Libyan beasts safely to fare, / except that she, though death gives her no pause, / for her good name must show some fear and care. / So now two great foes in her heart debate, / Honor and Love, her questionable state (70).][27]

The difficulties which she has already faced have made her strong and independent. Her love for Tancredi urges her to be bold, but she is subject to an internal conflict between the voices of honor (71–72) and love (73–77). She uses her friendship with Clorinda to "borrow" her armor, momentarily regretting that she has never trained in war as her friend has done (82–86); she organizes a maid and a squire to assist her, leaves the city, and sends the squire ahead to find Tancredi to tell him that she has come to heal him. Left alone, she begins to realize what she has undertaken, fears that the squire must have been captured, leaves her hiding place to ride toward the camp, is seen and taken for Clorinda, and then is pursued (102–11). Throughout this sequence, the reader follows Erminia's thoughts and emotions, her determination, her doubts, and her growing understanding of the risk she has taken in riding into an enemy camp alone. Tasso creates a situation which enables him to explore Erminia's responses to the conflicting pressures and emotions she faces. She flees through the rest of the night and wanders all the next day (VII.2–3). Waking, she finds herself in an idyllic valley among shepherds whose modest and humble manner of life protects them from the tempests which afflict the mighty. Attracted by the resigned and respectful philosophy and life-story of the shepherd, she remains there and adopts the life of a shepherdess, diverting herself (in another echo of Angelica) by carving her name and Tancredi's name on local trees (19–22), in the hope that one day he may learn of her love for him. It is a delightful sequence, and Erminia is a person whose innocent goodwill is very attractive to the reader, made more remarkable by the way Tasso has adapted motifs associated with characters from previous epics who knew and used their sexual attractiveness more than she does. She will remain in our minds until she returns to the story in the Egyptian camp in canto XIX, when she will assist the Christian spy Vafrin, discover the mortally wounded Tancredi, and bring him back to life and health.

Unfortunately for Erminia, Tancredi is in love with the Muslim warrior princess Clorinda (I.45–49, III.21–28). Their story reaches its climax in canto XII, perhaps the most moving section of the poem and arguably the greatest of all epic night raids.[28] Feeling outshone by the deeds of Argante and Solimano on the first day of the defense of Jerusalem, Clorinda offers, and is permitted to launch, a night attack on the siege engines, which had played such a successful part in the attack. As she disguises herself and waits for the right moment to sally from the city, her Muslim servant Arsete tells her the story of her birth and upbringing. Her mother had been queen of the Christian kingdom of Ethiopia but secretly sent her daughter away because she was mysteriously born white-skinned. After miraculous escapes from a tigress and a dangerously flooded river, Arsete brought her to his home in Egypt and educated her as a Muslim, despite her mother's wishes and the warnings of a protecting angel (XII.20–38). The previous dawn the angel had appeared to him again and demanded that he carry out his promised duty of having her baptized. Although she has had similar dreams herself, Clorinda resolves to maintain her feudal duty and carry out the raid (39–41).

Parts of Clorinda's early life (29–36) seem to be adapted from Virgil's account of the upbringing of Camilla (*Aeneid* 11.539–86), whom Clorinda also resembles in her generally carefree attitude. The raid is a great success; she and Argante set fire to the siege engines and kill many Christians. Unlike other night raiders in epics, they are never distracted from their main purpose by greed for treasure, equipment, or slaughter. But when the time comes to return, she, like Hector in *Iliad* 22, is mistakenly shut outside the walls and pursued around part of the city by Tancredi. After a terrible fight in which they are both severely wounded, Clorinda, at the point of death, begs him to baptize her (52–66). When he opens her visor to put the water he has collected in his helmet on her head, he realizes that he has killed the one person he most wanted to save. He forces himself to speak the text and watches her joyful response.

> Non morì già, ché sue virtuti accolse
> tutte in quel punto e in guardia al cor le mise,
> e premendo il suo affanno a dar si volse
> vita con l'acqua a chi co 'l ferro uccise.
> Mentre egli il suon de' sacri detti sciolse,
> colei di gioia trasmutossi, e rise;
> e in atto di morir lieto e vivace,
> dir parea: "S'apre il cielo; io vado in pace."
>
> D'un bel pallore ha il bianco volto asperso,
> come a' gigli sarian miste viole,
> e gli occhi al cielo affisa, e in lei converso
> sembra per la pietate il cielo e 'l sole;
> e la man nuda e fredda alzando verso
> il cavaliero in vece di parole
> gli dà pegno di pace. In questa forma
> passa la bella donna, e par che dorma. (XII.68–69)

[He did not die outright, but set guards so / strong on his heart, his woe was forced beneath. / Numb to his grief, he hastened to make flow / life-giving water where his steel gave death. / He spoke the holy text. She smiled. A glow / of bliss transformed her face, while her last breath / seemed to proclaim, at life's joyful release: / "The heavens open; I depart in peace" (68). A lovely pallor overspreads her face, / like violets mixed with lilies. On the sky / she fixes her fair gaze, and from that place / the sun seems to gaze back with pitying eye. / She does not speak, but, as if to embrace / the knight, she lifts her naked, cold hand high, / giving the pledge of peace. And in this way / resting, as if in sleep, the fair maid dies (69).][29]

Tasso manages an extraordinary balance of motivations. Tancredi struggles with his wounds and his emotions to keep himself sufficiently alive to save spiritually the person whom he has just before mortally wounded with his sword. The religious words he speaks open the heavens to her and she looks toward them while reaching in gratitude to him, dying in a wonderful tableau of peace and contentment. Then Tasso brings the readers into the tormented mind of Tancredi, overwhelmed with loss and regret, longing only for death. Tasso gives Tancredi speeches of overwhelming grief and responds to them with Piero's determined but kindly consolation (75–89). The canto is crowned by Clorinda's reappearance in a dream; she assures Tancredi of her happiness in heaven and of her gratitude and love toward him in a way which recalls and draws on the dead Laura's appearances to Petrarch (91–94). Tasso's handling of the unfolding situation of both characters and of the mixture of erotic, compassionate, and religious emotions is incomparable. His reading has enabled him to create situations of internal conflict which he explores and develops in masterly fashion.

With the destruction of the siege engines, Goffredo must dispatch carpenters to the forest to obtain the wood for their replacements. Ismene the pagan magician has forestalled them by raising spirits from hell to possess the trees in a passage of amazing menace (XIII.5–11) which exploits two passages from Lucan's *Pharsalia*.[30] First carpenters and then Christian knights are driven back by nameless fears or by the appearance of a wall of fire and a horde of monsters (18–31). After three days of such attempts, and after his burial of Clorinda, Tancredi confronts the wood. He passes through the wall of fire, but when he begins to cut down a tree, it bleeds and the voice of Clorinda seems to tell him that her soul and the souls of the others who have fallen in the battle now inhabit these trees. Even though he suspects that this must be an illusion, the thought of it is so fearful that Tancredi has to flee (32–46). Confused and amazed by Tancredi's report, Goffredo fears that he will need to counter the sorcery or obtain the wood he needs from much further off (50), until Piero the hermit explains that the task of chopping down the trees has been assigned to another hand and that even now the predestined hour approaches and the chosen warrior, who is not at this point named as Rinaldo, is beginning his journey (51).

As with Achilles at Troy, the return of Rinaldo is required before Jerusalem can be captured. Providence has chosen Goffredo to lead the crusaders to victory but has also selected Rinaldo as the prime executor of his commands (XIV.13). The location and rescue of Rinaldo is organized by Piero, with the help of the venerable old man of Ascalona (with his amazing underwater palace), the lady Fortune, who sails the ship, and the knights Carlo and Ubaldo. Tasso's account of the imprisonment of Rinaldo by Armida and his rescue from her idyllic pleasure-garden is evidently based on Ariosto's account of the rescue of Ruggiero from Alcina (*Orlando Furioso*, VI–VII), but with the important difference that Armida has been partially deflected from her wider task of harming the Christian cause (IV.20) by falling in love with Rinaldo (XIV.67). But at the crucial moment of parting, as we shall see, Tasso adds the Virgilian intertext of Dido (*Aeneid* 4), which will eventually enable him to change our view of Armida and to present Rinaldo as a more complete Aeneas. After sailing across the Mediterranean and into the Atlantic, Carlo and Ubaldo find Rinaldo lying in Armida's lap and holding the mirror so that she can do her makeup.

> Con luci ella ridenti, ei con accese,
> mirano in vari oggetti un solo oggetto:
> ella del vetro a sé fa specchio, ed egli
> gli occhi di lei sereni a sé fa spegli.
>
> L'uno di servitú, l'altra d'impero
> si gloria, ella in se stessa ed egli in lei.
> "Volgi," dicea "deh volgi" il cavaliero
> "a me quegli occhi onde beata bèi,
> ché son, se tu no 'l sai, ritratto vero
> de le bellezze tue gli incendi miei;
> la forma lor, la meraviglia a pieno
> più che il cristallo tuo mostra il mio seno. (XVI.20–21)

[With laughing eyes she, he with eyes aflame, / one object both in diverse objects see. / For her the glass displays herself; for him / her limpid eyes with Love's own image brim (20). In slavery one, the other in mastery / glories, she in herself, and he in her. / "Turn," said the knight, "ah! turn," he said, "on me / those eyes that bliss on other men confer! / For though you know it not, my fires shall be / of all your beauties the true portraiture. / Their form and all their marvels in my breast / better than in your mirror lie expressed" (21).][31]

Her eyes laugh while his are on fire. As she looks at herself, he looks at her. He glories in his servitude, she in her mastery. Like a Petrarchan poet, Rinaldo begs Armida to turn her eyes to his heart, where she will find her beauty more truly reflected than in any mirror. The true portrayal of her beauty is the fire it arouses within him. After she has left for her day of magical study, leaving him confined to the pleasure-garden until she returns in the evening, the two knights confront him with what he has become. Rinaldo awakes to his shame, and repentance creeps over him (XVI.31). As Armida realizes that he is leaving and that her spells are now impotent, her experience of love changes entirely.

Corre, e non ha d'onor cura o ritegno.
Ahi! dove or sono i suoi trionfi e i vanti?
Costei d'Amor, quanto egli è grande, il regno
volse e rivolse sol co 'l cenno inanti,
e così pari al fasto ebbe lo sdegno,
ch'amò d'essere amata, odiò gli amanti;
sé gradì sola, e fuor di sé in altrui
sol qualche effetto de' begli occhi sui.

Or negletta e schernita in abbandono
rimasa, segue pur chi fugge e sprezza;
e procura adornar co' pianti il dono
rifiutato per sé di sua bellezza. (XVI.38–39)

[She runs, all honor lost, all decency. / Ah! Where are all her boasts and triumphs now? / Love's reign, however powerful he might be, / she made or unmade with nods of her brow, / her scorn so equal to her pride that she / loved to be loved, but spurned the lover's vow. / She pleased herself alone; others she knew / only as proofs of what her eyes could do (38). Cast off now, scorned, neglected, see her go / in chase of him who flees and spurns her sight, / as though intent to make her tears of woe / adorn the gift of beauty he did slight (39).][32]

Whereas before she could make love turn and turn again with a toss of her head and could disdain the lovers even as she enjoyed being loved, now she runs after the one who has forgotten and rejected her. Her eyes formerly helped her enjoy her effect on others; now they try to adorn her disdained beauty with their tears. Tasso presents the change in her experience as beautifully and sympathetically as her sexual dominance over Rinaldo. He avoids copying Ariosto's revelation of Alcina's true ugliness under her false beauty (*Orlando Furioso*, VII.72–74), instead presenting Armida's arguments to win him back (XVI.43–51) and her desperate offer to follow him as a trophy and a servant rather than be left behind.

Me fra l'altre tue spoglie il campo veda
ed a l'altre tue lodi aggiunga questa,
che la tua schernitrice abbia schernito
mostrando me sprezzata ancella a dito.

Sprezzata ancella, a chi fo più conserva
di questa chioma, or ch'a te fatta è vile?
Raccorcierolla: al titolo di serva
vuo' portamento accompagnar servile.
Te seguirò, quando l'ardor più ferva
de la battaglia, entro la turba ostile.
Animo ho bene, ho ben vigor che baste
a condurti i cavalli, a portar l'aste. (XVI.48–49)

[Make whole your triumph, let your army see / one final trophy on your glorious way. / To scorn your scorner, bid me be displayed, / pointing your finger, your despised handmaid (48). Despised handmaid, for whom shall I now save / these curls, since they are worthless in your eyes? / I'll crop them and so make the name of slave / with slavish looks conform and sympathize. / When fires of battle hottest blaze, I crave / to be with you when war or havoc cries. / I have the courage, have sufficient force / to bear your lance for you, or lead your horse (49).][33]

She imagines his return to the Christian camp as a Roman-style triumph where his glory will be enhanced because he will have out-tricked the person who aimed to trick him. She will give up her glorious long hair for the short hair of the slave and follow him into the thick of the battle. This fantasy of humiliation and assistance is the reversal of her earlier fantasy of dominance, and it entails a reversal in the strategy of beauty. Like Aeneas, Rinaldo attempts to pacify her and explains that his duty calls him back to the Christian camp. In speeches based on Dido's (*Aeneid* 4.365–87), she denounces him, rejects his good advice, and threatens revenge (XVI.57–60). Tasso here uses Virgil to rewrite Ariosto.

Rinaldo returns with Ubaldo and Carlo, first to Ascalona, where the venerable old man advises him and presents him with his new armor (his shield, like Aeneas's, prophesies the great deeds of the d'Este family; XVII.65–81; *Aeneid* 8.626–731) and Carlo presents him with Sveno's sword. Rinaldo expresses his repentance to Goffredo and is forgiven, provided that he performs great deeds for the Christians (XVIII.1–2). Piero the hermit hears his confession, absolves him, and advises him to pray on the Mount of Olives before undertaking his first task of freeing the wood from its curses (XVIII.6–10). At the mount, Rinaldo displays the same kind of contempt for the world that Goffredo had learned from his dream-vision (XVIII.13, XIV.9–11), and like Goffredo, Rinaldo seems to be transfigured (XVIII.15–17, VIII.78). This remaking of Rinaldo as Christian knight—at the start of the poem he had been interested only in fame (I.10)—reminds us of the role which providence has assigned to him in the freeing of the wood and the capture of Jerusalem (XIV.13–14, 23). At first the wood offers itself to him as a place of delight protected only by a stream over which a bridge magically appears (XVIII.17–21); later the trees are inhabited by a hundred welcoming nymphs and then by Armida herself, who appears to emerge from a myrtle tree. As she invites him to embrace her (26–33), he remembers Piero's advice to scorn beauty and flattery (10). He persists in attempting to cut down the myrtle, and she transforms into a giant with fifty swords and fifty shields. Nothing daunted, he cuts down the myrtle, which had changed into a walnut tree, and frees the wood of its curse (34–37). The curse of the wood is powerless against the man who has been freed of illusions about the world, love, and fear (38). In the concluding siege and battle, Goffredo directs the Christian onslaught (XVIII.54–56, XX.8–20) and Rinaldo takes a leading role (XVIII.72–79, 97–99, XIX.31–37,

49–50, XX.53–60, 101–3, 113–16), but the courage and strength of many knights is required for success.

When Armida meets Rinaldo in the final battle, she is appalled at how little effect either her violent hatred or her love seems to have on him (XX.66–67), but later, when he prevents her from committing suicide, offers to help her win back her kingdom, and hopes that God will give her the grace to convert to Christianity (XX.127–28, 135), her anger dissolves into love and the phrase about the handmaid returns, this time with religious as well as amatory overtones.

> Sì parla e prega, e i preghi bagna e scalda
> or di lagrime rare, or di sospiri;
> onde sì come suol nevosa falda
> dov'arda il sole o tepid'aura spiri,
> così l'ira che 'n lei parea sì salda
> solvesi e restan sol gli altri desiri.
> "Ecco l'ancilla tua; d'essa a tuo senno
> dispon," gli disse "e le fia legge il cenno." (XX.136)

> [So speaks he and so prays, and with his sighs / and precious tears warms and anoints his prayers; / and as a shower of snowflakes melts and dies / in burning sunlight or the warm spring airs, / so now her violent rage dissolves and dies, / to leave her only other passions' cares: / "Behold your handmaid," says she, "let your will / dispose of her and be her master still."][34]

His Petrarchan tears and sighs as he makes his speech dissolve her anger, just as sunshine melts snow, and she submits to his direction in words which echo the words of the Virgin Mary (Luke 1:38). The *Lettere poetiche* in which Tasso responded to his critics in the 1570s indicate that he had decided to suppress the reconciliation between Rinaldo and Armida as part of his campaign to reduce the erotic part of the poem.[35] Although that causes problems for the dynastic project of the poem—in which Rinaldo is presented as one of the forbears of the Este family (X.75–78, XVII.65–81)—the poetic impulse to revise the rejection of Dido and to revalue Armida (in comparison with Alcina) by maintaining her humanity and allowing readers to see her point of view and feelings is a generous and ambitious invention, and it is impressively executed. Reading and working against Ariosto's Alcina helps Tasso present a Christian concept of forgiveness and rescue Rinaldo's apparently misplaced love, and reading Virgil prompts him to revisit and revise Aeneas's callousness to Dido, permitting him to present Rinaldo, finally, as a man who can love and fulfill his duty.

Although historically Tasso seems to have realized the idea for his poem by using his reading of Homer and Aristotle to formulate a critique and transformation of romantic epic, in our experience of the poem it feels more as if Tasso has enriched a historical narrative and structured it with reference to Homer and with episodes and motifs from Virgil, Ariosto, Petrarch, and other Italian poets. Whereas Ariosto's multiplicity of narrative lines leaves the reader uncertain and open to surprise, Tasso's delightful episodes and questioning characterizations always seem to find a place in a weighty, clear, and unified central narrative in which readers are always sure of their bearings. He manages to integrate the inventiveness and emotion of the episodes with a strong investment in a few key characters whose roles contribute to the central narrative but are not exhausted by it. Tasso also transforms material taken from the stories of Angelica, Helen, and Dido in ways which reveal at the same time as they surprise. His astonishing gifts in the very different directions of description, prayer, oratory, and lyric glitter in service to his sustained and serious purpose. We respond both to the triumph and the horror of Goffredo's achievement, and to Tasso's presentation of the characters, and especially the anguish, of Erminia, Clorinda, Tancredi, Armida, and Rinaldo. *Gerusalemme Liberata* portrays both the harsh obligations of duty and the simultaneously harrowing and growth-promoting experiences of emotion. Tasso's critical reading of Homer, Virgil, and Ariosto helps him write a work which is both profoundly Catholic in its teaching and open to understanding a wide range of human feelings and experiences.

Spenser's The Faerie Queene

Edmund Spenser (?1552–1599) constructed *The Faerie Queene* out of his reading of Ariosto and Tasso, Arthurian romance, the Bible, Chaucer, Homer, Virgil, Ovid, and many other classical and modern writers. His conception of the task of writing a heroic poem in English encouraged him to read, and where appropriate incorporate material from, the major epics and romances available to him. Because so many models were available, no one of them was strictly obligatory, in the way that Ariosto and Virgil were obligatory for Tasso. Yet from the start, the narrative structure of the poem reveals a strong reliance on, and adaptation of, Ariosto. At the time he began the poem, Spenser could not have had access to *Gerusalemme Liberata*, but soon after he read it he must have realized that the desire to outdo Tasso would provide him with a particularly strong stimulus. In the "Letter to Ralegh" (1590), which is a preface to the poem, he mentions Ariosto and Tasso alongside Homer and Virgil as the four historical poets who had created exemplary figures and whose approach he was going to follow.[36] We learn from Gabriel Harvey's reply, published in 1580, when Spenser had already written parts of the poem, that Spenser had written to Harvey of emulating and hoping to overgo Ariosto.[37] He used what he read in Ariosto and Tasso, but he did something different with it. Besides writing the kind of exemplary poem which he took the epic to be, he added other aims: to provide a comprehensive moral education suitable for a nobleman, to write an encyclopedia of English religious culture, and to tell a mythical national history focused both on the legendary British hero King Arthur and on Queen Elizabeth I.

From Ariosto, Spenser took over the principle of interlaced narratives and the location of a deserted woodland in which wandering knights encounter monsters, castles, caves, and gardens, which Ariosto had developed from medieval romances.[38] He also borrows magical objects—such as Arthur's shield (I.7.33–36), which is very similar to the shield which Atlante passes to Ruggiero—and individual episodes.[39] For example, Spenser takes the story of Phedon (II.4.17–36), which will later form the main plot of Shakespeare's *Much Ado about Nothing*, from Ariosto's story of Ariodante and Ginevra.[40] The risqué story of Fiordiligi falling in love with Bradamante (which in Ariosto is exploited by her brother Riciardetto, who presents himself to Fiordispina as a Bradamante who has miraculously become male) seems to underlie the response of Malecasta to Britomart (III.1.45–67).[41] Ariosto's inclusion of misogynistic and scurrilous episodes and inset narratives in his romance epic may have encouraged Spenser to follow suit—for example, in the story of the Squire of Dames (III.7.53–61) and the episode of Hellenore (III.9.26–10.20, III.10.44–53).

Spenser also seems to respond to some of Tasso's criticisms of Ariosto, and in particular to Tasso's idea of the epic as a little world combining variety with unity. Like Ariosto, Spenser tells multiple narratives, often interlacing them, especially in books III and IV, but Spenser's multiple heroes and narratives are easier to follow and to keep apart than Ariosto's because he divides his poem into books, each generally dominated by one main hero. Most of the books tell the almost complete story of a single hero who represents a particular virtue. Books III and IV are the most similar to Ariosto, but even they involve four main narratives which are essentially all complete by the end of the book (Britomart, Scudamour and Amoret, Marinell and Florimell, and Belphoebe and Timias), with the allowance that Britomart must also be involved in the story of her lover Artegall in book V. Local unity is provided by telling the story of the hero of each book and describing allegorical locations related to the nature of that virtue (such as the Houses of Pride and Holiness and the Cave of Despair in book I). Unity over the whole poem is promoted by the idea that the educated nobleman must learn all these virtues, by the presence of Prince Arthur assisting the hero in each book, and by the notional frame of the feasts at the Faerie Queene's court; this frame sets each narrative in motion and will end only with the final feast. Arthur's vision of the Faerie Queene (I.9.13–16) hints that this final feast may have been intended to include their marriage, which would have brought many of the strands of the poem together. This is a much weaker overall narrative unity than Tasso achieves in *Gerusalemme Liberata*, but it allows for greater variety and surprise while maintaining a strong thematic focus for each book and remaining much easier to remember and comprehend as a whole than *Orlando Furioso*.

To understand the ways in which Spenser used and transformed what he took from the Italian epics we must look in more detail at some episodes inspired directly by Ariosto and Tasso. His reading often prompted Spenser to reconsideration, to complication of ideas, and to wider applications. His account of the chaste Belphoebe's cure of the wounds of Arthur's squire Timias and his falling in love with her (III.5.27–51) owes a surprising amount to Ariosto's description of the curative powers of a very different heroine, Angelica, discussed earlier.[42] Timias had been severely wounded as he defeated three brothers in the forest (III.5.12–26). Belphoebe follows his trail of blood (which she thinks belongs to an animal she has wounded), finds him, and is amazed.

> Saw neuer liuing eie more heauy sight,
> That could haue made a rocke of stone to rew,
> Or riue in twaine: which when that Lady bright
> Besides all hope with melting eies did vew,
> All suddeinly abasht shee chaunged hew,
> And with sterne horror backward gan to start:
> But when shee better him beheld, shee grew
> Full of soft passion and vnwonted smart:
> The point of pitty perced through her tender hart. (III.5.30)

Like Angelica, Belphoebe feels an unexpected pity at the sight of the wounded knight. Like her, she rushes into the forest to find herbs which will staunch his bleeding and help him recover strength (32–33). As in Ariosto, the cure takes place in a delightful pastoral landscape. Unlike Ariosto, there is no moralizing sense of Cupid taking revenge on Belphoebe for her disdain of lovers. And also unlike Ariosto, as the cure develops it is Timias, not Belphoebe, who is exposed to the paradox of curing one wound only to fall into a more serious one.

> Daily she dressed him, and did the best
> His grieuous hurt to guarish, that she might,
> That shortly she his dolour hath redrest,
> And his foule sore reduced to faire plight:
> It she reduced, but himselfe destroyed quight.
>
> O foolish Physick, and vnfruitfull paine,
> That heales vp one and makes another wound:
> She his hurt thigh to him recurd againe,
> But hurt his hart, the which before was sound,
> Through an vnwary dart, which did rebownd
> From her faire eyes and gratious countenaunce.
> What bootes it him from death to be vnbownd,

To be captiued in endlesse duraunce
Of sorrow and despeyre without aleggeaunce?

Still as his wound did gather, and grow hole,
So still his hart woxe sore, and health decayd:
Madnesse to saue a part, and lose the whole. (III.5.41–43)

When Angelica notices her festering wound of love, she takes action to cure herself, leaving Ariosto to lament the lack of success of her nobler pursuers (XIX.27–33); in comparison, Timias is more timid and Belphoebe more determined in her refusal of love. Spenser confirms the contrast by making a different use of the rose of virginity theme which Ariosto had introduced again at this point (III.5.51–54; compare *Orlando Furioso*, XIX.33 and I.42–43). Where Ariosto had praised the rose of virginity as a prize for the man who takes it, Spenser treats its cultivation as a guarantee of virtue, exemplified by Belphoebe's "perfect loue and spotlesse fame" (III.5.54.3). Timias's thigh wound evokes Adonis, whom we will meet in the next canto. The cause of the wound is allegorically suggested to be lust of the flesh, lust of the eyes, and pride of life ("the three temptations").[43] At the same time, the poet has taken care to show us in stanza 30 that Belphoebe is in fact moved by the sight of Timias, so that the contrast is not absolute, and in fact the recollection of Angelica may help prepare us for Belphoebe's jealous reaction to Timias's apparent interest in her sister Amoret at IV.7.35–36. Spenser uses Ariosto here for ideas and for contrast but also to plant ideas and expectations in the intertextual reader's head. The preference for implication over direct assertion is acute here, since Belphoebe is the image of Queen Elizabeth in her private person and the episode alludes to the period in which Ralegh fell out of favor with the queen.

From Tasso, Spenser takes ideas, phrases, stanzas, and suggestions for episodes.[44] His seriousness of tone resembles Tasso more than Ariosto. Sir Calidore's arrival among the shepherds in book VI owes a good deal to Erminia's welcome from the shepherds in *Gerusalemme Liberata*, canto VII, though with the important difference that whereas Erminia is fleeing from armed pursuit and apparently insurmountable problems, Calidore chooses to remain among the shepherds and neglect his quest because he has seen Pastorella and wants to attract her attention (VI.9.7–12). When Erminia asks the old shepherd how he and his flock can live peacefully in the midst of war, he replies that they are safe because of their humility and their low estate, whereas the lightning strikes the high peaks. His simple food and clothing and the water from the brook are precious to him because his family's modest wishes and needs enable them to live contentedly (VII.8–11). Sir Calidore and Spenser's shepherd Meliboe use similar arguments but amplify them a little.

> How much (sayd he) more happie is the state,
> In which ye father here doe dwell at ease,
> Leading a life so free and fortunate,
> From all the tempests of these worldly seas,
> Which tosse the rest in daungerous disease?
> Where warres, and wreckes, and wicked enmitie
> Doe them afflict, which no man can appease,
> That certes I your happinesse enuie,
> And wish my lot were plast in such felicitie.
>
> Surely my sonne (then answer'd he againe)
> If happie, then it is in this intent,
> That hauing small, yet doe I not complaine
> Of want, ne wish for more it to augment,
> But doe my self, with that I haue, content;
> So taught of nature, which doth litle need
> Of forreine helpes to lifes due nourishment:
> The fields my food, my flocke my rayment breed;
> No better doe I weare, no better doe I feed. (VI.9.19–20)

By sharing the shepherd's arguments between the two speakers, Spenser can point up the contrast between Calidore's envy of the other's happiness and Meliboe's contentment with what he has got. The hint that it is his mental attitude that needs adjusting, not his station in life, underlines the idea the reader already has that Calidore may be making a mistake in neglecting his quest. Both Meliboe and Tasso's shepherd contrast their present happy state with the treacherous life of the court, where both earned their living as a gardener for a time (in Meliboe's case ten years) before leaving in disgust and returning to their native country (VI.9.24–25; *Gerusalemme Liberata*, VII.12–13). The biggest contrast between the two episodes emerges later. Whereas Erminia apparently remains with the shepherds until she reappears in the Egyptian camp in canto XIX, in Spenser's canto 10 the peaceful world of the shepherds is destroyed by the brigands who take Pastorella captive (VI.10.39–43). In Spenser the peace of the pastoral world is fragile and needs to be secured and rescued by heroic activity.

Spenser further complicates the reader's response to this episode by placing Calidore's vision on Mount Acidale within it. In a version of the earthly paradise, Calidore sees one hundred naked maidens dancing while Colin Clout plays his pipe. At the center of the dance are first the three graces and then the poet-shepherd's own beloved. This dance is presented as an image of the cosmic harmony which poetry creates and which Calidore is privileged to see, before he interrupts and unintentionally destroys it (VI.10.5–30). Such visions of harmony are fleeting. The representation of the graces enshrines courtesy and civility (VI.10.23–24) as a kind of mystery of delicacy which can be broken at any moment, even by the well-intentioned. In portraying the graces, Spenser draws on Thomas Cooper's "Dictionarium Historicum Poeticum" in his *Thesaurus linguae Romanae et Brittanicae* (London, 1565), which in turn draws on Hesiod, *Theognis*, 907–11. Spenser admires and uses Tasso, but his reading of Tasso also prompts him to express something different. Where Tasso is delighted by the pastoral interlude, Spenser is strongly attracted but deeply wary. Calidore receives a precious vision, but he neglects his task and witnesses (and in one case contributes to) the destruction of harmony and contentment.

Spenser draws on Tasso at another key moment of the poem in book I, in Redcrosse's vision of the new Jerusalem on Mount Contemplation (I.10.51–67). In canto XIV of *Gerusalemme Liberata*, God sends Goffredo a dream in which he gains a sight of heaven and is advised by the spirit of his old companion Ugone. Goffredo's first reaction is to want to enter heaven at once. Ugone reminds him of the tasks he must first complete on earth and further strengthens his resolve with a vision of the intricate workings of the heavens and the corresponding triviality of the earth. Tasso is probably drawing here on both Dante's *Paradiso* and Cicero's *Dream of Scipio* (XIV.4–19). Spenser picks up some of these ideas in the dialogue between the hermit Contemplation and Redcrosse.[45]

> Vnworthy wretch (quoth he) of so great grace,
> How dare I thinke such glory to attaine?
> These that haue it attaynd, were in like cace
> As wretched men, and liued in like paine,
> But deeds of armes must I at last be faine,
> And Ladies loue to leaue so dearely bought?
> What need of armes, where peace doth ay remaine,
> (Said he) and bitter battailes all are fought?
> As for loose loues they'are vaine, and vanish into nought.
>
> O let me not (quoth he) then turne againe
> Backe to the world, whose ioyes so fruitlesse are;
> But let me heare for aie in peace remaine,
> Or streight way on that last long voiage fare,
> That nothing may my present hope empare.
> That may not be (said he) ne maist thou yitt
> Forgoe that royall maides bequeathed care,
> Who did her cause into thy hand committ,
> Till from her cursed foe thou haue her freely quitt. (I.10.62–63)

Contemplation brings Redcrosse to understand both the insignificance of worldly concerns in relation to heaven and his obligation to fulfill his duties in the world before he can turn to the religious life. Immediately prior to this moment, he had told Redcrosse his true name and nation and his future role as Saint George, patron saint of England (60–61). In Tasso, too, the vision had come with an obligation, the reminder of Goffredo's need to recall Rinaldo before Jerusalem could be won. Again Spenser turns to a memorable passage from Tasso at a key moment of his poem and uses his own ideas to make a point which is in harmony with Tasso's but which he extends in a crucial nationalistic direction. The religious lesson remains the same—that even those who focus on reaching heaven may have earthly obligations which must first be fulfilled—but the future earthly road outlined for Redcrosse seems longer, humbler, and more easily applicable to the reader, as Spenser's project requires.

Spenser's most extended use of Tasso, the episode of the Bower of Bliss (II.12.38–84), which is based on Armida's Garden (*Gerusalemme Liberata*, XV.53–XVI.10), also draws on Homer's Circe (*Odyssey* 10) and Ariosto's account of Alcina's island (*Orlando Furioso*, VI.29–VIII.18).[46] Among the numerous borrowings from Tasso in this section, it is important to point out how closely Spenser imitates the song of Tasso's bird.

"Deh mira" egli cantò "spuntar la rosa
dal verde suo modesta e verginella,
che mezzo aperta ancora e mezzo ascosa,
quanto si mostra men, tanto è più bella.
Ecco poi nudo il sen già baldanzosa
dispiega; ecco poi langue e non par quella,
quella non par che desiata inanti
fu da mille donzelle e mille amanti.

Così trapassa al trapassar d'un giorno
de la vita mortale il fiore e 'l verde;
né perché faccia indietro april ritorno,
si rinfiora ella mai, né si rinverde.
Cogliam la rosa in su 'l mattino adorno
di questo dì, che tosto il seren perde;
cogliam d'amor la rosa: amiamo or quando
esser si puote riamato amando." (*Gerusalemme Liberata*, XVI.14–15)

The whiles some one did chaunt this louely lay;
Ah see, who so faire thing doest faine to see,
In springing flowre the image of thy day;
Ah see the Virgin Rose, how sweetly shee
Doth first peepe foorth with bashfull modestee,
That fairer seemes, the lesse ye see her may;
Lo see soone after, how more bold and free
Her bared bosome she doth broad display;
Loe see soone after, how she fades, and falls away.

So passeth, in the passing of a day,
Of mortall life the leafe, the bud, the flowre,
Ne more doth florish after first decay,
That earst was sought to decke both bed and bowre,

Of many a Lady', and many a Paramowre:
Gather therefore the Rose, whilest yet is prime,
For soone comes age, that will her pride deflowre:
Gather the Rose of loue, whilest yet is time,
Whilest louing thou mayst loued be with equall crime. (II.12.74–75)

This is as close and as good a translation as one could imagine, until the final word with which Spenser makes his moral point rather crudely. It will do both as a model for Spenser's attraction to, and ability at composing, the kind of sensual poetry which Tasso writes so well and as an emblem for his moral suspicions about it. Cutting off the delightful flow of the sensual music so abruptly also prepares us for the "rigour pitiless" (II.12.83) with which Guyon and the Palmer set about destroying the garden. Both Ariosto and Tasso had emphasized the importance of rescuing a valuable knight from the trap of sensual indulgence. In Spenser the emphasis is on imprisoning the witch Acrasia and the dangerous temptation posed by her garden of delights for all men. There can be no question for Spenser of following Tasso's lead in offering the possibility that Armida can be redeemed because she loves. And yet the destruction which Guyon undertakes (in contrast to the vanishing of Alcina's bower and Armida's destruction of her own palace) troublingly opposes his own virtue of temperance. Guyon is disturbingly like the iron man Talus of book V here. Part of the problem may be Spenser's overall aim of fashioning a gentleman. Viewed in that light, sensual indulgence must seem like something which should simply be abolished. For Tasso, on the other hand, the redemption of Armida could be something of a special case, though a special case which he decided to remove in his final version of the poem.

Readers of Spenser may seek to connect their unease at Guyon's response to the bower with the torments which Amoret undergoes in the House of Busirane and which afflict even Britomart (III.12.19–23, III.1.65, III.2.35–47). The disturbing dialectic of mastery and subservience which Tasso made explicit in the relationship of Rinaldo and Armida (and which Spenser copies at II.1.52–54) cannot be wished away with the stroke of Guyon's sword. Instead, Spenser faces up to the cruelty and selfishness implied in even the most conventional forms of love. The selfish demand for pleasure is mysteriously and secretly twisted into the heart of the stories of love and marriage which dominate book III of the *Faerie Queene*.

To explore the very difficult moment of Amoret's torment Spenser exploits a further resource, one familiar to Chaucer and to medieval writers of romance. The thirteenth-century allegorical dream-vision the *Roman de la Rose* was composed in two rather different sections by Guillaume de Lorris around 1230 and by Jean de Meun around 1275. Spenser makes three major references to the *Roman de la Rose* in books III and IV.[47]Spenser outlines six stages of love among the seekers of ease and pleasure in Castle Joyeous, the six courtiers who accompany Malecasta (Gardante, Parlante, Iocante, Basciante, Bacchante, and Noctante; III.1.39, 45). In this sequence, Britomart, even though she conquers the knights, is wounded by Gardante (III.1.65–66). Here the allegory of love is strongly associated with the corruption of Malecasta's court but is also presented as something to which even the strong and virtuous heroine Britomart may be subject. The Masque of Cupid in the House of Busyrane is introduced by Ease (III.12.4; Oiseuse in the *Roman de la Rose*), and several of the performers in the Masque (for example, Daunger, Reproch, Shame) resemble characters from the *Roman*. Again Britomart is wounded (III.12.33), and the supposition must be that this wound is related to the one she suffered at Castle Joyeous. When Scudamour tells of winning Amoret from the Temple of Venus, he relates his success in overcoming Doubt, Delay, and Daunger (IV.10.12–21), who again resemble delaying characters from the *Roman*. Since Scudamour's narrative aims to explain how Cupid took power over Amoret, the implication may be that both Britomart and Amoret have in some sense suffered at the hands of Cupid and that this is what enables Britomart's sympathetic rescue of Amoret, where Amoret's husband Scudamour fails.[48] Through rewriting episodes from Tasso and also using the *Roman de la Rose* within his own narrative, Spenser found a way to make explicit the connections between virtuous love, cruelty, and sexual experience. Reading a range of earlier writers prompted a rewriting and complication of their ideas.

From Ariosto, Spenser took a frame and certain objects and episodes, and from Tasso lines and sometimes stanzas of poetry, ideas, and episodes, as well as something of his serious religious tone. Even allowing for the incompleteness of *The Faerie Queene*, it appears that Spenser did not seek the kind of formal poetic unity that Tasso achieved. The individual episodes, whether narrative, descriptive, or didactic, make the greatest impression. Spenser leaves it to the reader to make comparisons between them and draw conclusions from the evidence which accumulates about the virtues.

Spenser's avoidance of Tasso's tight narrative unity enables him to create a greater role for the reader's work of comparison and reflection. Whereas in the earlier cantos readers following the knights are set problems in religion and ethics, from which they learn the right answers at the end of each episode, in later cantos and books that sense of certainty is attenuated as the problems of love and politics come to seem more deeply rooted in human life and history and less resolvable. Later "allegorical centres" like the Temple of Isis (V.7.2–24) and Mount Acidale (VI.10.5–31) seem to be more mysterious and less clearly didactic than the Houses of Holiness (I.10.3–68) and Alma (II.9.17–60). Spenser begins with a strong sense of the values which he must promulgate in the forest wilderness of his poem, only to discover that those values are more problematic than he thought and no longer secure in the country and the royal court he left behind. Ovidian myth and neo-Platonic philosophy help him to articulate the theory of persistence through change and through generation which, in the Garden of Adonis (III.6) and the Mutability Cantos (VII.6–7), is the strongest interpretative resource in the later books. By working out how he wants to differ from and adapt Tasso, Spenser discovers episodes and stanzas which enable him to work through the problems of human love, ethical behavior, and religious faith most troubling to him. Spenser makes his poem by appreciating and questioning the words and narratives of his predecessors and by comparing what they tell him with his own experience of the world.

In this chapter, I have tried to explore the different ways in which Ariosto, Tasso, and Spenser used their shared inheritance of epic and romance and each other's poems. The epic tradition and their chosen reading provided each author with situations and motifs which they could draw on or could choose to use differently. In all three poems one has a strong sense of inherited materials being exploited, combined, and rewritten to create a new work suited to each poet's situation and talents. Ariosto's *Orlando Furioso*, a triumph of narrative verve, is surprising, shocking, and funny. It develops the material inherited from Boiardo in new and inventive ways which sometimes reveal the strangeness and uncontrollability of the world. Readers of Ariosto are amused, amazed, and entertained. Tasso's *Gerusalemme Liberata* is more unified and serious, more deeply involved in the anguish of individual characters, but also more lyrical and more sensuous. His choice to read Homer and Aristotle alongside Virgil and Ariosto enables him to achieve a new balance between the unity of the siege epic and the emotional episodes of the romance epic. Spenser's *The Faerie Queene* aims at religious and ethical education, but it looks hard at the psychological and moral issues, refuses simple solutions, and is eventually more troubled, problematic, and unsure. Spenser pays conscious tribute to many of the authors he had read (think of his rewriting of *The Odyssey*, Virgil, and Tasso in book II, canto 12), but at key moments in the poem the choice to reuse materials from Tasso prompts him to understand his world in a more complicated way.

Reading and Community as a Support for the New in Elizabeth Gaskell's *Mary Barton*

Do they want to know why poor men, kind and sympathising as women to each other, learn to hate law and order, Queen, Lords and Commons, country-party, and corn-law leaguer, all alike—to hate the rich, in short? Then let them read Mary Barton. Do they want to know what can madden brave, honest, industrious North-country hearts, into self-imposed suicidal strikes, into conspiracy, vitriol-throwing, and midnight murder? Then let them read Mary Barton.[1]

Elizabeth Gaskell's first novel, *Mary Barton*, published in 1848, was highly original and made a huge impact on its readers.[2] The enthusiasm and the shock with which it was received is enough evidence of the novelty and force of her material. Her novel is exciting, well constructed in dramatic scenes, full of well-presented characters, and highly provocative of thoughts and emotions. The novel tells the story of John Barton's despair and his daughter Mary's growth into independent action and responsibility. Jem Wilson, an old family friend whose proposal Mary regrets having rejected, is accused of the murder of Harry Carson, the manufacturer's son, who has also approached her. When Mary realizes that her father committed the murder, she finds witnesses who can acquit Jem without incriminating John. Guilt-ridden and at the point of death, John Barton confesses the murder to Harry's father, who eventually forgives him. Mary and Jem marry and set off for a new life in Canada.

My aim in this chapter is to illustrate Elizabeth Gaskell's originality and success and show how she used her understanding of literary tradition to articulate and develop her new female point of view on the new urban poverty caused by industrialization. Her consciousness of isolation in her task led her to draw on both earlier and contemporary writers for support and motivated her to provide her successors and contemporaries with models and encouragement. Her use of earlier writers corresponded to a widespread change in thinking about the past after the French Revolution. For early nineteenth-century writers, as Peter Fritzsche asserts, the revolution emphasized the role of change in history and shattered the lines of historical continuity. The future seemed more threatening, and further violent revolutions were strongly imagined threats. Thus, as remedies against the melancholy of the present, writers had strong motives for reassembling fragments from the past and for asserting continuities.[3] As we shall see, *Mary Barton* emerged from Gaskell's wide reading, her habit of regular writing, a Unitarian sense of duty and the obligation to tell the truth, and the hope of distracting herself from the personal tragedy of her baby son Willie's death in 1845.[4] At the same time, Gaskell made tradition part of the subject matter of her novel when she showed Mary Barton throwing off the expectations about female behavior which had constrained her and when she dramatized John Carson's religious obligation to forgive John Barton.

How to Write

Elizabeth Gaskell was very well read. At Avonbank School she studied English reading and composition, arithmetic, drawing, music, French and Italian, geography, and ancient and modern history.[5]

After she left Avonbank, her father encouraged her Latin studies and gave her the poems of Gray and Cowper. She regularly read Shakespeare, Spenser, Scott, and Thomson. Her aunt's home at Knutsford, where she mostly resided as a young woman, had copies of Cervantes, Defoe, Fielding, Sterne, Smollett, Richardson, and Goldsmith.[6] In her letters of 1836, she mentions "getting up" Wordsworth, Coleridge, Crabbe, Dryden, and Pope.[7] Her letters show an easy familiarity with Italian, French, Rossini's *The Barber of Seville* in Italian, and Chaucer in Middle English, which she clearly expected her correspondents to share.[8] They frequently mention her reading of Tennyson and of contemporary novels by, for example, William Massie, Susan Ferrier, and Bulwer-Lytton.[9] She mentions frequent reading of Carlyle's *Sartor Resartus*, from which she always takes away the axiom, "Do the duty that lies nearest to thee."[10] At Avonbank, she had been encouraged to write stories and descriptions, and she probably continued to write throughout her youth, which would explain her husband's suggestion that she should embark on her novel to distract her from her overwhelming grief at her son's death.[11]

Her letters explain her approach to writing. To her friend Eliza Fox she explains in 1849 that nobody and nothing is real in *Mary Barton*, apart from the character and some of the speeches of John Barton, based on "a poor man I know." Instead, she imagines the incidents which she will describe to the point where they become real.

> I told the story according to a fancy of my own; to really SEE the scenes I tried to describe, (and they WERE as real as my own life at the time) and then to tell them as nearly as I could, as if I were speaking to a friend over the fire on a winter's night and describing real occurrences.[12]

In an 1859 letter to her daughter Marianne which sketches an answer she wants Marianne to write on her behalf to the budding novelist "Herbert Grey," she advises on an approach which must be close to her own.

> I think you must observe what is *out* of you, instead of examining what is *in* you. . . . Just read a few pages of De Foe &c—and you will see the

healthy way in which he sets *objects* not *feelings* before you. I am sure the right way is this. You are an Electric telegraph something or other.[13]

She advises Grey to study some situation which he knows very well from daily life and to construct a plot which emerges from that situation and study it hard. He can learn about this by studying how Shakespeare works up plots from early Italian tales.

> Really make this sketch of your story an object of labour & thought. Then set to & imagine yourself a spectator & auditor of every scene & event! Work hard at this till it become a reality to you,—a thing you have to recollect & describe & report fully & accurately as it struck you, in order that your reader may have it equally before him. Don't intrude yourself into your description. If you but think eagerly of your story till *you see it in action*, words, good simple strong words, will come,—just as if you saw an accident in the street that impressed you strongly you would describe it forcibly.[14]

Gaskell evidently thinks of this method as her own special technique: working up her scenes in imagination until she seems to be a witness of the actual events, and then describing these events simply and powerfully in the most natural language which comes to her. At the same time, she is happy to be able to bolster that advice with references to Defoe (on the importance of external objects) and to Shakespeare (on working up the sketch of the plot). The works of these predecessors, rather than providing her with her method, have illustrated some aspects of it in such a way as to give her confidence in setting her method out for her reader.

Gaskell was neither the first writer nor the first woman writer to tackle northern industrial topics. As Angus Easson observes, Frances Trollope in *Michael Armstrong the Factory Boy* (1839–1840) describes the workings of textile factories and the role of child labor in them, arguing that all the evils of the system would be ameliorated if the bill limiting children to ten hours' labor a day was passed. Charlotte Elizabeth's *Helen Fleetwood* (1841) presents the terrible conditions faced by child workers, describes the impact of machines, and, as Easson says, proposes as solutions religious conversion and a reversion to the rural past. Elizabeth Stone in *William Langshawe, the Cotton Lord* (1842) contrives a Walter Scott–like romance based around Manchester and makes use of the historical murder in 1831 of the young manufacturer Thomas Ashton, which was also an inspiration for Gaskell.[15]

Stone takes a more positive view of the owners than Gaskell and despises the unions. Where Stone's Wolstenholme is an innocent victim, Gaskell presents Harry Carson as immoral, bad-tempered, and arrogant. For Stone, the murder acts as a proof of the evil of the unions; for Gaskell, it is a tragedy born of the inability of two groups of men to understand the viewpoint of the other.[16] Although Gaskell does not condone the murder, she understands the grievances which lead the workers into conflict with the millowners. For a novel-reading audience, being presented with the murderer of an unarmed son of the local manufacturing elite as a tragic figure was already a considerable shock. It is hardly surprising that her publisher insisted that the novel not be titled "John Barton," after the tragic murderer, as Gaskell had originally intended.[17] Much of the provocation of the novel stems from Gaskell's hard-hitting presentation of the injustices suffered by the laborers. Sometimes these resentments are spoken by John Barton.

> If I am out of work for weeks in the bad times, and winter comes, with black frost, and keen east wind, and there is no coal for the grate, and no clothes for the bed, and the thin bones are seen through the ragged clothes, does the rich man share his plenty with me, as he ought to do, if his religion wasn't a humbug? . . . No, I tell you, it's the poor, and the poor only, as does things for the poor.[18]

The force of this passage derives partly from the accumulation of descriptive detail, which is one of Gaskell's strong points. The actions of the novel bear out John's central contention that in times of suffering the poor are helped only by other poor people and are ignored and rejected by those who have the means to do real good. At crisis points in the novel, John and Mary interrupt their own intended actions to take food to someone in need or to return a child to his home (chap. 6, pp. 58–65; chap. 16, pp. 188–89; chap. 17, p. 198; chap. 20, p. 229). These actions of solidarity are sometimes presented in the novel as forms of mutual support which belong especially to women, but at other times working-class men are seen to engage in them as well. Gaskell sees the mutual help of the poor as a real resource for improvement as well as an indictment of the behavior of the wealthy.

Personal Observation and Description

At times, and with some caution, Gaskell uses her own voice to make the point that the poor understandably resent the fact that, during periods when trade is restricted, the owners remain comfortable while the workers starve.

> Large houses are still occupied, while spinners' and weavers' cottages stand empty, because the families that once filled them are obliged to live in rooms or cellars. Carriages still roll along the streets, concerts are still crowded by subscribers, the shops for expensive luxuries still find daily customers, while the workman loiters away his unemployed time in watching these things, and thinking of the pale, uncomplaining wife at home, and the wailing children asking in vain for enough of food—of the sinking health, of the dying life, of those near and dear to him. The contrast is too great. Why should he alone suffer from bad times? (chap. 3, p. 24)

She allows that there may be times when trade is difficult, but argues that it would be easier for the workers to understand that the situation of the economy has forced them into hardship if they could see that the owners share their suffering. Then she uses concrete detail to develop the contrast between the large houses, carriages, concerts, and shopping of the owners and the destitution and starvation of their workers' families. Once she has drawn this description to a rhetorical conclusion, she imagines the worker drawing from his observations: "Why should he alone suffer from bad times?" Although she softens the point a little, allowing that a more objective view of the situation might be different, the accumulated detail has already made her stronger point. She is trying to describe the feelings of the poor. These feelings may not always be justified, and they may dissipate with the return of prosperity. She even allows that some of the workers' suffering may be attributable to a lack of foresight on their part, but she continues to insist that serious and long-suffering men feel this way and that they have not forgiven those who have caused this suffering. This argument is part of her characterization of John Barton's state of mind, but she articulates it as a widespread reaction among a whole class of earnest, enduring people. A little later she goes further in linking the ways in which the destitute workers react to what she has heard and seen in visiting their homes.

> And when I hear, as I have heard, of the sufferings and privations of the poor . . . of parents sitting in their clothes by the fireside during the whole night for seven weeks together, in order that their only bed and bedding might be reserved for the use of their large family, . . . of others being compelled to fast for days together, uncheered by any hope of better fortune, living moreover, or rather starving, in a crowded garret, or damp cellar, and gradually sinking under the pressure of want and despair into a premature grave, and when this thing has been confirmed by the evidence of their careworn looks, their excited feelings, and their desolate homes,—can I wonder that many of them in such times of misery and destitution, spoke and acted with ferocious precipitation? (chap. 8, p. 85)

With her personal knowledge of the accumulating details of the workers' suffering, she is unsurprised that some of them should speak and act desperately. She does not quite say that such a reaction is justified, but she strongly implies that almost anyone would react in that way to such provocation. When she reports in inverted commas the views expressed by the millowners who are preparing to meet the workers, she allows herself a bracketed intervention to point out the inconsistency of blaming the workers for behaving cruelly.

> "If it were only for that, I'll stand out against them, even if it is the cause of my ruin."
>
> "Ay, I for one won't yield one farthing to the cruel brutes, they're more like wild beasts than human beings."
>
> (Well, who might have made them different?) (chap. 16, p. 182)

In that local moment, her comment attacks the way the owners talk about their employees, but the broader implication is that the cruelty of the owners and their failure to educate their workers makes them responsible for the behavior of the men.

Description is one of the key skills of narrative art and one which Gaskell executes and deploys very effectively. Though some of Gaskell's readers would have come across descriptions of working-class housing in government blue books, newspapers, and pamphlets, her grasp of the domestic detail of the street and the cellar where John Barton and Wilson visit the Davenports brings the issue home to novel-readers in a particularly powerful way.[19]

> As they passed, women from their doors tossed household slops of every description into the gutter; they ran into the next pool, which overflowed and stagnated. Heaps of ashes were the stepping-stones, on which the passer-by, who cared in the least for cleanliness, took care not to put his foot. Our friends were not dainty, but even they picked their way, till they got to some steps leading down to a small area, where a person standing would have his head about one foot below the level of the street, and might at the same time, without the least motion of his body, touch the window of the cellar and the damp muddy wall right opposite. You went down one step even from the foul area into the cellar in which a family of human beings lived. It was very dark inside. The window-panes, many of them, were broken and stuffed with rags, which was reason enough for the dusky light that pervaded the place even at mid-day. After the account I have given of the state of the street, no one can be surprised that on going into the cellar inhabited by Davenport, the smell was so foetid as almost to knock the two men down. Quickly recovering themselves, as those inured to such things do, they began to penetrate the thick darkness of the place, and to see three or four little children rolling on the damp, nay wet brick floor, through which the stagnant, filthy moisture of the street oozed up; the fire-place was empty and black; the wife sat on her husband's lair, and cried in the dark loneliness. (chap. 6, p. 60)

One could analyze in relation to the rhetorical doctrine of amplification the way in which this passage moves step by step from one appalling picture to the next even worse one. The whole sequence of the observation and then action of the two unemployed men in seeking to ameliorate the even worse suffering of their friend powerfully engages the reader's sympathy for the victims and admiration for those who help them. The "two rough men" are described as "tender nurses" (p. 61) as John pawns his coat for the money which will buy fuel and fire for this cellar. Gaskell forcefully contrasts these scenes with views of the richly provisioned shopping streets and the elegant and well-provided homes of the wealthy. These contrasting descriptions underline her observations about inequality and the acute consciousness of the poor about the easy life which some lead amid their deprivation. In a parallel way, Gaskell provides us with a sequence of descriptions of John Barton's house which map his decline after his wife's death and as his situation becomes more desperate. Chapter 2 provides an almost idyllic description of the room crammed with furniture in which the tea party will take place.

> Two geraniums, unpruned and leafy, which stood on the sill, formed a further defence from out-door pryers. In the corner between the window and the fireside was a cupboard, apparently full of plates and dishes, cups and saucers, and some more nondescript articles, for which one would have fancied their possessors could find no use—such as triangular pieces of glass to save carving knives and forks from dirtying table-cloths. However, it was evident Mrs. Barton was proud of her crockery and glass, for she left her cupboard door open, with a glance round of satisfaction and pleasure.... The place seemed almost crammed with furniture (sure sign of good times among the mills). Beneath the window was a dresser, with three deep drawers. Opposite the fire-place was a table, which I should call a Pembroke, only that it was made of deal, and I cannot tell how far such a name may be applied to such humble material. On it, resting against the wall, was a bright green japanned tea-tray, having a couple of scarlet lovers embracing in the middle. The fire-light danced merrily on this, and really (setting all taste but that of a child's aside) it gave a richness of colouring to that side of the room. It was in some measure propped up by a crimson tea-caddy, also of japan ware. A round table on one branching leg, really for use, stood in the corresponding corner to the cupboard; and, if you can picture all this, with a washy, but clean stencilled pattern on the walls, you can form some idea of John Barton's home. (chap. 2, p. 15)

Food must be purchased and an extra tea cup borrowed to avoid the embarrassment of the young Mary having to share a cup with their friend's son Jem, but the description speaks of pride and organization.[20] Even a few pages later the scene is more chaotic, with the unwashed plates left for the morning now given higher relief by the desperate and ultimately failed attempts to save Mrs. Barton's life (chap. 3, p. 21). In chapter 10, the house is gradually being stripped of all its little ornaments. Mary takes the smart tea tray and caddy and the blankets, because it is summer, to the pawn shop in order to provide John with the occasional meal. By chapter 34, Mary returns from Liverpool to find John sitting in an almost bare room.

> He sat by the fire; the grate I should say, for fire there was none. Some dull, grey ashes, negligently left, long days ago, coldly choked up the bars. He had taken the accustomed seat from mere force of habit, which ruled his automaton body. For all energy, both physical and mental, seemed to have retreated inwards to some of the great citadels of life, there to do battle against the Destroyer, Conscience. . . .
>
> She had some money about her, the price of her strange services as a witness; and when the lingering dusk grew on she stole out to effect some purchases necessary for her father's comfort.
>
> For how body and soul had been kept together, even as much as they were, during the days he had dwelt alone, no one can say. The house was bare as when Mary had left it, of coal, or of candle, of food, or of blessing in any shape. (pp. 353–54)

The room calls forth a judgment but also prompts Mary's practical care for John, which echoes his actions in the Davenports' cellar.

Gaskell shows her readers the histories, thoughts, feelings, and emotional development of a range of working-class characters. In so doing, she invites her readers to respond to her characters as people like themselves. Like other novelists of the 1840s, she was influenced by Carlyle's ideas from *Past and Present* (1843) and *Chartism* (1839). Three of these ideas seem to be reflected in *Mary Barton*: the notion of an almost unbreachable divide between workers and factory owners; the belief that severe social disturbance was imminent in the north; and the idea that the workers had been so badly let down by the wealthy that their resentment and rebellion was quite understandable.[21] But the concrete detail through which Gaskell explores these ideas is always based on her own experience, her visits to impoverished households, and her reaction against the system which made such deplorable conditions possible. The way her imagination works on this deep local knowledge enables her to give her readers human and recognizable characters instead of the rather depersonalized picture of the masses on the verge of insurrection which she found in Carlyle.[22]

John, Jem, and Mary

One strong focus of Gaskell's attention is John Barton. In the early stages of the novel, she presents him as a warm, good, optimistic, self-reliant figure who uses his small resources to take care of others. We see the leadership role which his colleagues expect him to play and which he fulfills. We see his sense of duty to his family and to his fellow workers and his human feeling in providing for others' needs even at times of crisis and of personal want. At the same time, as we have seen, Gaskell attends to, develops, and sympathizes with his resentment at the difference between the owners' and workers' experience of hard times in trade. When his wife Mary dies, Gaskell tells us both of his determined care for his daughter Mary and of his growing harshness and obstinacy.

> The neighbours all remarked he was a changed man. His gloom and his sternness became habitual instead of occasional. He was more obstinate. But never to Mary. Between the father and the daughter there existed in full force that mysterious bond which unites those who have been loved by one who is now dead and gone. While he was harsh and silent to others, he humoured Mary with tender love; she had more of her own way than is common in any rank with girls of her age. (chap. 3, p. 23)

In chapter 15, Gaskell draws together the different types of pressure John feels. He never gets over the disappointment of the trip to London and Parliament's rejection of the Charter, described in chapter 9, and because of his notoriety as a Chartist, he is unable to find work and his consequent bodily privations sour his mind. Gaskell compares his situation with the Italian torture in which the walls of the room gradually move in and crush the prisoner. The morbid strength of his thoughts is intensified by the opium which he takes to forget his need for food. While Gaskell regrets his recourse to opium, she also understands it (chap. 15, p. 169). In his distress over the difference in the experiences of rich and poor, "the only feeling that remained clear and undisturbed in the tumult of his heart, was hatred to the one class, and keen sympathy with the other." She compares the actions of the uneducated workers with those of Frankenstein, "that monster of many human qualities" which is yet unable to tell the difference between good and evil.

> The people rise up to life; they irritate us, they terrify us, and we become their enemies. Then, in the sorrowful moment of our triumphant power, their eyes gaze on us with mute reproach. Why have we made them what they are: a powerful monster, yet without the inner means for peace and happiness?
>
> John Barton became a Chartist, a Communist, all that is commonly called wild and visionary. Ay! but being visionary is something. It shows a soul, a being not altogether sensual; a creature who looks forward for others, if not for himself.
>
> And with all his weakness he had a sort of practical power, which made him useful to the bodies of men to whom he belonged. He had a ready kind of rough Lancashire eloquence, arising out of the fullness of his heart. . . . And what perhaps more than all made him relied upon and valued, was the consciousness which every one who came into contact with him felt, that he was actuated by no selfish motives; that his class, his order was what he stood by, not the rights of his own paltry self. (chap. 15, p. 170)

Gaskell prepares for the meeting between workers and owners, from which Barton is absent on a mission of mercy, by explaining the different pressures which Barton was under and recalling his strong and heroic characteristics. In the men's anger at the meeting and at Harry Carson's caricature of their famished thinness, John counsels against further violence directed at fellow workers, proposing and supporting instead the plan of vengeance on the owners agreed to at the end of chapter 16. Motives of loyalty and duty combine with his anger to compel him to carry out the murder which he has been chosen by lot to commit. Even as he makes his way to carry out his task, Gaskell shows us his considerate side when he hears the cry of a child, who reminds him of the son he has lost. He returns the child to his mother and receives an Irish blessing from her before continuing (chap. 17, p. 198).

Gaskell works hard to remind us of John's qualities of human concern, both to enhance the reader's sense of the tragedy and to prepare for his extreme remorse after committing the murder, which leads into the final section of the novel. Because she needs to maintain suspense and danger around Jem's fate in order to develop the heroic role for Mary of saving Jem while not incriminating her father, Gaskell finds herself compelled to conceal a secondary problem: since John felt such remorse, and since he knew that Jem was being tried for his life on circumstantial evidence, why did he not reveal his guilt to save Jem? Although he was in Glasgow for part of the time, there surely would have been news of the inquiry into the murder. He had returned to Manchester some days before his not entirely adequate apology to Jem, in chapter 35, for "the meanest thing I ever did." Perhaps Gaskell intends us to think that he was so preoccupied by his own feelings of guilt that he failed to draw the necessary conclusion. Or perhaps she hopes that by the time readers have understood the problem, they are too relieved and delighted at Mary's skill in reconciling apparently conflicting obligations to mind much.

We are introduced to Jem Wilson as the family friend of Mary Barton's childhood. He is excessively free in his behavior toward her and too open about his growing affection for her (chap. 2, pp. 14, 16; chap. 5, pp. 44, 56). He shows a conventional heroism in crossing the ladder-bridge twice to rescue his father and another man from the blazing factory. The firemen remark on his enthusiastic insistence on performing both rescues in spite of their more experienced presence (pp. 52–56). He is also shown to be a new kind of heroic worker in his mastery of machines and in the engineering innovations he brings about. He is the willing breadwinner for his family when his father becomes unemployed, and he settles the reward for his invention as a pension for his mother and aunt (chap. 12, pp. 142, 145). When Mary rejects his proposal of marriage, he takes the refusal as final, out of a possibly misconceived consideration for Mary's feelings (chap. 11, pp. 129–30; chap. 12, p. 139). Also, Jem and Mary are the only ones who listen to Esther and who try to improve her lot (chap. 14, pp. 163–65; chap. 21, pp. 236–42; chap. 38, pp. 390–92).

Faced with the charge of murder, Jem is inactive and unresourceful, partly because he is unwilling to incriminate John Barton and partly because of a sort of fatalism. He is persuasively confident of his own innocence but does not help his lawyer and indeed writes to reject his legal representation (chap. 32, pp. 317–18). He is seen as someone who tries to save other people (for example, his mother and John Barton) at the cost of his own interests. He is presented to us as desperately in need of Mary's assistance, indeed as helpless without her. On his acquittal, he is once again a victim of social expectations, as some of his coworkers refuse to accept his presence in the factory (chap. 34, p. 359; chap. 36, pp. 375–76). He cooperates with his employer to make a success of the opportunity which Canada presents.

Mary initially resists Jem's advances, resenting both the liberty that he takes with her and the assumption among their families and acquaintances that he might expect to marry her. She is conscious of her beauty and worries that Jem is in love with her, but she recognizes his good qualities. Gaskell presents Mary as resourceful and autonomous beyond her years when she has to take over her mother's role of managing the family's money, possessions, and food. Revealing an interesting mixture of worldly calculation and naïveté, she sees herself as an independent agent and dreams of using her attractiveness to create power and wealth to sustain her father in his trouble. As soon as she has knowingly and deliberately rejected Jem, Mary realizes what a terrible mistake she has made, not on rational grounds but as a result of a paroxysm of unexplained grief and the realization of both her own true nature and of the fundamental nature of her bond with Jem.

> To return to Mary. Her plan had been, as we well know, to marry Mr. Carson, and the occurrence an hour ago was only a preliminary step. True; but it had unveiled her heart to her; it had convinced her that she loved Jem above all persons or things. But Jem was a poor mechanic, with a mother and aunt to keep; a mother, too, who had shown her pretty clearly that she did not desire her for a daughter-in-law: while Mr. Carson was rich, and prosperous, and gay, and (she believed) would place her in all circumstances of ease and luxury, where want could never come. What were these hollow vanities to her, now she had discovered the passionate secret of her soul? (chap. 11, p. 131)

This realization gives her the strength to accept the anger of Jem's mother as justified and to resist the ever more forceful but also more openly damaging offers and threats from Harry Carson. Although she now realizes the mistake she has made and her obligation to put it right, Mary still, partly on Margaret's advice, clings to the conventionally female role of waiting patiently to be asked again rather than speaking on her own account. She is restrained from speaking or writing to Jem about her new understanding of her true feelings by "maidenly modesty" and by the conventional belief that men like to have all the courting to themselves (chap. 11, pp. 132–33; chap. 12, pp. 142–43).

When she realizes that her father is the murderer of Harry Carson, she understands that she has to put an end to maidenly modesty and inaction. Only she can save Jem without incriminating John. From this point on, she takes on a heroic role, marshaling her resources and drawing on the knowledge and contacts of other people without revealing her knowledge to them.[23] As Margaret realizes (chap. 25, pp. 280–81), Mary will trust only herself to do everything that may be required in order to establish Jem's alibi: "No one could have her motives; and consequently no one could have her sharpened brain, her despairing determination" (p. 280). She needs her absolute determination, her sharp brain, and a little luck with the wind in order to pull through and rescue Jem. She also needs, once again, to put aside "feminine shame" and speak in public of what she really feels.

> Perhaps I liked Mr. Harry Carson once—I don't know—I've forgotten; but I loved James Wilson, that's now on trial, above what tongue can tell—above all else on earth put together; and I love him now better than ever, though he has never known a word of it till this minute. For you see, sir, mother died before I was thirteen, before I could know right from wrong about some things; and I was giddy and vain, and ready to listen to any praise of my good looks.... [After I rejected James's proposal] he took me at my word and left me; and from that day to this I've never spoken to him, or set eyes on him; though I'd fain have done so, to try and show him we had both been too hasty; for he'd not been gone out of my sight above a minute before I knew I loved—far above my life. (chap. 32, p. 325)

One could write a short essay on Mary's blushes and her shame at being spoken about as a lover or admitting her feelings to herself (chap. 8, p. 83; chap. 12, p. 145; chap. 32, p. 325; chap. 34, pp. 349, 355), but her understanding places her in a position where she has to act with courage and candor in spite of the internalized social expectation that she should not. Circumstances, intelligence, and her certainty of her love for Jem bring out a heroic character and a heroic action. However inclined she is to blush, she realizes instantaneously that blushes and shame will have to be put aside in order to play her part in putting the world right. Speaking in her own voice, Gaskell endorses and encourages this kind of exertion.

> Of all trite, worn-out, hollow mockeries of comfort that were ever uttered by people who will not take the trouble of sympathising with others, the one I dislike the most is the exhortation not to grieve over an event, "for it cannot be helped." Do you think if I could help it, I would sit still with folded hands, content to mourn? Do you not believe that as long as hope remained I would be up and doing? I mourn because what has occurred cannot be helped. (chap. 22, pp. 244–45)

Gaskell's deep personal understanding that there are some griefs, such as the death of a child, for which no reaction is possible except mourning strengthens her sense of the obligation to act to ameliorate a situation where improvement is possible. Mary Barton is her exemplar of this duty of active intervention.

Plotting and Ending

Throughout the book, Gaskell's management of the plot is impressive. She arranges a series of intense and contrasting scenes in the earlier, slower-moving part of the plot and then keeps a tense narrative drive through the second half, in which one crisis succeeds another. Her portrayal of Mary and the legal and social difficulties which she faces in saving Jem owes something to Shakespearean heroines like Viola, Portia, and Isabella, while the geographical aspects of her struggle may draw on Scott's Jeannie Deans from *The Heart of Midlothian*.[24] We know that she read Scott and that she recommended Shakespeare's plots as models for novelists. In *Mary Barton*, she keeps a wide range of characters in the reader's mind but can also introduce new figures of interest later in the novel, such as Ben Sturgis and Mrs. Sturgis. Readers have always admired the comic portrayal of Job Legh, the amateur entomologist, who represents a strain of working-class curiosity and empirical knowledge and who tries to console Barton with the wonderful story of rescuing his orphaned granddaughter Margaret from London and bringing her back to Manchester (chapter 9).[25] In a very different vein, the meddling paid matchmaker, Mary's coworker Sally Leadbitter, is also presented and deployed very effectively.

The most difficult task which Gaskell sets herself is the ending, where she aims to coordinate the expectations of different inherited genres. She ends the romance plot somewhat happily with a new and successful life for Mary and Jem, which must be led far away from Manchester because Jem has been expelled from the city's factories by the continuing suspicions of his coworkers. She allows the tragic plot to run its course to the death of John Barton, but then attempts to move on from the pessimism of the desolate battle between the classes with a scene of personal forgiveness, a growth of understanding between masters and men, and a gradual amelioration of the condition of the workers. Presumably Gaskell saw it as her duty both to represent in a moving way the desperate circumstances of the workers and their families, through the destruction of John Barton, and to suggest that there were possible roads to improvement which lay beyond suffering.

The first steps in this process are taken by John Barton when he summons Jem and John Carson, the mill owner, to his home to hear his confession, which is motivated by conscience and by the hope for some sort of internal peace before death. Through Carson's response, John Barton understands the further effects of the murder and the consequential suffering of the victim's father. This reminds him of his own sorrow when his son Tom died because of their living conditions. Gaskell puts a strong emphasis here on John's awareness of a suffering shared by millowner and worker.

> The eyes of John Barton grew dim with tears. Rich and poor, masters and men, were then brothers in the deep suffering of the heart; for was not this the very anguish he had felt for little Tom, in years so long gone by, that they seemed like another life? (chap. 35, p. 366)

The last book of *The Iliad,* in which Priam reminds Achilles of the grief which his father will feel, might have been an inspiration here.[26] Achilles puts aside his anger and his desire to be revenged on the body of Hector for the death of Patroclus, and the king and the hero are united in shared sorrow. Homer prepares this reconciliation through Zeus's instructions to both humans about how they should act, whereas Gaskell chooses to use her characters' shared heritage of Bible reading. To Barton's first plea for mercy and his insistence that he did not understand what he was doing, Carson replies, understandably in the light of the character which has been developed for him, with an almost Satanic preference for revenge over forgiveness: "Let my trespasses be unforgiven, so that I may have vengeance for my son's murder" (p. 367, clearly contradicting the Lord's Prayer, Matthew 6:9–15). In the street, Carson sees the dainty wealthy child ask her nurse to forgive the rough errand-boy who has knocked her over and at home he reads the story of Christ's prayer on the cross: "Father, forgive them, for they know not what they do" (Luke 23:34). The repetition of the motif of forgiveness for those who know not what they do prompts his extraordinary gesture of returning to Barton's home to forgive him. Gaskell expects her readers to understand both that this forgiveness is extremely difficult and that the divine command is clear to Carson and must be obeyed by him. She takes the unusual step of requiring that the millowners live up to their Christian principles in order to achieve improvements in society.

Her next task is to bring this personal religious transformation to the outside world. The agency for this transfer is another summons, from Carson to Job Legh and Jem. Carson's aim is to learn more about the circumstances of his son's death and to satisfy himself that only Barton, who is dead now and was already dying when he made his confession, was responsible. What results is an unusual exchange of views between the men, represented here by Job, and the owners.[27] Neither side yields to the other, and Job is not really satisfied with what he has been able to say, but although they do not change each other's views, they do hear each other. This mutual listening, Gaskell tells us at the end of chapter 37, is the beginning of a slow change in Carson's attitude through which he will become the pioneer of "many of the improvements now in practice in the system of employment in Manchester" (p. 388).

I would argue that the plot and unity of *Mary Barton* turn on the question of responses to tradition. To save Jem, Mary must cast aside the traditional role assigned to women and become independently active. She must turn her back on "feminine shame," and in the public trial she must declare the strength of her feelings. John Carson, by contrast, must move beyond his rejection of the Lord's Prayer and obey the Christian injunction to forgive. He must live up to the traditions which before he followed only nominally, and he must reject revenge in order to have a chance of building a better future.

Metafiction

That many readers find this change in Carson impossible to accept is a kind of compliment to the success of Gaskell's realistic representation of Manchester life. Gaskell, however, continually makes us aware that she is writing fiction and that she is depending on the particular power of stories to help people reflect on events in the hope of changing things in the future.[28] Gaskell's comment about Carson's participation in the improvements "now in practice" in Manchester employment (p. 388) is one among several in which Gaskell alludes in an almost Chaucerian way to the connections between stories and life. Pointing to such connections within a story always prompts readers to think about the status of fiction. One very telling instance occurs in the trial when Gaskell, in the middle of entering the minds of many of the characters involved, explains to us that she was not actually there.

> I was not there myself; but one who was, told me that her look, and indeed her whole face, was more like the well-known engraving from Guido's picture of "Beatrice Cenci" than anything else he could give me an idea of. He added, that her countenance haunted him, like the remembrance of some wild sad melody, heard in childhood; that it would perpetually recur with its mute imploring agony. (chap. 32, p. 324)

In part this intervention serves to distance the author slightly from the comparison she introduces. "Reader, you may, if you wish, think

Guido Reni dipinse.   Auguste Guglielmi dis.   Vincenzo Salandri inc. in Roma.

BEATRICE CENCI

There are many engravings of this portrait, formerly attributed to Guido
Reni. They are reasonably similar to each other. This one is by Vincenzo
Salandri, active in Rome around 1835. We do not know exactly which
engraving Gaskell has in mind, but she accurately describes the image as well
known. Copyright © UCL Art Museum, University College London.

of her as looking like the engraving of the supposed portrait of Beatrice Cenci (who was beheaded for arranging the murder of her abusive father), which you may know, but I admit that this comparison is secondhand." In another way, her intervention serves to emphasize her scrupulousness as an author. "Some of the things I tell you I saw for myself; for others I am reliant on the witnesses I have spoken to." Because she is scrupulous in telling us that she was not present at the trial, we ought perhaps to trust the rest of her narration even more. But this intervention surely also has a contrary effect: by telling us how she has constructed her scene, she reminds us, at this crucial moment, that the whole story is a fabrication, a fiction based on some social-historical facts but involving many scenes invented for the purpose of influencing a reader.

Soon after Mary has realized her father's guilt, Gaskell intensifies her sense of oppression and conflicting duties by describing how the buildings of the court where she lives crowd in on her as she goes out to fetch water for relief.

> The hard square outlines of the houses cut sharply against the cold bright sky, from which myriads of stars were shining down in eternal repose. There was little sympathy in the outward scene, with the internal trouble. All was so still, so motionless, so hard! Very different to this lovely night in the country in which I am now writing, where the distant horizon is soft and undulating in the moonlight, and the nearer trees sway gently to and fro in the night-wind with something of almost human motion; and the rustling air makes music among their branches, as if speaking soothingly to the weary ones, who lie awake in heaviness of heart. The sights and sounds of such a night lull pain and grief to rest. (chap. 22, p. 246)

To some extent Gaskell's intervention here amplifies the oppression of the urban scene through contrast. Not all nights are like the one Mary is experiencing; not all environments press in on human beings. There is another way to live. But again the intervention has the effect of reminding us that Gaskell is sitting in a peaceful room writing and that the scene and the emotions she has just described are her invention and that they are very different from her own experience as she writes, and perhaps very different from the personal experiences of all women of her social position. There may even be an implied reminder to readers that they too are reading this scene in circumstances (probably involving comfort and leisure) very different from Mary's. Fiction helps readers to share experiences, but it can also, as here, remind them of differences.

In chapter 33, Gaskell describes the various reasons why Jem does not immediately greet John Barton when he sees him return to his home after his extended trip to Glasgow.

> If you think this account of mine confused, of the half-feelings, half-reasons, which passed through Jem's mind, as he stood gazing on the empty space, where that crushed form had so lately been seen,—if you are perplexed to disentangle the real motives: I do assure you it was from just such an involved set of thoughts that Jem drew the resolution to act as if he had not seen that phantom likeness of John Barton—himself, yet not himself. (p. 347)

This passage foregrounds the role of the reader. "If you find the way that I have written about Jem's thoughts to be confusing, then I assure you, you are experiencing just the kind of confusion that Jem felt in thinking through these questions." It is as if the writer acknowledges a writerly failure in not being able to present the reader with a clear account of Jem's thoughts, but then redeems the situation by claiming that a feeling of confusion will bring the reader closer to what Jem is feeling. Gaskell sets up an idea of three levels of experience and expression. She contrasts what Jem feels with the way in which she has been able to express these feelings and with what readers can learn from her words. She fears that she will have failed by inducing confusion, but then claims that this confusion she has created in the minds of readers will give them the best possible idea of how Jem in fact feels. One part of the effect of this rather self-conscious maneuver is to remind us that this is fiction and that all the words of the novel are inventions aimed at prompting a response from readers. My argument is that we need to see the invocation of Carson's change of heart and his constructive role in the future of Manchester in chapter 37 as a self-conscious appeal to the nature of fiction. To put it oversimply, the terrible events of the story could be ameliorated if the owners could come to understand the workers' point of view and if the workers could enjoy improved conditions and better education.

A Woman's Point of View

When Thomas Carlyle, who disliked novels, replied via the publisher to thank the then-anonymous author for sending a copy of *Mary Barton*, he identifies the author as a woman before praising her achievement.

> Dear *Madam* (for I catch the *treble* of that fine melodious voice very well),—We have read your Book here, my Wife first and then I; both of us with real pleasure. A beautiful, cheerfully pious, social, clear and observant character is everywhere recognisable in the writer . . . your field moreover is new, important, full of rich materials (which, as is usual, required a soul of some *opulence* to recognize them as rich); the result is a Book deserving to take its place far above the ordinary garbage of Novels,—a Book which every intelligent person may read with entertainment, and which it will do every one some good to read.[29]

Even without the mind-set and the insight of a Victorian sage, it is possible to feel that some of the particular excellences of the novel are connected to the expression of a woman's point of view. When Gaskell considers Mary's career choices, one strong reason given for her unwillingness to go into service is that she has become accustomed to her independence and to "the dear feminine privileges of gossiping with a merry neighbour, and working night and day to help one who was sorrowful" (chap. 3, p. 26). Mary claims the right to talk merrily with other women but also to have the freedom to give her time to assisting those who are in need. When Jem reaches Mary's sickbed in chapter 34, Gaskell describes the difficulty he faces.

> And now Jem found the difficulty which every one who has watched by a sick-bed knows full well; and which is perhaps more insurmountable to men than it is to women,—the difficulty of being patient, and trying not to expect any visible change for long, long hours of sad monotony. (pp. 347–48)

It may also be women whom she has in mind in her reference to the writer's and the reader's experiences of the sickroom in chapter 25.

> The room at Mrs. Wilson's had that still, changeless look you must have often observed in the house of sickness or mourning. No particular employment going on; people watching and waiting rather than acting . . .

what little movement is going on, so noiseless and hushed . . . you fall back into the same train of thought with all these associations, and forget the street, the outer world, in the contemplation of the one stationary, absorbing interest within. (pp. 277–78)

The sickroom demands a special kind of patience and a warmth of solidarity which Gaskell seems to rate among the "feminine privileges," which include mingling duty with a kind of pleasure in doing practical good. When Jem has brought his mother back to Manchester to comfort Alice in her final hours, and after Alice has died, he understandably wants to return to Mary's bedside in Liverpool. Initially his mother expresses her distress at taking second place so soon and, "with an air of injured meekness on her face" (chap. 33, p. 343), tries to make it difficult for him to go. He is impatient at her lack of understanding, but then he hits on a line of conversation.

> "Mother! I often think what a good man father was! I've often heard you tell of your courting days; and of the accident that befell you, and how ill you were. How long is it ago?"
>
> "Near upon five-and-twenty years," said she, with a sigh.
>
> "You little thought when you were so ill you should live to have such a fine strapping son as I am, did you now?"
>
> She smiled a little and looked up at him, which was just what he wanted.
>
> "Thou'rt not so fine a man as thy father was, by a deal!" said she, looking at him with much fondness, notwithstanding her depreciatory words. (p. 343)

He leads her back to thinking of the happiness which she enjoyed with his father before bending "the subject round to his own case" (p. 343) by hoping that she would want him to be as happy as she had been.

> "I did not make him as happy as I might ha' done," murmured she, in a low sad voice of self-reproach. "Th'accident gave a jar to my temper it's never got the better of; and now he's gone, where he can never know I grieve for having frabbed him as I did."
>
> "Nay, mother, we don't know that!" said Jem, with gentle soothing. "Anyhow, you and father got along with as few rubs as most people. But for *his* sake, dear mother, don't say me nay, now that I come to you to

ask your blessing before setting out to see her, who is to be my wife, if
ever woman is; for *his* sake, if not for mine love her whom I shall bring
home to be to me all you were to him: . . ."

The hard look left her face; though her eyes were still averted from
Jem's gaze, it was more because they were brimming over with tears,
called forth by his words, than because any angry feeling yet remained.
(pp. 343–44)

By evoking memories and by drawing comparisons, Jem brings his
mother round to seeing the question of his return to Liverpool in a
different light and to blessing Mary rather than feeling jealous of
her. It is a highly effective passage of persuasion combining narrative with comparison, and it is spoken by a man, and yet this very
effective line of conversation seems to me more likely to have been
thought up by a woman than by a man. Gaskell's woman's understanding of Jane Wilson's feelings and memories helps her give Jem
a kind way of bringing her round. Patsy Stoneman has pointed out
that Gaskell often puts her male heroes in situations where they
carry out historically female roles of childcare and nurturing.[30]
Jem's argument prepares the scene of Mary's return to his home.

> Could his mother mar it? Could she break into it with her Martha-like
> cares? Only for one moment did she remember her sense of injury,—
> her wasted trouble,—and then her whole woman's heart heaving with
> motherly love and sympathy, she opened her arms, and received Mary
> into them, as shedding tears of agitated joy, she murmured in her ear:
> "Bless thee, Mary, bless thee! Only make him happy, and God bless
> thee for ever!" (chap. 35, pp. 362–63)

Gaskell describes this act of forgiveness intended to promote others'
happiness as a product of Jane Wilson's "woman's heart." Gaskell's
introduction of a woman's point of view in such an original discussion of crucial public themes significantly enlarges what she and her
novel can represent.

Using and Making Tradition

When Gaskell faced up to the storms aroused by the publication of
Mary Barton and *Ruth,* she made her defense on lines closely related to her method of authorship.

Some say the masters are very sore, but I'm sure I *believe* I wrote truth. (*Letters*, p. 66)

I am almost frightened at my own action in writing it. . . . I can only say I wanted to represent the subject in the light in which some of the workmen certainly consider to be *true*, not that I dare to say it is the abstract absolute truth. (p. 67)

Whatever power there was in Mary Barton was caused by my feeling strongly on the side which I took. . . . I know, and have always owned, that I have represented *but one* side of the question. . . . I believe what I have said in Mary Barton to be perfectly true, but by no means the whole truth. . . . I believe that there is much to be discovered yet as to the right position and mutual duties of employer, and employed; and the utmost I hoped from Mary Barton has been that it would give a spur to inactive thought, and languid conscience in this direction. (p. 119)

"An unfit subject for fiction" is *the* thing to say about it [*Ruth*]; I knew all this before, but I determined notwithstanding to speak my mind out about it; only how I shrink with more pain than I can tell you from what people are saying, though I wd do every jot of it over again to-morrow. . . . Of course it is a prohibited book in *this*, as in many other households; not a book for young people, unless read with someone older (I mean to read it with MA [her daughter Marianne] some quiet time or other;) but I have spoken out my mind in the best way I can, and I have no doubt that what was meant so earnestly *must* do some good, though perhaps not all the good, or not the *very* good I meant. I am in a quiver of pain about it. I can't tell you how much I need strength. (pp. 220–21)

I think I have put the small edge of the wedge in, if only I have made people talk & discuss the subject a little more than they did. (p. 226)

In both novels she has taken a subject close to her own personal experience, as she advises Grey to do, and worked it up into a story, imagined to the point where it presents itself as real to her. She acknowledges that other people see the issues raised in a different way, but she believes that she has expressed her view of the events truthfully and powerfully. At the very least, her writing has prompted people to think and speak further about the issues she raises. Behind her powerful and original directness on social issues lies her

Unitarian background and education, which encouraged her to sympathize with people worse off than herself and to speak her convictions. Carlyle's discussion of the "two nations" in *Past and Present* may well have helped her formulate her idea in *Mary Barton* of the need for workers and owners to understand each other better. In an important letter on her new house and the difficulty of reconciling her different selves, she sees herself as a sort of Christian socialist.

> You *must* come and see us in it, dearest Tottie, and try to make me see "the wrong the better cause," and that it is right to spend so much ourselves on *so* purely selfish a thing as a house is, while so many are wanting—thats the haunting thought to me; at least to one of my "Mes," for I have a great number, and that's the plague. One of my mes is, I do believe, a true Christian—(only people call her socialist and communist), another of my mes is a wife and mother, and highly delighted at the delight of everyone else in the house, Meta and William most especially who are in full extasy. Now that's my "social" self I suppose. Then again I've another self with a full taste for beauty and convenience whh is pleased on its own account. How am I to reconcile all these warring members?[31]

Although one might like to imagine Gaskell thinking of Montaigne here, the presumption must be that the idea of the war between her different selves is her own. When she can, she likes to support her original perceptions with suggestions that earlier writers have expressed similar ideas. The epigraphs in *Mary Barton* usually predict the contents of the chapter which will follow. Several of them are taken from workers' poetry in order to give evidence of a literary tradition of writing about the workers' suffering and to substantiate her claim throughout the novel for the overlooked intellectual accomplishments of farm and factory workers (chap. 1, p. 5; chap. 4, pp. 35–37; chap. 6, p. 57). In chapter 9 (pp. 111–12), she quotes Samuel Bamford's "God help the poor" in its entirety to reinforce her own descriptions and to assert the sensitivity of the workers in writing and in responding. Other epigraphs come from Crabbe, the Romantics, and the seventeenth-century poets. In the footnotes, she cites Shakespeare, Chaucer, and Langland to justify and dignify her reporting of Lancashire dialect words (chap. 4, pp. 32, 33; chap. 5,

p. 47; chap. 6, p. 59; chap. 7, p. 76). Within the text of the novel, she makes easy allusions to phrases and situations from Shakespeare (chap. 6, p. 70; chap. 15, p. 177; chap. 16, p. 184; chap. 27, p. 288). She gives particular prominence on the title page to a quotation from Carlyle's essay "On Biography," which pronounces the foolishness of fiction while allowing that it may do good. None of these literary references indicates a substantial personal debt in terms of thought or plot. Rather, they serve to justify and encourage her own originality by suggesting parallels for some elements of her work in older and greater writers.[32]

The pain caused to Gaskell by hostile criticism from friends and reviewers (and even, in the case of *Ruth*, book-burning) was to some extent assuaged by the support she received from correspondents. Several of her letters express her gratitude for people writing to express their understanding and admiration for what she was trying to do. The support of other writers and other women was particularly helpful. In a business letter to Edward Chapman, she says:

> In the midst of all my deep & great annoyance, Mr. Carlyle's letter has been most valuable; and has given me almost the only unmixed pleasure I have yet received from the publication of MB.[33]

Even though she was confident of her powers of observation, of the truth of what she wrote, and of the good that could arise from saying what she thought, words of approval from strangers and friends were a very welcome, and sometimes a necessary, form of encouragement for her. Gaskell seems to have appreciated that other writers might find the same kind of support and admiration equally helpful and that she could be in a position to provide this to them. Pauline Nestor writes about her sense of belonging to a community of women writers and of her friendships with her peers.[34] One example would be her comic letter of admiration to George Eliot in 1859, expressing her delight that she had been taken for the real author behind the pseudonym.

> Dear Mr. "Gilbert Elliott,"
>
> Since I came up from Manchester to London I have had the greatest compliment paid me I ever had in my whole life, I have been suspected of having written "Adam Bede." I have hitherto denied it; but

really I think, that as you want to keep your real name a secret, it would be very pleasant for me to blush acquiescence. Will you give me leave?

Well! If I had written Amos Barton, Janet's Repentance & Adam Bede I should neither be to have nor to hold with pride & delight in myself—so I think it is very well I have not.[35]

When Gaskell discovers that George Eliot is in fact Marian Evans, she writes again.

Since I heard, from authority, that you were the author of Scenes from "Clerical Life" & "Adam Bede," I have read them again; and I must, once more, tell you how earnestly fully, and humbly I admire them. I never read anything so complete, and beautiful in fiction, in my whole life before.[36]

George Eliot responds in the warmest possible terms about the good which reading Gaskell's letter and her novels have done her.

I shall always love to think that one woman wrote to another such sweet encouraging words—still more to think that you were the writer and I the receiver. I had indulged the idea that if my books turned out to be worth much, you would be among my willing readers.

Eliot tells Gaskell how much she admires *Mary Barton* and *Cranford* and relates that she had been reading the former as she was writing *Scenes from Clerical Life* and the latter during the composition of *Adam Bede*.

I like to tell you these slight details because they will prove to you that your letter must have a peculiar value for me. . . . And I cannot believe that such details are indifferent to you, even after we have been so long used to hear them: I fancy, as long as we live, we all need to know as much as we can of the good our life has been to others.[37]

We have no reply to this letter and no further letters between Eliot and Gaskell. We know that the two women never met, but this letter, with its anticipation of the ending of *Middlemarch*, is the strongest imaginable confirmation that Gaskell's achievement and example served to encourage Eliot, just as Gaskell generously acknowledged Eliot's superiority. Jenny Uglow argues that the two writers shared an egalitarian impulse and a sense of the practical good which writing could do in the world. Both wanted women to have intellectual and personal freedom without losing what both saw as feminine strengths: "a lightness, a lack of pomposity, an easy imaginative sympathy, above all a language of their own."[38]

Gaskell was fully conscious of her own originality, but she also knew that in the difficult times which followed the publication of *Mary Barton* and *Ruth*, the encouragement and appreciation of other writers had been sustaining for her art. She came to hope that she could help other writers in the same way. This idea she developed that writers, and especially women writers, might be a source of strength and encouragement to each other may have been prompted by her friend Lady Kay-Shuttleworth, who first introduced her to Charlotte Brontë. In a letter of 1850, Gaskell discusses Brontë, whom she has not yet met.

> I think I told you that I disliked a good deal in the plot of Shirley, but the expression of her own thoughts in it is so true and brave, that I greatly admire her. I am half amused to find you think I could do her good, (I don't know if you exactly word it so, but I think it is what you mean,) I *never* feel as if I could do anyone good—I never yet was conscious of strengthening anyone, and I do so feel to want strength, and to want faith. I suppose we all *do* strengthen each other by clashing together, and earnestly talking our own thoughts and ideas. The very disturbance we thus are to each other rouses us up, and makes us more healthy.[39]

Just as she found in her letter on Carlyle's response to *Mary Barton*, part of the encouragement came from disagreement and from commenting on possible mistakes.[40] From Charlotte Brontë's letters we know that she was fortified by Gaskell's 1849 comments on a prepublication copy of *Shirley*. "Her note brought tears to my eyes. She is a good—she is a great woman—proud I am that I can touch a chord of sympathy in souls so noble." "When Mrs. Gaskell tells me that she shall keep my works as a treasure to her daughters . . . I feel the sting taken from the strictures of another class of critics."[41]

Charlotte Brontë's death on 31 March 1855 was a shock to Gaskell, who had not even known that Brontë was ill. On 31 May, writing to her publisher George Smith to request a copy of Brontë's portrait, she explained that one day she would like to write about her.

> I can not tell you how I honoured & loved her. I did not know of her illness, or I would have gone straight to her. It seems to me that her death was as sad as her life. Sometime, it may be years hence—but if I live long enough, and no one is living whom such a publication would hurt, I will publish what I know of her, and make the world (if I am but strong enough in expression,) honour the woman as much as they have admired the writer.[42]

Her appreciation of the role which her letters had played in supporting other writers perhaps prompted her to the more public task of making people understand how a writer could overcome adverse circumstances both in her writing and in how she lived her life. On 16 June, annoyed by the mistakes in press accounts of Charlotte's death, Patrick Brontë wrote to Gaskell to ask her to "write a brief Account of her life."[43] By 18 June, Gaskell had already written to agree. She was well aware that in writing so soon she would have to suppress some details of Charlotte's life to avoid giving offense to her father and to Arthur Nicholls, her husband.[44] On some issues which became controversial, such as the school at Cowan Bridge and Branwell Brontë's disastrous love affair, she took the family line, which also coincided with the portrait she wished to paint. But the conception of the biography remained her own: to present Charlotte as a heroine who stoically and bravely carried out her duties in the face of great suffering on behalf of her family. She knew that everyone admired Charlotte Brontë's novels, but she wanted them also to honor and to be inspired by the woman who wrote those books out of a life of misery.

In spite of the changes which Gaskell was compelled to make for the third edition, *The Life of Charlotte Brontë* has always been regarded as one of the great Victorian biographies.[45] Patrick Brontë called the portrayal of his family "full of truth and life." "Indeed all the Pictures in the work have vigorous, truthful, and delicate touches in them, which could have been executed only by a skillful female hand." He regarded it as "every way worthy of that one Great Woman, should have written of Another."[46] The anonymous review in *The Economist* of 18 April 1857 declares, "We have before us the life of a truly great and noble woman, written by one who has sufficient moral sympathy to understand her character and sufficient intellectual insight to appreciate her genius."[47]

The Life of Charlotte Brontë inspired later women writers but also provoked their consideration of other ways in which women might write and live.[48] Mary Taylor, Charlotte's school friend whose early letters to Gaskell had helped fix her idea of Charlotte, admired the "true picture of a melancholy life" but was also unhappy and unsurprised that of the two reviews she had read,

> [n]either of them seems to think it a strange or wrong state of things that a woman of first-rate talents, industry, and integrity should live all her life in a walking nightmare of "poverty and self-suppression." I doubt whether any of them will.[49]

Jenny Uglow suggests that Gaskell's title-page quotation from Elizabeth Browning's *Aurora Leigh* places before the reader's eyes a different response to a domineering father, hinting at a "different kinship, the sisterhood of women writers."[50] The kind of personal support which Gaskell had found through letters and reviews and which she had given to other writers through her correspondence was now extended into a more public model, a sort of proclamation of a tradition of women writers.

The public response to Gaskell's novels showed how original she was. In *Mary Barton*, she presented her leisured readers with a sympathetic picture of the realities of working-class life in Manchester, of the resourcefulness and capability of the people who lived in those near-impossible conditions, and of the need for workers and employers to listen more carefully to honest accounts of the problems each side faced. She knew that she would be attacked, but she firmly believed in the value of speaking the truth to those in a position to effect change. At the same time, she always sought ways of disarming possible prejudice, for example, by disclaiming any knowledge of political economy in the preface (p. 4) and by presenting her story as told from a woman's point of view. By disarming resistance and acknowledging the limitations of her point of view, she hoped to make the truth she aimed to tell even more persuasive to her audience.

In spite of her courage and originality, Gaskell was highly conscious of needing to assert from time to time that earlier writers, both great and ordinary, had expressed some of the same ideas and used some of the same words as she had. When she encountered fierce criticism for telling the truth in the best way she could, she was strengthened by other writers' acknowledgment of what she had achieved. In time she came to offer a similar support to others, both privately through her correspondence and publicly through *The Life of Charlotte Brontë*. Although literary tradition was an important feature of her own education, and although she recommended the reading of novels and plays as a way to learn to develop plots, the main material for her writing came to her from recent events, from her visits to Manchester homes, and from her imagination. But as she developed plots, her reading of Shakespeare, the Bible, and other novelists (and perhaps also Homer) shaped her sense of what she was doing. She was sympathetically aware of the power of stories to change lives. Her sense of a tradition of literature reassured her and gave her a sense that other people had noticed and written about some of the problems she proposed to confront. She needed this reassurance because the generality of the novels she read did not address such urgent subjects of the present. Her confidence in and understanding of her own writing methods were strengthened by her feeling that other writers had employed some of them.

Gaskell's consciousness of having been helped by other writers suggested to her that she could provide encouragement to other authors in their work, even to authors, like Charlotte Brontë and George Eliot, whom she regarded as having more talent and knowledge than she had herself. As Gill Frith suggests to me, she may well have shared with Brontë and Eliot a concern with widening the horizons of her readers, of helping them to understand and sympathize with predicaments and actions which they would otherwise have condemned. With the success of Austen, the Brontës, and George Eliot before them, later women novelists perhaps needed Gaskell's example less than they might previously have done, but her social concerns, her earnest truthfulness, her courage, and her personal kindness continue to recommend her to readers.

European and African Literary Traditions in Ngũgĩ wa Thiong'o's *Wizard of the Crow*

WIZARD OF THE CROW is a comic novel on a deeply serious subject, the fate of African nations after their victories over colonial powers. It combines two main plots: a love story and a narrative of political intrigue. The love story is a survival plot in which Nyawĩra and Kamĩtĩ escape from being public enemies of a corrupt dictatorship, grow to understand each other better, and develop a resistance movement against the regime. The political plot is centered on a nameless dictator, the Ruler, who struggles to maintain his power in the face of internal threats and international pressures; whose ministers Machokali and Sikiokuu intrigue against each other to increase their power; and who is eventually replaced by an equally corrupt, ruthless, and improvisatory underling, Tajirika, who begins his rule with a slightly mutated version of the same Western economic and military connivance which established the Ruler's dictatorship. Pessimistic about national and international politics, the novel encourages faith and hope in individuals and communities. Outrageous in its satire, the novel stages a deeper comedy in the unexpected consequences of improvised actions, both better and worse than the improviser intended. Laughter and tears, the senses, and the body and bodily functions are central to the preoccupations of this richly entertaining and deeply thought-provoking novel.

Combining African and Western traditions to make something new, Ngũgĩ wa Thiong'o (1938–) incorporates Kenyan political history and Gikuyu folktales into the European and international form of the postmodern novel. By writing from a sort of exile to his own people, he also addresses a worldwide audience. I begin this chapter by discussing Ngũgĩ's incorporation of African history and traditional stories and storytelling methods into the form of the Western novel. Then I consider the political plot, focusing on the figure of the Ruler. Finally, I turn to the plot of love and resistance, discussing Nyawĩra and Kamĩtĩ in turn.

As a late colonial-era pupil at Alliance College in Nairobi and Makerere University College in Kampala, Ngũgĩ followed an essentially British curriculum in English literature. In his memoirs of his education, he particularly mentions his studies of the novelists Stevenson, Dickens, Austen, Emily Brontë, George Eliot, Hardy, Lawrence, and Conrad—he specialized in Conrad's works in his final year—but he also drew inspiration from the African and Caribbean writers he read outside the curriculum, such as Chinua Achebe, Wole Soyinka, Cyprian Ekwensi, Peter Abrahams, and George Lamming.[1] He was personally inspired and helped in the publication of his first novels by the support of Achebe.[2] He also mentions his reading of Tolstoy's *Childhood, Boyhood, Youth* and acknowledges Gabriel Garcia Márquez as a master.[3] At Leeds University, while he was already writing *A Grain of Wheat*, he began to read Frantz Fanon's *The Wretched of the Earth*, which was crucial to *Petals of Blood* and his later novels.[4] But when he reflects on what made him a writer, he gives equal or greater importance to the folktales which he heard at home and to Bible stories.

> Or did the miraculous conception begin years earlier in the evenings in my mother's hut where I first heard her stories of Swallow, who carried messages of those in distress; Hare, who fooled the biggies, Hyena, Lion, and Leopard, even arbitrating among them; Donkey, who brayed sorrow and shat mountains at the same time but also was so stubborn;

and the scary two-mouthed ogre who lured beautiful maidens into his lair up in baobab and sycamore trees? Or maybe it was a bit later, when I learned to read and lost myself among the biblical characters of Abraham, Cain, Abel, Isaac, Rachel and Leah, Goliath and David, his sling not too dissimilar to the one I used to scare away the hawk who swooped down from the sky and snatched chicks from a mother hen or meat from the hands of a baby? Was it when I was held captive by David's harp strings, which time and again calmed the unpredictable tempests in the soul of King Saul?[5]

Incorporating Gikuyu Traditions within the Form of the Novel

Wizard of the Crow uses many motifs and devices from folktales, from oral storytelling, and from the Bible. It explicitly raises the issue of the ambivalence of tradition in the use of proverbs by the Ruler and his associates and in their attempts to reinstate African traditions of obedience for their own advantage. Where the first wave of African novels in English tended to privilege African traditions as lost promised lands or ways of resisting the colonial intruders, Ngũgĩ understands the repressive aspect of some traditional beliefs and practices even as he uses the oral and literary traditions he knows.

Wizard of the Crow was written and first published in Gikuyu (sometimes Kikuyu), Ngũgĩ's mother tongue.[6] The local population, who would mostly have heard the book being read out loud, was the primary envisaged audience for whom Ngũgĩ wrote the novel. The novel has many immediate linguistic and political overtones for Kenyan Gikuyu speakers which international anglophone readers will miss or will appreciate only more slowly. Take, for example, the name of the heroine, Nyawĩra. On page 450, we learn that Tajirika and Vinjinia had considered the name Nyawĩra for their daughter (who is eventually named Ng'endo) but decided against it because it means "work" and they did not want to condemn their daughter to the life of a laborer. A Gikuyu reader or listener would have understood this from the time Nyawĩra introduces herself to the hero, Kamĩtĩ, on page 63. Prior to this, she was just Tajirika's secretary. The significance of the name would have been reinforced for these readers and listeners on page 78, where we learn that Nyawĩra had chosen that name from a much longer given and family name, En-genethi Nyawĩra Charles Matthew Mũgwanja Wangahũ. As Ngũgĩ told Ken Olende, the hero's name, Kamĩtĩ, means "of the trees."[7] This must have prepared Gikuyu readers for his interest in plants and his instinct for retreating to the forests at crucial moments, and it also would have enabled them to understand better the insulting dialogue of Tajirika's mocking "interview" of Kamĩtĩ, which first brings hero and heroine into contact (pp. 52–59, especially p. 57). Because the Gikuyu word *Mũgwanja* means "seven," Gikuyu read-ers would have picked up the connection between the "Seven Herbs of Grace"—the principles of healthy living which Nyawĩra and the Wizard give to their patients (p. 275)—and Nyawĩra's earlier name, Grace Mũgwanja (pp. 63, 78). This pun later enables her former husband, Kaniuru, to make the connection between the Wizard of the Crow and Nyawĩra after he visits the Wizard and is given one of their cards (pp. 360–63). When the American obesity specialist Professor Din Furyk hears the Ruler saying a word like "coral, or crawl or cruel" (pp. 472, 487), the Gikuyu reader will immediately suspect, as the Wizard does, that the Ruler is developing the disease of only being able to say "if," since *korwo* is the Gikuyu word for "if" (pp. 488–89, 490–91), as the footnote on page 490 explains. By the same token, the Gikuyu reader is likely to recognize some of the songs included in the novel or their political, religious, or folklore models.

Readers from outside East Africa should be aware that they are likely to miss many historical and political references. In his review of the novel, Simon Gikandi tells us that readers familiar with the politics of the Moi era (1978–2002) will recognize in the Ruler's banishment of his wife Rachael "the unnamed politician who, hav-ing felt slighted by his wife in public, had her confined to a rural farmhouse for thirty years, where she died alone, in abjection."[8] Gi-kandi also notes the connection to the story of Rachel from the Bible, "the Ur-text of African language written literature."[9] In his geographical and ecological study of the novel, Brady Smith com-pares the building project of Marching to Heaven with Moi's at-tempt to build Uhuru Park in downtown Nairobi.[10] In his memoir, *Birth of a Dream Weaver*, Ngũgĩ mentions the stories of the Ugan-

dan dictator Idi Amin feeding his opponents' bodies to the crocodiles while keeping their heads in a refrigerator. He also calls Daniel
arap Moi "the Kenyan Amin."[11] Understandably, Ngũgĩ does not in
this memoir of his earlier life refer to *Wizard of the Crow*, but the
Ruler's use of the crocodiles of the Red River (pp. 4–5, 453, 755) and
his charnel house of trophies of the bones and skulls of his enemies
(pp. 10–11, 522–23) must resonate with these political stories for an
East African reader. Ngũgĩ's main intended audience was a Kenyan
one; these readers would pick up much more rapidly than anglo-
phones on his games with the language and his historical and political allusions.

At the same time, *Wizard of the Crow* makes masterful use of the
form of the novel. There is an elaborate and well-managed plot,
divided between a sequence of very tense scenes of interrogation
and vast public set-pieces, such as the dedication of the site of the
Marching to Heaven skyscraper (pp. 245–54) and the Day of National Rebirth (pp. 666–91). Incidents which seem to be set aside at
an earlier point in the plot, such as the decision to send the five
motorcyclists to the different regions (pp. 164–65) and Kaniuru's
dealings with the bank employee Jane Kanyori (p. 344, 447–48),
return later with devastating effect (pp. 562–64, 711–15, 747). Like
Emily Brontë, to whom he often refers, Ngũgĩ makes use of a range
of narrators and compels the reader to reconstruct the story on the
basis of judgments about their differing viewpoints and credibility.[12]
Wizard of the Crow presents a range of strong characters through
whose eyes we see some of the events and whose point of view and
motivations the reader is made to inhabit and understand, even
when he or she may want to criticize them. There is an attractive,
amusing, and sometimes surprising group of minor characters, such
as the former policeman A.G., who tells much of the story; Gautama, the owner of the Mars Café, who always wants to talk about
space exploration; Nyawĩra's mother, Roithi, who refuses to have
anything to do with the pressure being placed on her daughter; and
her upwardly mobile father, Wangahũ, who laments women's lack
of understanding of the value of the property he is wriggling to con-
serve. As fiction, the novel is open to the strange, the irrational, and
the exaggerated. The dictator's discovery of SID, self-induced disap-
pearance (p. 697), has something in common with the spontaneous

combustion of Dickens's *Bleak House*, while the grand skyscraper project Marching to Heaven, which will enable the Ruler to speak with God, may recall the projects of Mr. Merdle from *Little Dorrit* or the Golden Dustman from *Our Mutual Friend*. *Wizard of the Crow* exploits the capaciousness of the novel form, which can embrace the Ruler and the beggars, the country and the city, allow readers access to the thoughts and schemes of a wide range of individuals, and enable them to make conclusions and judgments about their behavior and the structure of the society in which they live. The capaciousness of the novel, its ability to admit different kinds of language, is part of its nature as a form, though it may now be under threat.[13]

Wizard of the Crow incorporates Gikuyu folktales, songs, and proverbs, Bible stories, and other elements of Kenyan oral culture. Nyawĩra tells Vinjinia's children the well-known Kikuyu fable of the Ogre who torments the Blacksmith's wife (pp. 154–56).[14] The children join in with the song associated with this story, and they pick up from it the idea of the ogre with two mouths which becomes important later in the novel (pp. 733, 739–40). In Nyawĩra's telling of the story, the intermediary who calls the husband back to save his wife and child from the ogre is a weaver-bird, but in some traditional versions this intermediary is a dove. Nyawĩra and Vinjinia agree to use the word "dove" as a code word for seeking help from each other because, here adding a Bible reference to the folktale, "Dove is the messenger of peace and salvation" (pp. 465–66, 618–20, 740).[15] Simon Gikandi connects the moment when Vinjinia's daughter Gacirũ becomes trapped at the Lake of Tears (pp. 440–43, 736–38) with the folk story of the girl who was sacrificed in the lake.[16] In Ngũgĩ's adaptation of this tale, the daughter is freed from the lake by tears of laughter, because laughter conquers sorrow (p. 739). Gikandi also explains the baring of the bottoms of the women activists (p. 250) as "a traditional form of female protest, one drawn from Gikuyu oral traditions," and explains that the Wizard of the Crow is a character in traditional stories.[17] The invocation of the novel ("In the spirit of the dead, the living and the unborn . . .") and the naming of the six books of the novel after different kinds of daemon (Power Daemons, Female Daemons, Bearded Daemons, and so on) further evokes the prominence of spirits and representatives of the dead in

Gikuyu folklore.[18] The bearded spirits play a key role at the end of the novel.

Songs are a central feature of the performance of Gikuyu folktales. They often round off the tales and give them a wider meaning. The audience is sometimes expected to join in with the songs, even when they are spoken by a particular character.[19] Ngũgĩ frequently inserts songs into the narrative of *Wizard of the Crow*, sometimes echoing hymns (pp. 87, 655, 737) or love songs (pp. 451, 466), but also making points which the characters wish to underline. When the ruler addresses the nation on television after the protest at the birthday party, he denounces the protesters and their plastic snakes, saying that his Pharaonic snakes will swallow those who think they are the new Moses.[20] This results in the popularization of a snake dance and a song, which could almost be an epigraph for the whole novel:

> *The pot I made is broken*
> *Little did I know that freedom*
> *Would bear a viper and a devil* (p. 25, emphasis in original)

When Kamĩtĩ has returned from America and is searching for Nyawĩra among the queues, he comes across a better-organized procession of protesters, expressing their sense of purpose in a song:

> *The people have spoken*
> *The people have spoken*
> *Give me back my voice*
> *The people have spoken*
> *Give me back the voice you took from me* (p. 591, emphasis in original)

On the day of national rebirth, the students sing another version of this song.

> *Look in my eyes and see*
> *I don't fear death*
> *As I demand the voice*
> *You took from me* (p. 676, emphasis in original)

Songs express many of the key demands of the protesters throughout the novel (pp. 74, 253, 308, 310), but they are also used to introduce characters of the story, as when the church children adapt a

British nursery rhyme to introduce the cat of Maritha and Mariko (p. 30), which will later become one of the key symbols of consolation in the novel (pp. 588, 657–59, 731) and will be crucified by the "Soldiers of Christ" (pp. 663–64, 729).

Wizard of the Crow allots an important role to proverbs, viewed as acute summaries of traditional wisdom but also as arguments which can be exploited in different ways by different sides. Some proverbs are spoken by narrators to explain or naturalize events (pp. 51, 75), but they can also be spoken by characters or used to comment on their actions (pp. 51, 83). The main narrator uses an adage to introduce minister Sikiokuu's rage at having to repay to the Ruler some bribes he had not even received: "There is nobody quicker to anger than a thief who has been robbed" (p. 566). When the Ruler gloats over the demise of the other minister, Machokali, he announces: "A cunning robber may well meet his match in a stealthy thief" (p. 607). Ngũgĩ amuses us at the Ruler's expense when he creatively garbles an English proverb:

> "What do the English say? The price of internal vigilance is freedom."
>
> "Thank you, Your Mighty Excellency, for your faith in my abilities," said Sikiokuu, though he was sure that the Ruler had jumbled the words of the English proverb. (p. 559)

Whether or not freedom is protected by eternal vigilance, it is undoubtedly true that internal surveillance destroys freedom, as Ngũgĩ wants us to remember. Sikiokuu defends his inaction over the Movement for the Voice of the People with a proverb: "One does not rush to hit a snake before it has fully come out of its hole."

> Sikiokuu's attempt to defuse the Ruler's wrath by explaining that his statement was only a proverb made matters even worse. Was Sikiokuu suggesting that there were proverbs that superseded the Ruler's mighty sayings? The Ruler had power over all proverbs, all riddles in Aburĩria, and no proverb could bar him from hitting the hidden, even in the most inaccessible of holes. (p. 24)

Because proverbs aspire to encapsulate traditional wisdom, the Ruler regards them as threats to his power which must be overturned by his own "mighty sayings."

The novel makes many references to the Bible, which, as we have seen, Ngũgĩ regards as a primary source of inspiration and Gikandi views as the foundational text of African-language written literature. The project of Marching to Heaven recalls the project of building the Tower of Babel to reach the heavens, and Foreign Minister Machakoli mentions the comparison in proposing this wonder of the world (p. 17).[21] When the Ruler, inspired by stories of an ancient king of Babylon, decides to walk among the people and visit All Saints Cathedral, he chooses to ride there on a donkey, in imitation of Christ (p. 27).[22] When Tajirika is first interrogated, he annoys Njoya (here playing "good cop") by answering some of his questions, "You have spoken," the words of Jesus to Pilate (pp. 316, 322).[23] This inspires his interrogator Njoya to a biblical phrase of his own:

> "*And the truth shall make you free.* Is that not what the Bible says?"
>> "But you said I was not in custody."
>> "It is just a way of talking. Tell the truth and shame the Devil."
> (p. 323)[24]

His denial of the (unintended) implication of his ostentatious phrase reveals Njoya's cynicism. The Ruler's use of biblical language in congratulating Kaniũrũ on finding out the Wizard's hiding place ("You have done well. Go home and continue in your righteousness" pp. 655–56) inspires him to find a new use for his art in helping to conceal the Ruler's balloonlike weightlessness.

> He would place his chosen God in a tangible heaven, and it was then that he thought he knew the full meaning of the words of his namesake, John the Baptist, when he said: *And behold I saw a new heaven and a new earth. Amen.* (p. 656; Revelation 21:1)

This language of revelation and new life will return at the end of the novel when the four riders sent off in imitation of the apocalypse (pp. 164–65) return as the bearded spirits, fetched from death row to Tajirika, sitting on Sikiokuu's copy of the Ruler's raised chair.

> The riders assumed him a deity. Wonderful Tumbo said loudly, with absolute conviction: He is the chosen one, a man set apart by the gods. The four spirits abandoned themselves to newfound joy and gratitude for life restored, and there was nothing they would not do for their

savior. They listened with all their power to every word of what was
expected of them. They would conceal weapons under their hair when
they went to meet with the Ruler at the State House. (p. 752)

Biblical language and quotations from the Bible are so engrained in
these characters' consciousness that they are normal ways of responding to unusual situations. Ngũgĩ shows how they are used to
exalt existing holders of power but also to anoint and legitimize the
seizure of power. Equally disturbingly, the pious Vinjinia uses the
language of the incarnation ("To us is now born a savior, Baby D," p.
735) to explain why she no longer wishes to associate with Nyawĩra,
even before her husband seizes power. It may be worth pointing out
that much of this use of biblical language is associated with negative
figures in the novel.

The forcefulness of oral storytelling within the novel is emphasized by the figure of A.G., whose storytelling methods are described
retrospectively, close to the beginning of the novel.

> Later, after his own life had taken twists and turns defying all rational
> explanation even for him, a trained police officer, Constable Arigaigai
> Gathere always found himself surrounded by crowds wanting to hear
> story after story about the Wizard of the Crow. . . . If his storytelling
> took place in a bar, it was fueled to new heights of imagination by an
> endless supply of liquor. When the setting was a village, a marketplace
> or the crossroads, Constable Arigaigai Gathere felt charged with energy
> on seeing the rapt faces of the men, women and children waiting to
> catch his every word. But whatever the setting, his listeners came away
> with food of the spirit: resilient hope that no matter how intolerable
> things seemed, a change for the better was always possible. (p. 96)

Many of the confusions which were later evident in information
about the Wizard turned out to be the result of different ways in
which A.G. had told his stories (pp. 570–71, 586–87). Ngũgĩ even
allows himself to joke that the existence of the Ruler's chamber of
skulls might turn out to be no more than a rumor "or tale from the
mouth of Askari Arigaigai Gathere" (p. 11). The possibility of reaching a wide collective audience through oral storytelling is linked in
Ngũgĩ's practice with the decision to publish in Gikuyu (probably
with reference to his novel *Devil on the Cross*).

When the Kikuyu novel came out it was bought by families who would get someone who reads very well to read for everybody. In other words the novel was appropriated by the peasantry, it became a collective form and part of the oral tradition. Even the people who could read Kikuyu preferred to read it in groups, and I have been told that workers in factories during lunch hour would gather together and get one person to read the novel for them. . . . When [the novel] is appropriated by the peasantry and the working classes it may very well be transformed into a collective experience.[25]

Ngũgĩ fervently believes that stories can change people's attitudes and ultimately their lives and that a novel published in their own language can reach a wide public oral audience, both those who cannot read and those who prefer the collective experience of a story. Combining the capaciousness of the novel form with folktales, songs, proverbs, and biblical language, Ngũgĩ created a new form of writing which had a greater impact on his primary chosen audience.

The Ruler

Turning from form to subject matter, I shall consider first the political plot, which is bitterly satirical in its mode of presentation. The focus of *Wizard of the Crow* on the Ruler and his henchmen marks a new departure for Ngũgĩ, who has usually been more concerned with writing about workers and peasants. He uses the portrayal of the Ruler partly to arouse anger about the outcome of the struggle for independence and partly to help his audience understand how the forces of domination have operated. The Ruler is portrayed as vain, power-hungry, paranoid, devious, manipulative, and sexually predatory. At the same time, the reader is made to understand the pressures facing an African dictator in the global world, not just the usual problems of managing rival ministers, but also the difficulty of satisfying the global superpower, which is no longer content to applaud him for massacring socialists but demands that he adapt to a new world order or retire.[26] When the Ruler expects to receive an apology for the slights to him in New York (he is not even offered an appearance on GNN's *Meet the Global Mighty*), the American envoy instead counsels a move to democracy.

> The West and the civilized world are eternally grateful to you for your role in our victory over the evil empire. We are now embarking on a new mission of forging a global order. That is why I am now visiting all our friends to tell them to move in step with the world. To everything its season, says the preacher. There was a time when slavery was good. It did its work, and when it finished creating capital, it withered and died a natural death. Colonialism was good. It spread industrial culture of shared resources and markets. . . . We are in the post–cold war era, and our calculations are affected by the laws and needs of globalization. The history of capital can be summed up in one phrase: *in search of freedom*. Freedom to expand, and now it has a chance at the entire globe for its theater. It needs a democratic space to move as its own logic demands. So I have been sent to urge you to start thinking about turning your country into a democracy. Who knows? Maybe with your blessings, some of your ministers might even want to form opposition parties. (p. 580)

Ngũgĩ's satirical overemphasis reveals the cynicism of the American promotion of democracy for the benefit of multinational companies, but he also allows us to understand the Ruler's anger at being lectured and puzzlement at the change in American strategy. The Ruler is ruthless and cynical, but he joins the reader in astonishment at the envoy's grandiloquent hypocrisy. And then he adapts. Taking his cue from the Americans, he gives birth to a form of democracy, Baby D, which will satisfy their requests and his needs. There will be many political parties in Aburĩria, and the Ruler will be the leader of all of them (pp. 698–700). The Ruler is surprised and pleased at the ease and extent of his success. Soon the Global Bank loans are unfrozen and joint military exercises with the Americans and permanent American military bases are instituted (pp. 710, 744). Luckily, his now-discredited minister Machokali has provided him with the Ruler's *Political Theory*.

> There are no moral limits to the means that a ruler can use, from lies to lives, bribes to blows, in order to ensure that his state is stable and his power secure. But if he could keep the state stable through sacrificing

truth rather than lives, bending rather than breaking the law, sealing
the lips of the outspoken with endless trickeries rather than tearing
them with barbed-wire and hot wax, if he could buy peace through a
grand deception rather than a vast display of armored vehicles in the
streets . . . it would be the sweetest of victories. (p. 703)

This modernization and development of Machiavellianism gives the
Ruler a sense of wisdom and satisfaction, but it also perhaps high-
lights the risk of soft power. His new minister of defense (p. 717)
deposes the Ruler and seizes power by the traditional (European
and African) means of assassination of the Ruler, and the Americans
approve (pp. 752–55).

Ngũgĩ investigates the Ruler's personal life in two related ways:
the episode of the banishment of his wife Rachael and the disease
which the Ruler contracts in America and which Ngũgĩ uses to open
the novel. At one of their rare meals alone together, Rachael, who
in general had acquiesced in his infidelities, asks him not to take
schoolgirls as bed-makers:

> Are they not really our children? You father them today and tomorrow
> you turn them into wives? Have you no tears of concern for our tomor-
> row? (p. 6)

He is astonished at her accusation and banishes her to live alone, in
a house surrounded by a stone wall and an electric fence, and with
food, furniture, clothing, and clocks frozen at the moment of utter-
ing her question, to await his "second coming":

> On that day when he found that she had shed all the tears for all the
> tomorrows of all the children she had accused him of abusing, he would
> take her back to restart life exactly from where it had stopped, or rather
> Rachael would resume her life, which had been marking time, like a
> cinematic frame on pause. I am your beginning and your end. (p. 8)

He wants to show her that he controls everything, including time.
He never visits her, but he constantly receives reports on her moods
and activities, waiting for the moment of her tears, which she always
withholds. When the women protest against Marching to Heaven,
the accusation which most wounds him concerns his treatment of
Rachael.

A man who could so imprison his own wife in her home is a beast in human form! Rachael's fate speaks volumes: if a woman who had been at the mountaintop of power and visibility could be made to disappear, be silenced forever while alive, what about the ordinary woman worker and peasant? The condition of women in a nation is the real measure of its progress. *You imprison a woman and you have imprisoned a nation*, we sang in a song of celebration. (p. 253)

After the triumph of Baby D, under the delusion that he has routed all his enemies, the Ruler's thoughts turn again to Rachael. He is enraged by her defiant resistance to his attempts to make her beg for forgiveness. She roams the house of her imprisonment at night, like a ghost. Perhaps she throws the lantern at the Ruler, who has entered the house on his belly, like a snake, or perhaps she laughs in his face, collapses in her laughter, and sets light to the house. A ball of fire pursues him in his flight to the State House and gives him insomnia (pp. 707–8). The figure of Rachael requires symbolic elucidation: perhaps she stands for the part of the country that always defies the Ruler's attempts to dominate their minds, or perhaps for the resistance of women to his assaults on female bodies. Certainly she represents a mental or spiritual human limit on the godlike power which the Ruler assumes and which he can often enforce on his people's bodies.

The novel opens with a discussion of the five most popular theories for the cause of the Ruler's disease: anger, a botched scapegoating ritual involving the ruler's hair, aging, his longing for Rachael's tears, and the work of the daemons housed in the skulls and bones of his enemies kept in the State House (pp. 1–11). The disease first manifests itself in America (pp. 469–71) as a balloonlike expansion of the Ruler's body and (though this may be a separate disease, since the Wizard cures it, pp. 489–93) the inability to say any word but "if." The longer he stays in America and the more frustrated he is by his reception there, the more his body swells to the point where he has to be flown back to Aburĩria strapped to the floor of a specially adapted airplane (p. 508). Back home, the Ruler continues to swell, becomes almost weightless, floats upwards (pp. 650–52), and eventually occupies almost the whole volume of his large throne room.

On the Day of National Rebirth, his size gives him more and more pain (p. 689), to the point where "blasts of thunder like stealthy missiles had fired from each of his seven orifices and then exploded in turns" (p. 709), after which he returns to normal size. He now even believes that he might have incorporated the powers of the Wizard of the Crow (pp. 695, 707).

In its origin, the Ruler's disease should probably be linked (perhaps as a bodily reflection) with the insane expansionist project of Marching to Heaven and the mental attitude of equality with God which nurtured it. There must also be a strong connection with his experience in America, where the disease first manifests itself. He had traveled to America to address the General Assembly of the United Nations and in the hope of securing a new loan from the Global Bank. While he is in New York, he is unable to meet the president of the United States and is largely ignored by the state and the media. Anger at his treatment and his justified feeling that a white ruler would never be snubbed in that way would probably have played a part in his continued expansion. Perhaps the god-delusion of his return to Aburĩria could explain his conquest of gravity (p. 651), though the explicit link is to the Global Bank's public declaration (without prior notification) of its refusal of a loan and freezing of other funds. But the conclusion of the disease also seems to be connected to the idea of giving birth, and in particular to the arrival of Baby D. The Ruler suffers a kind of exposure and defeat when his plans for the Wizard's public confession fail and Nyawĩra and the Wizard escape, but he also manages a transformation: burning his enemies in effigy and then announcing their deaths, he secures continued power and global financial support through the travesty of democracy. The Ruler's powers are not unlimited—he can be resisted and he will eventually fall—but he has great resources of adaptation and an ability to incorporate his enemies in his project (pp. 20–21).

Along with his *Political Theory*, the Ruler promulgates a philosophy, *Magnus Africanus: Prolegomenon to Future Happiness, by the Ruler*. He has realized that the "real threat to Aburĩria's future lay in people's abandoning their traditions in pursuit of a stressful modernity" (p. 621). The center of this philosophy is a doctrine of obedience to patriarchal authority. Men should beat their wives and women should welcome this.

> Teachers would be strongly encouraged to impart to schoolchildren the virtues of the past, of unquestioning obedience. Instead of using the word *past*, they would talk about African modernity through the ages, and they should talk of the leading figures in Africa's march backward to the roots of an authentic unchanging past as the great sages of African modernity. (p. 622)

With outrageous comedy, Ngũgĩ satirizes the self-contradiction of an African modernity rooted in tradition, but he also reveals the corruption of this so-called tradition by focusing its beliefs on violence against women.[27] After Sikiokuu had extracted a confession from Tajirika which would damage Sikiokuu's ministerial rival Machokali, he orders him not to confront his wife Vinjinia with the doctored photographs which prompted the confession. Tajirika is outraged at the order not to touch her without permission. Sikiokuu agrees that an indefinite ban on wife-beating would be asking him "to give up what defines modern Aburĩrian manhood," but suggests a hotline: Tajirika should call him any time he feels the urge to beat his wife and Sikiokuu will tell him if the time is ripe (p. 404). The comedy of this twisted exchange is firmly rooted in Ngũgĩ's rejection of violence against women and his refusal of the regime's idea that African tradition should be defined by it. Ngũgĩ points out that neo-colonialist rulers can enlist elements of African tradition to reinforce their repressive politics.

Ngũgĩ's portrayal of the Ruler invites comparison with Shakespeare's depiction of tyrants like Richard III and Macbeth. Ngũgĩ quite often refers to *Macbeth* and was involved in an African dress production of the play at Makerere University College.[28] One of the Ruler's reactions to anxiety looks like an adaptation of a motif from *Macbeth*. An oracle in a neighboring country had assured the Ruler that

> only a bearded spirit could seriously threaten his rule. Though he read this as meaning that no human could overthrow him, for, since they had no bodily form, spirits could never grow beards, he became sensitive to

beards and then decreed . . . that all goats and humans must have their beards shaved off. (p. 5)

Just as Macbeth believes that the equivocating predictions of the witches about the man not born of woman and the moving forest mean that he can never be overthrown, so the Ruler is comforted by the oracle.[29] But at the end of the novel, the four motorcycle riders return, covered in long silver hair and beards. Their psychological and spiritual threat to the ruler is doubled by the social message they bring back from their long tour of the country.

> Now, despite years of lonely toil, they were glad to report that people in Aburĩria were catching up with the rest of the world; and that from north, south, east, and west, nay, from the remotest rural villages and urban centers, queues were forming and slowly marching toward the capital, singing an end to the causes of all the cries of the dispossessed. They want a clean atmosphere so that people can have clean air to breathe, clean water to drink, and clean spaces to live and enjoy. They reject the rule of the viper and the ogre. Their songs end up in chorus with the other parts of the globe: Don't let them kill our future. (p. 748)

The spirits bring back the central message of the novel: that city dwellers and peasants are united with people in other countries across the globe in the need for a share of the country's wealth, a clean environment, and an honest government. The Ruler sentences the bearded spirits / policemen to death, in spite of the fact that they can show that they were carrying out his orders (pp. 748–49). Tajirika reprieves them, and as the bearded daemons of the title of book 6, they kill the Ruler for him. So, as in *Macbeth*, the impossible oracle is fulfilled and a naturalistic explanation is offered for what could also be presented, this time on television, as magical:

> The four spirits calmly said that they had been sent by the dead, the living and the unborn to tell the nation that the Ruler and the official hostess . . . had been recalled by the ancestors that very morning. (p. 753)

Later the people of Aburĩria are informed that the Ruler himself had been aware of this summons and a few weeks before had secretly transferred all his powers to the new ruler, Emperor Titus Flavius Vespasianus Whitehead (pp. 753, 751), known to us as Tajirika, who had engineered the Ruler's assassination.

Nyawĩra

Turning now to the love plot and to the opponents of the regime, Nyawĩra, who is beautiful, intelligent, resourceful, independent, and determined, is presented like a heroine of a Shakespearean comedy. She disguises herself in many different forms, perhaps using her training in theater arts (p. 64). When Kamĩtĩ first meets her, she is linked to the scent of flowers (pp. 50, 61). She joins him in his humiliation outside Tajirika's office, sits down beside him, and begins to weep. Soon their shared tears turn to laughter, anticipating one of the novel's main themes. Nyawĩra introduces the idea that Tajirika may be an ogre with two mouths, like the ones in the stories (pp. 61–63). When they meet again in the dark without recognizing each other, they are again linked through laughter (p. 77). Like the heroine of a Shakespearean comedy, Nyawĩra takes the initiative in their love affair and their lovemaking (pp. 89–91, 202–6, 723–24). She is in control but also playful, as in her use of the plastic snake to frighten and then arouse Kamĩtĩ (pp. 89–91). She collaborates with the Wizard in the foundation and operation of the shrine, and she continues his work of healing in his absence (pp. 274–76, 296, 428). She protects him from danger. Even though the Wizard instructs her to stay under cover, she emerges and ritually threatens the policemen arresting him, temporarily paralyzing them and making them afraid to mislay even a hair of his head (pp. 372–73), with later comic consequences when they take the instruction literally (pp. 418, 427, 660, 755). Twice Nyawĩra devises ways of rescuing him from government custody, and she lies over him to protect him when he has been shot and takes him to a secret hospital where he can be treated (pp. 626–31, 676, 688–91, 759).

Nyawĩra is also a strong feminist and a modern woman. When she first meets Kamĩtĩ, she gives him a list of African and Indian women writers to read (p. 83). She interrupts their first scene of attempted lovemaking to criticize Kamĩtĩ for not carrying a condom and provides one herself on the next occasion (pp. 91–93, 203). She takes the initiative in organizing the women to avenge the beating of Vinginia (pp. 428–39). Nyawĩra's political creed emphasizes the need to overturn the oppression of women:

> "I believe that black has been oppressed by white; female by male; peasant by landlord; and worker by lord of capital. It follows from this that the black female worker and peasant is most oppressed. . . . Three burdens she has to carry. Those who want to fight for the people in the nation and in the world must struggle for the unity and rights of the working class in their own country; fight against all discriminations based on race, ethnicity, color, and belief systems; they must struggle against all gender-based inequalities and therefore fight for the rights of women in the home, the family, the nation, and the world." (p. 428)

Protests by women form an important part of her political repertory. In the protest against the dedication of the site for Marching to Heaven, Nyawĩra and her companions use a traditional African form of women's protest, baring their behinds to the dignitaries, while shouting their slogan, "MARCHING TO HEAVEN IS A MOUNTAIN OF SHIT" (pp. 246–50, all caps in original). For the protest at the opening of Kaniũrũ's office, they equip themselves with traditional women's clothing of leather skirts and red-ochered tops to frame Vinjinia's demand for news of Tajirika's imprisonment, and they sing songs about the sanctity of the family and the need to fight for the progress of the people and the land (pp. 304–10). Nyawĩra uses African traditions to make arguments against oppression and in favor of women's rights.

An active member of the dissident political organization, the Movement for the Voice of the People, Nyawĩra has to interrupt other activities to attend meetings (pp. 64, 125). The movement employs traditional African beliefs to increase the effect of their protests, particularly in their use of snakes (pp. 22, 24–25, 64). Nyawĩra takes part in, and probably inspires, the distribution of leaflets and snakes (p. 127). She helps to fortify the beggars' protest with stronger political slogans, such as "Marching to Heaven Is Marching to Hell," "Your Strings of Loans Are Chains of Slavery," and "The March to Heaven Is Led by Dangerous Snakes" (p. 74). She takes part in discussions about protests and tactics (pp. 428, 666, 669–70). Only at the end of the novel do we learn that Nyawĩra is in fact the leader of the movement (pp. 756–60). The imperative to reject "customs" which oppress women is enunciated by Nyawĩra in her statement of the aims of her political movement.

> Biology is Fate. Politics is choice. No, the life of even the least among us should be sacred, and it will not do for any region or community to keep silent when the people of another region and community are being slaughtered. The wealth of science, technology, and arts should enrich peoples' lives, not enable their slaughter. We oppose the tendency to make women carry the weight of customs that have outlived the contexts that may have made them necessary or even useful earlier. (p. 726)

Nyawĩra's choice of political engagement can be a source of tension between her and Kamĩtĩ. When he asks her to remain with him in the forest to find themselves and learn from the trees and the animals, she replies that she needs to be involved in the fight against Marching to Heaven and leaves him (pp. 207–13). After she has been put on the most-wanted list and seeks refuge in the forest, he changes his mind, arguing that they will be safer among the people and that there is a foulness inundating their society which they need to fight (pp. 215–16, 264–66). At different points in the novel, she expresses irritation with his spiritual preoccupations, but she also recognizes that he has changed her and that without him there is something missing in her life (pp. 196, 427).

The Wizard of the Crow

Kamĩtĩ's is the first (at first unnamed) consciousness that the reader enters in the novel. We witness an out-of-body experience as, lying on a pile of garbage, he imagines being a bird flying over all five regions of Aburĩria. Huge wealth sits beside poverty, and everywhere people are hungry, thirsty, and in rags. He realizes that he is not alone. Luckily, and much to the consternation of the dustmen, he returns to his body before it is carried to the dumpsite (pp. 38–41). We follow his thoughts as he looks for a job, at first leaping with joy at the attention Tajirika pays to his qualifications, and then groaning in despair at his humiliation (pp. 50–59).

Kamĩtĩ becomes the Wizard of the Crow as an act of improvisation to escape from a policeman, and then to escape the possible consequences of the first lie (pp. 77, 98–99). He calls himself a make-believe wizard (p. 125), but readers may not be quite so sure, because we are introduced to him almost as a corpse returning to life, because his out-of-body experiences recur, and because when he returns home he learns from his parents that he was born into a line of healers and seers and with the sign of the seashell in his hand (pp. 294–95). He has a physical aversion to the stench of corruption and of money, which seems to echo his father's observation that the healer-seer can never possess more than food, clothes, and shelter (pp. 122–23, 208–10, 295). People who visit him seem to be impressed by his personality, and even Nyawĩra, who witnessed the original improvisation, is struck by his ability to see into people's souls and entice them to do things they would normally resist. She finds that her skepticism about magic is being shaken (p. 196). Ngũgĩ is careful to offer readers both traditional African and more empirical Western explanations for the Wizard's powers.

Apart from his initial attempt to frighten away the policeman searching for him, Kamĩtĩ's practice as a wizard is generally marked by the techniques of the counselor or the psychotherapist. He questions people; he listens acutely to what they tell him; he tries to draw out their hidden fears and motivations; and he persuades them to enact scenes involving their desires in order to lead them beyond the point of impasse (pp. 171–88, 489–92). He dispenses moral advice and precepts of healthy living (pp. 274–80, 359–60). His use of the mirror in his consultations may be intended to impress people, or it may be an indication of a semi-occult power (pp. 117–19, 490–91). On one occasion, Kamĩtĩ relies on this assumption of its occult power to trick Sikiokuu (pp. 408–11). Certainly he seems to have an uncanny knack for knowing when people are lying to him and what it is they are trying to conceal.

When Kamĩtĩ is in New York, he has a second vision during a sleep that lasts a week (pp. 496–97). A voice tells him to visit all the dwelling places of black people around the world and find the sources of their power. In the shape of a bird, he travels to Egypt, to East, South, and West Africa, to the Caribbean, and to New York, alighting everywhere to glean wisdom (p. 494). This incident is recalled at the end of the novel, when Kamĩtĩ looks at a map on the wall of the headquarters of the Movement for the Voice of the People and sees a moving, neon-lit arrow tracing his journey across Africa and stopping and flickering at centers of ancient black civilization that he should remember, whereas the others present see only a map with red arrows attached to it (p. 757).

Earlier in the book, Kamĩtĩ has been characterized as a person interested in ancient Indian literature and religion (pp. 55). He mentions the teachings of Buddhism, Jainism, and Sikhism alongside traditional African beliefs (pp. 210–11), discusses the tenets of Taoism (p. 266), and retells stories from the *Mahabharata* (pp. 382–83, 723). *The Ramayana* and the teachings of the Buddha return at the end of the novel in the words of the former proprietor of the now-closed Mars Café, the aptly named Gautama (p. 765). Kamĩtĩ describes what he has learned from nature, solitude, and a study of the properties of plants, under the influence of Indian healers. This culminates in his display to Nyawĩra of the African deities he has carved in his pan-African pantheon of the sacred (pp. 267–68). Ngũgĩ links Kamĩtĩ's outlook and powers to the Indian and African deities and philosophies which he has studied. He is very much a global figure of the woods, a postcolonial sorcerer (p. 405).

Kamĩtĩ's emotions and beliefs are expressed most clearly in the great virtuoso set-piece scene of the novel, the appearance of the Wizard before the People's Assembly. The Ruler has preempted the Movement for the Voice of the People's planned national strike and Day of National Self-Renewal by announcing that that same day will be the celebration of his birthday, a national holiday, and the day on which the Wizard of the Crow will make a public confession to the People's Assembly. The students preside over the assembly, Minister of Information Big Ben Mambo officiates, and the Wizard will speak. The reader observes different groups watching the proceedings and preparing to act: Kaniũrũ plans to assassinate the Wizard, Sikiokuu has been instructed by the Ruler to kidnap the Wizard, and Nyawĩra and the movement are waiting for their moment to intervene in order to rescue him from imprisonment. The Ruler, now grossly expanded, is watching on television, directing events as best he can. At the same time, he is being filmed and observed by the American and African doctors who are trying to heal his "self induced expansion" (pp. 492, 669–80). The Wizard has been instructed by the Ruler to confess his part in the rumor of the Ruler's pregnancy, to reveal the whereabouts of Nyawĩra, to remove the daemons of queuing, and to cleanse the crowd of defiance against the state (pp. 667, 682), but he has no idea what to say.

> Kamĩtĩ did not know how to begin or what to tell the gathering. Again he wished he had had a chance to speak with Nyawĩra. But, as that was not meant to be, he was now on his own. A loner by nature, he disliked public speaking, and here was a multitude in rapt attention! He had taken on the identity of the Wizard of the Crow as a cover, a joke, and now he was expected to be true to that identity. . . . He hated lies and lying, even for private gain, and now he was expected to lie publicly for another's gain. He had wanted to root his life in truth—even as a diviner he had tried his best to avoid falsehood—and here he was, his life hanging on a false confession! (p. 679)

He begins by retelling the story of his flight around Africa and telling a parable of how humans surrendered control over their lives to the blind deity of money and market.

> "Why did Africa let Europe cart away millions of Africa's souls from the continent to the four corners of the wind? How could Europe lord it over a continent ten times its size? Why does needy Africa continue to let its wealth meet the needs of those outside its borders and then follow behind with hands outstretched for a loan of the very wealth it let go? How did we arrive at this, that the best leader is the one who knows how to beg for a share of what he has already given away at the price of a broken tool? Where is the future of Africa? I cried. . . .
>
> "Don't cry despair at those who sold the heritage; smile also with pride at the achievements of those that struggle to rescue our heritage. . . . What kind of tomorrow was Aburĩria pregnant with? Of unity or murderous divisions? Of cries or laughter? Our tomorrow is determined by what we do today. Our fate is in our hands." (p. 681)

As Kamĩtĩ speaks the Ruler's painful contractions intensify, and he eventually loses his ability to control events. Again Kamĩtĩ tries to think of what Nyawĩra would do in this situation. He calculates that the Ruler will not want to execute him on television. He smashes all the foreign mirrors which Sikiokuu has provided to help his divination.

"Since true divination is about revealing the hidden," he said, "I want to share with you the secrets of my heart. I know Nyawĩra. I love her and will never betray her, even if I must go to the land of no return. Nyawĩra, I know, will be there with me, for she found me in pieces and made me whole. . . . Nyawĩra is you. Nyawĩra is you and me and others. . . . If you know that you are Nyawĩra, please rise so that those who have been looking for you, calling you an enemy of the state, may see you. Nyawĩra, show us the way."

A woman stood up; I am Nyawĩra, she said. Hardly had the eyes of the people turned to her than a man stood up and said, I am Nyawĩra; he was followed by every other woman and man until the entire assembly proclaimed itself Nyawĩra. (pp. 687–88)

The policemen in the crowd are confused. People start to sing and dance about building a beautiful land with knowledge and the heart. The Ruler, in desperate pain, gives the signal for the kidnapping; Kaniũrũ shoots the Wizard and is wrestled to the ground. Different groups invade the assembly; there are seven explosions, and a mushroom cloud appears. Everyone flees, assuming that a coup has taken place. Nyawĩra shields Kamĩtĩ's wounded body (pp. 688–91).

The scene of chaotic bloodshed is very reminiscent of a penultimate scene from an Elizabethan tragedy, like *The Spanish Tragedy*, *The White Devil*, or *Hamlet*, in which everyone is watching everyone else watching a performance, but the performance goes wrong and the audience witnesses the actual deaths of some of the protagonists. In another way, it is reminiscent of a Shakespearean comedy, or of the trial scene in *Mary Barton*, in which the heroine (but this time the hero) makes a public declaration of love. It also evidently echoes American popular culture in the recollection of "I am Spartacus." Probably Ngũgĩ knows all of these works, but none of them is strictly speaking a source for the scene. Still, the idea of the watchers being watched by other audiences and the idea of the mass declaration of solidarity must have been part of what inspired the development of this scene. Ngũgĩ wants us to understand that all workers are enemies of this kind of state and that security and hope lie in collective action and the solidarity each individual displays as she stands up and identifies with work (Nyawĩra). The conclusion of the chaos is optimistic in the sense that Kamĩtĩ is saved from certain death and reunited with Nyawĩra, but also realistic in that the Ruler retains control by embracing fake democracy, Baby D.

At the end of the novel, Kamĩtĩ moves toward Nyawĩra's position by returning to the city, joining the movement, and realizing that organized collective action is required to heal the land (p. 725). But Nyawĩra comes to understand the vital role of his gifts when she appoints him to head the clinic, to develop it as a nursery of health and clean living, and to complete his carvings of the African deities (pp. 759–60). The Wizard's visions of pan-African deities are offered as a better substitute for Christian imagery and biblical language, which had been tainted by association with the neocolonialist power of the Ruler and his supporters. Kamĩtĩ's studies of the achievements of black people around the world and his carvings of pan-African deities are presented as ways to use traditions positively and internationally in order to complete the process of political change. Kamĩtĩ is determinedly internationalist and pan-African, whereas Nyawĩra is preoccupied with the economic and political situation in Aburĩria. This conclusion functions as a resolution of their debate in the middle of the novel, when she temporarily leaves him, arguing that she is concerned with the ministry of wounded bodies while he is preoccupied with wounded souls (pp. 212–13). This is also the point which Ngũgĩ emphasizes at the end of his 2006 interview with Ken Olende for *Socialist Worker*:

> In my view the goal of human society is not just to feed and clothe and shelter. There must be a spiritual dimension. For me religion is an expression of our desires and our spiritual being. There is no reason why art will not always express our ethics or ideals. Stories will always be there. The struggle to transform ourselves will always be there and that struggle will always be expressed in art.[30]

Critics have noted that *Wizard of the Crow* picks up ideas (including sculpture) from Ngũgĩ's earlier works and does something new with them.[31] Part of what is new is the comic lens through which events are exaggerated to the point of absurdity. *Wizard of the Crow* looks forward and confronts the issues raised by the globalization of capital, which the Ruler calls "corporonialism" (p. 747). Ngũgĩ incorporates African history, folktales, and traditions in the European form of the novel to write about an African present and future reality. He uses indigenous African traditions alongside imported ones, such as biblical stories and phrases, but he is suspicious of both kinds, and he shows that both can be misused for opportunistic purposes. More than his other works, *Wizard of the Crow* is concerned with the ongoing psychological consequences of colonialism and displays Ngũgĩ's understanding of how the political machine of tyranny functions and how it distorts reality. In incorporating the songs, magic, and teaching of the Gikuyu folktale, the novel entertains and offers personal hope while also teaching harsh and realistic lessons. *Wizard of the Crow* is the novel which, together with his lifetime of creative work, should win Ngũgĩ the Nobel Prize. If it does, it will fittingly be the first novel written in an African language to achieve this honor.

Writers' and Readers' Traditions

THE STUDIES IN THIS book have suggested seven ways in which authors have used their reading of previous writers. In the first place, writers may treat their reading as a model. We find this very strongly in Chaucer's rewriting of Boccaccio's *Il Filostrato* as *Troilus and Criseyde*. Chaucer took over the plot, many of the incidents, suggestions for characters, and even many phrases, but he used the earlier work to make something that was distinctively his own. Petrarch's uses of the writings of the troubadours and the earlier Italian poets for ideas about the form, content, and approach of his poems serve as a further example.

Second, a slightly weaker but parallel approach is to take over more limited elements of material from one's reading. Thus, Petrarch never based an entire Italian poem on a classical Latin model, but he often took over phrases and ideas from Ovid and Virgil. Tasso and Spenser sometimes based a whole episode on a passage of Virgil or Ariosto, but their overall plans and their major characters were mostly decisively different. Gaskell and Ngũgĩ sometimes took ideas for an incident from, or based phrases on, the Bible or, in Ngũgĩ's case, African folklore. Chaucer's use of Dante or Ovid might fall into this category. The use of material from one's reading is so common in literature as to be almost universal.

In the third place, writers may learn how to write and pick up elements of method from their reading. Thus, Chaucer learned from his reading of Boccaccio's poetry ways in which he could adapt and develop Boccaccio's original text, and those lessons in turn influenced his approach to writing *The Canterbury Tales*. Ngũgĩ learned about how to use multiple narrators from his studies of Brontë and Conrad. Gaskell believed that she had a distinctive approach to writing fiction, but when she tried to explain her method to aspiring writers, she used the examples of Defoe and Shakespeare for support.

Fourth, reading an earlier author may stimulate a writer to do things differently. Reading Aristotle and Homer prompted Tasso to take a different approach to writing epic from his admired (and obligatory) models, Virgil and Ariosto; at the same time, Tasso chose to express that difference by adding episodes and motifs based on Ariosto to a structure taken from history but organized on Homeric lines. Spenser based the overall structure of *The Faerie Queene* on a reorganization of Ariosto's world picture prompted by Protestantism and the aim of moral education, but he added episodes based on Ovid, Plato, and Tasso.

The sense of a literary and moral tradition, both in the past and in the present, may provide a writer with support and encouragement in undertaking something new. Gaskell wrote of the strength which she received from the words of Carlyle. She bolstered *Mary Barton* with quotations from workers' poetry and from classic English literature in order to emphasize the historical roots of the new work she was attempting. Ngũgĩ was encouraged to write by his early reading of African and Caribbean writers, and he was helped into print by the personal support of Chinua Achebe. Chaucer sought to associate *Troilus and Criseyde* with the great writers of classical antiquity and with the personal support of learned contemporaries such as Gower and Strode.

Sixth, many of our writers combine elements from different national traditions. Chaucer and Spenser both looked to Italian models to help them write the first great long poem and the first epic, respectively, in English (apart from *Beowulf*, which neither of them knew). Ngũgĩ deliberately combined what he had learned about novel writing from writers across the world with local Gikuyu traditions such as proverbs, biblical language, and political mythology. Petrarch drew on classical Latin poetry to enrich forms and elements which he took from the Provençal troubadours, the Sicilian poets, and recent Italian poetry.

Finally, tradition itself may become a site of struggle within the text, as when Gaskell contrasts traditional expectations of female behavior with what Mary needs to do, or when she describes John Carson's understandable and habitual way of responding with the obligation laid on him by the Bible. Ngũgĩ reveals the way in which some African proverbs and practices are distorted by the Ruler and his associates to promote their divisive ideology. Eventually the movement entrusts to the Wizard of the Crow the task of investigating pan-African religious stories, beliefs, and practices as the basis for a new social framework.

My aim in this book has been to study enough examples to indicate the richness, the spread, and the variety of uses of literary tradition. The examples I have discussed show both that great original work often involves heavy reliance on previous authors and traditions and that this reliance has different aspects and forms. It is not unthinkable that there could be a new work which relies not at all on literary tradition, but the balance of the historical record is probably against such instances. There may be some moments at which a particular national literature is more open to ideas of renewal from the past or to external influences, but in practice the success or failure of a particular influence depends mainly on the quality of the individual writer's work and the readiness of an audience to embrace that work.

All the examples studied have shown the role of free choice in a writer's possession of tradition. Within literary tradition, freedom plays a far more significant role than obligation. Even where certain previous writers seemed to be unavoidable—for example, Ariosto for Tasso, or Dante for Petrarch—there turned out to be freedom in the way the inheritance could be employed. Writers have, and need, considerable freedom both in their choice of models and in how they adapt those models. Yet the underpinning offered by an awareness of tradition is also very valuable. Reading and working from previous works makes it possible to learn from the past. Previous texts and traditions may provide readers with expectations which give the writer further ways to make meanings—for example, through surprise changes of outcome or reassertions of expectations. Free choice is closely related to play, a crucial aspect of an author's use of earlier texts. If the play is overt, it may itself extend the range of possible meanings which can be conveyed to the reader. Chaucer's case is the most complicated. Probably his audience had no knowledge of Boccaccio's *Il Filostrato*. If they had known it, his game of calling the previous poet Lollius would have seemed pointless. Still, he explicitly alerts readers to the existence of a prior text and to his intention to add to it. When he describes himself as having found Troilus's very words and then translates a sonnet by Petrarch, Chaucer may assume that his audience will not know the poem, but it would still be a good joke if they did know. On other occasions, such as in *The Clerk's Tale*, Chaucer does admit to translating Petrarch.

The Bible and Christian tradition are used in different ways by the writers we have studied. In the *Canzoniere*, Petrarch adopts phrases from the Latin Bible and alludes to many religious practices, including pilgrimage and veneration of sacred images. In *Troilus and Criseyde*, Chaucer presents Troilus's final turn away from the human world mainly through Boethius, Dante, and the Christian commonplace of the enduring love of God. In *The Canterbury Tales*, he uses Bible stories, such as Noah's flood and Judas's betrayal of Jesus, for comic effect, but he employs Christian ideas, such as the prisonlike inferiority of human life, for serious purposes. In Tasso, liturgical phrases and practices frequently appear. God expresses his views through angels and dreams rather than through Bible texts, but Tasso twice alludes to the New Testament episode of the transfiguration. The key transformation of Armida is conducted through two allusions to the phrase "handmaid of God" (*ancilla Dei*), which appears in Luke 1:38 but is also frequently heard in the liturgy through the canticle *Nunc dimittis*. Spenser makes very strong use of the Bible in book I of *The Faerie Queene*, especially the Revelation to John, for his depiction of Duessa, and of baptism, holy communion, and Christ's passage from the crucifixion to the resurrection in the battle between Redcrosse and the dragon. In *Mary Barton*, Gaskell first marks Carson's crucial move toward forgiveness and understanding through his blasphemous reference to the Lord's Prayer and later through his contemplation of Christ's prayer on the cross (Luke 23:34), prompted by the girl he watches in the street. Gaskell strongly asserts that a more truly Christian response from the mill owners is a precondition of the improvement of society. Ngũgĩ's characters frequently imitate phrases from the Bible. The Ruler's project of Marching to Heaven is inspired by the Tower of Babel, while Sikiokuu models his response to the Ruler on the Revelation to John. Like some African traditions, the Bible is presented as a source of the tricks by which the postcolonial ruling class keeps the populace in its place, and there is at least a suggestion at the end of the novel that the apparatus of Christianity should be replaced, or at least moderated, by the pan-African pantheon of deities which the Wizard is carving.

A confrontation with tradition makes writers aware of how one learns to write. Both Petrarch and Gaskell write letters about the training of writers. For Petrarch, the key is the right kind of imitation, whereas for Gaskell the central point is to imagine concrete situations as vividly as possible and to develop plots on the basis of one's reading. We have seen how Chaucer improved his skills in writing by translating Boccaccio and by using Boccaccio's methods to adapt *Il Filostrato*. Renaissance poets believed that the epic was the pinnacle to which their craft aspired, and from their reading of Virgil they understood that writing an epic required both the use of existing models and bold innovation related to contemporary conditions. Meditating on the work of Ariosto enabled Tasso and Spenser to write their own very different epics. Studying the ways in which writers have used their reading helps readers understand how old books can be used to make new meanings.

An interest in literary tradition focuses attention on the role of the reader in creating the significance of a book. The moral education of the reader is the guiding structural principle of *The Faerie Queene*. Spenser wants us to think about the right answer to the episodes faced by his knights and to learn from the houses they visit and the books they read about religious and ethical principles and English history. For Chaucer in *Troilus and Criseyde*, the reader's role is to correct his alterations to his source in order to abbreviate or expand his words so that they reflect the reader's better understanding of love. At the same time, readers' awareness of Chaucer's use of antifemale texts to write "The Wife of Bath's Prologue" can help them understand both Chaucer's methods and the uses of critical reading of a tradition. Gaskell wants her readers to feel the contrasts between the lives of the rich and the poor in Manchester. Her metafictional interventions remind those readers of the differences and connections between their own lives and those of her characters in order to urge them to learn from reading how to improve society, as Carson does in her novel.

My case studies have confirmed the need to enlarge our sense of the traditions available to a writer. Against the largely national traditions of his predecessors, E. R. Curtius in *European Literature and the Latin Middle Ages* insists that the literature of Europe is a unified field, created in the world of medieval Latin writing between the end of classical antiquity and the composition of Dante's *Divine Comedy*.[1] Elena Ferrante's comments and my last two examples insist on the importance of extending Curtius's focus on European tradition and to set beside it knowledge of the literatures of other cultures and of the works of women writers, both of which have been marginalized by male European critics.[2]

Turning now to the related question of the uses of literary tradition for readers, I would suggest that the study of earlier texts provides readers with a pragmatic context for understanding and discussing what they are reading and how it might relate to their lives. Previous literature provides a range of possibilities for understanding an author, a series of models, and a set of examples of roads not taken which define the meaning of the road chosen. Some of what we are doing when we compare Tasso with Homer may have nothing to do with Tasso's procedures of writing and everything to do with our own ways of understanding what we read, even if we need to imagine what we are doing as a story about Tasso's writing. We feel that we grasp Chaucer in a different and better way when we see how he changed the text of Boccaccio or how he responded to old French models, even though Chaucer had no intention that we would compare the two texts and may even have sought to mislead his readers about his sources.

Any text can be read without any awareness of the texts which seem to precede and underlie it, but most readings which incorporate a prior and comparative understanding of the earlier text will seem to the reader more satisfying and revealing. The key here is to be cautious about the kind of claims we make for these contextual readings. They are our own readings, and we may be able to use them to persuade other readers. They are unlikely to constitute an unquestionable truth about the text we are reading, however, even if they almost always help us to make meaning from the text by showing us things about the local choices an author was making. Just as in language elements of context and delivery contribute to our understandings (and misunderstandings) of what we hear, so a knowledge of prior related texts (literary traditions) helps our interpretations. Some prior texts may seem of greater importance to the understanding of a particular work than others—for example, because we know that the author had read them or because they belong to the same genre—but the introduction of more surprising comparator texts may offer new and exciting ways of thinking about a text, even if we need to treat the connections and comparisons with greater dashes of skepticism.

Both for readers and for writers, there is a danger that the adoption or study of a tradition may bring with it hidden assumptions which foreclose on some kinds of meaning. Even people who find it very helpful to work from earlier texts or to read later texts in the light of earlier ones will always need to be critical of such texts' potential to help us accept unexamined assumptions or to neglect to criticize ideological prejudices that are somehow bound up in the earlier text or genre.

At some moments in the writing of this book, I have wondered whether it would be better to avoid using the word "tradition" altogether, since its association with literature is relatively recent and since some of its implications and connotations may be unhelpful. On reflection, I decided to resist this move. In some respects, it can be advantageous to have a term which can refer both to the use of a prior text by an individual author and to that author's absorption of a much wider and less defined range of phrases, stories, characters, and beliefs. The slightly misleading impression that "tradition" is somehow already present in the world is in fact part of the explanation for the word's success. As long as we remember that the idea of tradition is almost always called upon when something new is being attempted or resisted, and as long as we maintain the connection between tradition and the expectation of new work, it seems to me that the word is too useful to avoid. Using the word also helps us to think about the connections between readers' and writers' uses of tradition even as we recognize that there will also be differences. To insist that the writer (or reader) in the present always make a choice about whether and how to use a particular model may embolden us to criticize the repetition of questionable earlier beliefs and may help us see how their incorporation contributes to a strategy of meaning-making. We could wish for a word which conveyed more sense of the author's will in choosing an example to follow, but Chaucer's game-playing suggests that authors may prefer to conceal the role which their decision plays in what is evidently not a completely free choice. The examples we have studied have shown how much, and in how many different ways, reading previous texts can help to make new writing. As readers, we must also be aware of the ways in which models can both make possible a range of intertextual meanings and close down other ways of thinking. If we forswore either the word "tradition" or the reading of old books, our losses would be much greater than our gains.

Canons and Nationalism

I now need to turn to two issues which I mentioned in the Introduction and then parked: canons and nationalism. What has our study of literary traditions suggested about what students should be expected to read as part of their literary education? We can use the distinction between readers' and writers' traditions which has emerged from these studies to address the question of the literary canon. How would we define the literary traditions which writers can benefit from studying? What would be a good canon of reading for someone who wants to write? In the first place, I would emphasize that there is always a degree of freedom in the choice of authors and, even more, in how writers use their reading. Tasso probably had to use the work of his Este epic predecessor Ariosto, but he made very good choices about how to use him. On the other hand, Tasso's very moving and important descriptions of the horror of attempting to cut down the enchanted grove of trees in cantos 13 and 18 of *Gerusalemme Liberata* are derived from Lucan, an available but not well-known model which Tasso chose freely. Sometimes writers work from a particular author or book because that model seems to be present in the minds of their audience, as some poets of early twentieth-century urban life felt obliged to invoke Baudelaire, or some innovative novelists might feel that an awareness of the achievement of Joyce is required. At other times, using a model, like Oedipus or Medea, might enable writers to address neglected, shameful, or irrational currents in the life of their culture. Some parts of the literary past appeal to a writer as making visible something which they feel to be alive in the present.

The limitations on writers' freedom in choosing models may be related to genre and to place and time. For some novelists, the foundational novels of the European past stand as peaks to be scaled and as resources of narrative technique. For writers of Latin prose during the Renaissance, attempting to write like Cicero was part of the experience of learning the tools of the trade which was always also there in the minds of reader and writer. For sixteenth-century European love poets, Petrarch's vocabulary and his repertoire of images provided attractive materials which were easier to use or satirize than to avoid. But there can also be times—and Gaskell is a good example here—when the novelist's experience of life tells her that there are new subjects which have been ignored by previous writers and which must be addressed in new ways.

A second canon-related conclusion could relate to the international element of the choices we have observed. Especially in the early stages of the literature of a particular language, writers have found it fruitful to choose their models from other languages and other cultures. Perhaps writers in training would gain from being systematically exposed both to writings from another culture and to examples of how authors in their own tradition have made use of motifs and ideas taken (sometimes indirectly) from that culture. The migration of folktales from Asia to Europe would furnish abundant examples. Since writers aim to use language sensitively, perhaps one could suggest that their awareness of the possibilities of their own language could be enhanced by studying another language, together with its literature, especially including a comparison between poetry of their native and their acquired languages.

Since one cannot write in any genre without some awareness of how other writers have exploited the genre, it would also seem important for writers to study a range of poetry, plays, novels, and stories, both great technical models from the past and recent authors, for a sense of the development of the genre and its possibilities for the writer today. In lyric poetry, a preference for recent writing in one's own language may be more justifiable; in novels and drama, a more international perspective acquired via translations would seem more fruitful. Reading in current affairs, social research, and across a range of subjects, together with attention to other art forms, may provide a writer with new and useful subject matter. Immersion in the discoveries and the great issues of the present may give writers subjects and themes to use in developing their talents. Some writers are made by the events they witness or participate in; for others, the transfer of ideas between disciplines may provide new ways of envisaging the world. Vassily Grossman's inside experience of both the siege of Stalingrad and the Russian army's discovery of the extermination camp at Treblinka, together with his understanding of physics, made possible his extraordinary achievement in *Life and Fate*. Evidently his use of Chekhov and Tolstoy as models and inspiration was another factor. A writer's sense of the possibilities of writing may be enlarged by study of the greatest writers of the past, even those, like Homer, Dante, Shakespeare, Tolstoy, and Dostoevsky, who seem largely beyond the scope of imitation.

Readers benefit from both a sense of the variety of ways in which an issue can be confronted in literature and a sense of the ways in which literary forms and the ideas they express change over time. They also gain understanding by reading books written at different places and times, in different genres, and from different points of view. It may be helpful for them to think about the ways in which authors respond to and sometimes bring about historical change in society. Readers need to follow their own instincts in reading, but they should also take note of suggestions made by literary history or their contemporaries about books to read. The degree of compulsion in the arrangement of reading should be relatively small, but it should include literature from a wide range of earlier periods as well as from the very recent past. It should include some of the greatest achievements of world literature and the appropriate national literature as well as texts written in different countries, by women as well as men, and by representatives of different social groups. Students of literature would benefit from acquiring a mastery of at least one language other than their native language, ideally one belonging to a rather different culture.

Readers benefit from acquiring cultural, historical, and religious knowledge which assists their understanding of texts. We always learn more about what an author has done by thinking about the expectations which the audience of a particular genre would have had at a particular historical moment. Criticism which we might want to make of, for example, the extravagant description of a new year's feast at King Arthur's court may usefully be tempered by the knowledge that a certain type of romance traditionally begins with such a scene and the suggestion that in such a case the author's intention may be more to surpass other feast descriptions than to attack the court's excessive consumption. At the same time, there is a risk that such observations about literary tradition may be harmfully normalizing and make us overlook conclusions which we would otherwise wish to draw. In a reading of Chaucer's *The Prioress's Tale*, we may want to register that the tale's casually anti-Semitic assumptions were usual among English Christians of the fourteenth century but we would not want to soften our critical reaction to their hostility.

In some cases, knowledge about religious or cultural beliefs can seem essential to reading the text. The ending of *The Prioress's Tale* depends on the audience believing that it is a good thing to end the sort of half-life that the child endures so that he can fully leave the world and go to Christ in heaven. As a reader, one may need to share such a belief, even temporarily, in order to appreciate the tale. Evidently this religious conclusion is also crucial to our final understanding of the Prioress herself, since her prologue portrays her as an aristocratic lady who had been placed in a convent by her family and who may have been more interested in clothes, romances, and dogs than the life of a bride of Christ. The audience's understanding of her will presumably deepen with the shock of the strong religious conviction of her tale. At the same time, of course, the strong belief demonstrated by the ending of the tale connects, through Christian fundamentalism, with the deplorable anti-Semitism which is the basis of the story and the way the Prioress tells it.

Reading must also contribute to more than the formation of a pattern of reading or the composition of new books. Reading is a crucial way of looking outwards, of confronting and coming to terms with the considered expression of another human being, another mind. Reading makes us aware of what other people think, by giving us access to words written and spoken in the past. Readers can uncover both their connectedness to and their differences from language users of other times, places, and beliefs. Reading texts from the past, from other cultures, or from writers of different genders, different formations, and different politics makes us face up to differences of belief and helps us identify both the nature of our own beliefs and their limitations. Hearing the words of others and looking at the world through their eyes brings out our own identity and makes it possible for our identity to develop through contact with what other people say and think. Working at interpreting texts, at sympathetically supplying the information we need to hear what they are saying, shows us where we are and gives us an example of what we could choose to do and to be.

Canons of literary texts and conceptions of tradition have long been linked to issues of national pride and national identity. We need to understand both the political motivations of those who promote ideals of national culture and the reasons which underlie some of their arguments. Every book is written in an individual language. All languages are connected to political systems based on the (modern) idea of the nation. So every nation, like every tribe, has a national literature which is (mostly) written in one of the languages of the nation. Therefore, it is entirely reasonable that nations claim to possess their own literatures. Benedict Anderson treats language as one of the constituents of the imagined community of the nation, and he proposes national literatures as one explanation for the otherwise puzzling phenomenon of love of the nation.[3] Because writers are often immersed in the details of everyday national life, and because they often observe the historical travails of a nation, at least as a backdrop, a group of literary works is often thought of as defining a nation. Writers and oral performers are also central to the process of the development of languages.

Against this, we must draw particular attention to the real histories of nations. People who now live in a certain place are the descendants of people who migrated there at different stages and under different conditions. Almost all modern languages are compounds of elements originally brought or taken from languages of places of origin, of trade routes, of holy books, and of sources of knowledge. We must insist on the role of people who break the link between nation and literature: the colonized who write in the language of their oppressors; the cosmopolitans who choose to write in a language different from their mother tongue; and the traders who live their lives and express themselves in an international form of a language. In Sainte-Beuve, the beginnings of the study of a national modern literature are seen to be bound up with the process of recognizing literary tradition. At the same time, our studies of Petrarch, Chaucer, and Ngũgĩ have emphasized the interlingual and international characteristics of the creation of a national literary tradition. It would be foolish to deny the effect of nationalism on how people think about their lives, but we must remember that in most cases the international component of a national literary tradition forms both a foundation and a prompt for renewal. Particularly in the face of modern methods of communication, events and discoveries made in one part of the world quickly find resonance and responses elsewhere. The narrowing context of present-day nationalism suggests the usefulness of reading outside literary traditions, in ethnography and prehistory, in botany and zoology, and in geography and history. The familiar maps and ethnic configurations which fuel nationalistic imaginations were brought into existence by movements of landmasses, plants, and peoples. Today and in the future we all have to negotiate a world where traditions are plural and where all of us will need to understand more than one culture, more than one economy, and more than one system of beliefs. Carefully and individually chosen reading can open us to the fruitfulness of looking outward.

The chief danger of literary tradition is that it may blind us to our choices and motivations and lead us to accept ideas or patterns of behavior which we should condemn. These real and pressing dangers can be mitigated by emphasizing the importance of new work and new readings of older work. As long as we are at least partly reading older books with a view to writing new ones, we should be able to see that some of what they celebrate, however strongly rooted in history, is wrong and needs to be changed. Like Ferrante, we may find that there are things from our past that we cannot change, even in our own writing. Like Gadamer, we may realize that an encounter with earlier prejudices is a key part of the process of coming to understanding.

Traditions die through military force, through inward-looking, through indifference, through imperviousness to change, through a narrow focus on external details, and for many other reasons.[4] Some aspects of any tradition need to be changed. But the consequences of ignoring or rejecting tradition are immense. We lose our memory and our ability to learn from and build on what has happened before. To deny a role for tradition is ultimately to deny the force of reading and writing. Traditions keep ideas, texts, and expressions alive through being chosen by individuals as the context in which new texts can be composed, using the social and linguistic expectations of the audience to stimulate them in new ways. Without the reading of older texts and texts from other places, our resources for thinking and writing are impoverished. Without new writing and reading, our capacity to adapt tradition so that it can become fruitful is reduced.

So I would like to end this book on a warily optimistic note. We know that people continue to write very well about books, ideas, people, and events that matter to them. We also know that reading older books provides writers with subjects, languages, and conventions they can work with. To speak of this process as "tradition" is not misleading as long as we remain aware of the degree of free choice involved, the ways in which traditions are created and used in the present, the likelihood that a tradition will blind us to some alternatives as well as opening us to others, and the need to write and read new texts.

Preface

1. R. W. Burchfield's loan to me of Curtius's *European Literature and the Latin Middle Ages* in lieu of a couple of Chaucer tutorials in 1975 stimulated my interest in rhetoric and many other literary issues.

Introduction. Ideas of Literary Traditions

1. Charles Augustin Sainte-Beuve, "Qu'est-ce-que c'est la tradition littéraire?," in Sainte-Beuve, *Causeries du lundi*, 16 vols., 3rd ed. (Paris, 1857–1870), vol. 15, pp. 356–82.

2. T. S. Eliot, *Selected Essays* (London, 1972), p. 13.

3. T. W. Adorno, *Minima Moralia: Reflections from Damaged Life*, trans E.F.N. Jephcott (London, 1978), no. 32, p. 52: "One must have tradition in oneself, to hate it properly." Neil Lazarus, *Nationalism and Cultural Practice in the Postcolonial World* (Cambridge, 1999), pp. 1–8.

4. Robert Conn, *The Politics of Philology: Alfonso Reyes and the Invention of the Latin American Literary Tradition* (Lewisburg, PA, 2002). Conn's account of literary tradition was inspired by Peter Uwe Hohendahl, *Building a National Literature: The Case of Germany 1830–1870*, trans. Renate Baron Franciscono (Ithaca, NY, 1989).

5. Arnold Schoenberg, "National Music (2)" (1931), in *Style and Idea* (London, 1984), p. 174.

6. Elena Ferrante, *La Frantumaglia*, 2nd ed. (Rome, 2016), p. 132: "Scrivere è anche la storia di ciò che abbiamo letto e leggiamo, della qualità delle nostre letture, e un buon racconto alla fine è quello scritto dal fondo della nostra vita, dal cuore dei nostri rapporti con gli altri, dalla cima dei libri che ci sono piaciuti." *Frantumaglia*, trans. Ann Goldstein (London, 2016), p. 140. I am grateful to Gill Frith for suggesting this book.

7. Ferrante, *La Frantumaglia*, pp. 260, 333, 336–37; Ferrante, *Frantumaglia*, trans. Goldstein, pp. 269, 343, 347.

8. Ferrante, *La Frantumaglia*, pp. 347–48: "Abbiamo bisogno, tutte, di costruirci una nostra—diciamo—genealogia che ci inorgoglisca, ci definisca, ci permetta di vederci fuori dalla tradizione in base a cui gli uomini da millenni ci guardano, ci rappresantano, ci valutano, ci catalogano. È una tradizione potente, ricca di opera splendide, ma che ha tenuto fuori molto, moltissimo, di noi. Raccontare a fondo, con libertà—anche provocatariamente—il nostro 'di più' è importante, tende a comporre una mappa di cosa siamo o vogliamo essere." Deborah Orr, "Elena Ferrante: In a Manner of Speaking" (interview with Elena Ferrante), trans. Daniela Petracco, *The*

Gentlewoman, 19 February 2016, reprinted in *Frantumaglia*, p. 361. (The Italian and English versions of this interview are different in organization.)

9. Harry Levin, "The Tradition of Tradition," *Hopkins Review* 4, no. 3 (1951), reprinted in Levin, *Contexts of Criticism* (Cambridge MA, 1957), pp. 55–66; Raymond Williams, s.v. "Tradition," in *Keywords: A Vocabulary of Culture and Society*, rev. ed. (New York, 1985), pp. 124–25.

10. Francis Bacon, *The Advancement of Learning*, ed. Arthur Johnston (Oxford, 1974), II.XVII.2, p. 134.

11. Augustine, *Epistles*, 54.1.

12. Milton, *Complete Poems and Major Prose*, ed. Merritt Y. Hughes (Indianapolis, 1975), p. 739; cf. *Paradise Lost*, XII.512. Dryden, *The Hind and the Panther*, II.70–175.

13. Edward Shils, *Tradition* (London, 1981), p. 325: "The Enlightenment was antithetical to tradition."

14. Anthony Giddens, "Reith Lectures 1999: Runaway World," lecture 3, "Tradition," 21 April 1999, downloads.bbc.co.uk/rmhttp/radio4/transcripts/1999_reith3.pdf (accessed 25 April 2017), pp. 2–3.

15. George Eliot, *The Spanish Gypsy, The Legend of Jubal, and Other Poems, Old and New* (Edinburgh, n.d.), book 2, p. 169, quoted in Levin, *Contexts of Criticism*, p. 59.

16. Karl Marx, *The Eighteenth Brumaire of Louis Bonaparte* (Moscow, 1972), p. 10. I am grateful to Carolyn Steedman for this reference and the next.

17. Thomas Paine, *Rights of Man*, in Paine, *Political Writings*, ed. Bruce Kuklick, rev. ed. (Cambridge, 2000), p. 64: "I am contending for the right of the *living*, and against their being willed away, and controlled and contracted for, by the manuscript-assumed authority of the dead."

18. Max Weber, *Economy and Society*, 2 vols. (Berkeley, 1978), vol. 1, pp. 215–16, 226–41.

19. Williams, s.v. "Tradition," *Keywords*, p. 125.

20. Anthony Giddens, "Living in a Post-Traditional Society," in Ulrich Beck, Anthony Giddens, and Scott Lash, *Reflexive Modernization: Politics, Tradition, and Aesthetics in the Modern Social Order* (Cambridge, 1994), p. 63.

21. Alasdair MacIntyre, *Whose Justice? Which Rationality?* (London, 1988), pp. 6–7, 12. I am grateful to Maria Devlin McNair for this reference.

22. MacIntyre, *Whose Justice?*, p. 22.

23. MacIntyre, *Whose Justice?*, pp. 340, 350–64.

24. L. D. Reynolds and N. G. Wilson, *Scribes and Scholars*, 4th ed. (Oxford, 2013), provides a clear introduction to this topic and has a good bibliography.

25. Andrew George, "Introduction," in *The Epic of Gilgamesh* (London, 2003), pp. xiii–xxx.

26. Charles Augustin Sainte-Beuve, "Qu'est-ce-que c'est la tradition littéraire?" (1858), in Sainte-Beuve, *Causeries du lundi*, vol. 15, pp. 356–82, 357: "Il y a une tradition—En quel sens il la faut entendre—En quel sens il la faut maintenir—." Christo-

pher Prendergast, *The Classic: Sainte-Beuve and the Nineteenth-Century Culture Wars* (Oxford, 2007), pp. 5–17, 62–70, 92–95, 261–64, 278–80.

27. Sainte-Beuve, *Causeries du lundi*, vol. 15, p. 358: "Elle consiste en un certain principe de raison et de culture qui a pénétré à la longue, pour le modifier, dans le caractère même de cette nation gauloise."

28. Sainte-Beuve, *Causeries du lundi*, vol. 15, p. 372.

29. Charles Augustin Sainte-Beuve, "Qu'est-ce qu'un classique?" (1850), in Sainte-Beuve, *Causeries du lundi*, vol. 3, pp. 38–55, 42: "Un vrai classique, c'est un auteur qui a enrichi l'esprit humain, qui en a réellement augmenté le trésor, qui a fait faire un pas de plus . . . qui a rendu son pensée, son observation ou son invention, sous une forme n'importe laquelle, mais large et grande, fine et sensée, saine et belle en soi; qui a parlé à tous dans un style à lui et qui se trouve aussi celui de tout le monde, dans un style nouveau sans néologisme, nouveau et antique, aisément contemporain de tous les âges." Antoine Compagnon, "Sainte-Beuve and the Canon," *Modern Language Notes*, 110 (1995): 1188–99.

30. Sainte-Beuve, *Causeries du lundi*, vol. 3, p. 40: "L'idée de *classique* implique en soi quelque chose qui a suite et consistance, qui fait ensemble et tradition, qui se compose, se transmet, et qui dure."

31. Sainte-Beuve, *Causeries du lundi*, vol. 3, p. 49.

32. E. R. Curtius, *European Literature and the Latin Middle Ages (Princeton, NJ, 1953)*, pp. 249–51.

33. T. S. Eliot, "Tradition and the Individual Talent" (1919), in Eliot, *Selected Essays*, p. 14.

34. Eliot, *Selected Essays*, p. 15.

35. David Morley, *The Cambridge Introduction to Creative Writing* (Cambridge, 2007), pp. 25–33.

36. Eliot, *Selected Essays*, pp. 15, 20.

37. F. R. Leavis, *The Great Tradition: George Eliot, Henry James, Joseph Conrad* (London, 1973), p. 2.

38. Leavis, *The Great Tradition*, p. 5.

39. Rosemary Ashton, *The German Idea* (Cambridge, 1980); John Rignall, ed., *George Eliot and Europe* (Aldershot, 1997).

40. Edward Shils, *Tradition* (London, 1981), pp. 4–7. I am grateful to Gordon Fyfe for this reference. See also Struan Jacobs, "Edward Shils's Theory of Tradition," *Philosophy of the Social Sciences* 37, no. 2 (2007): 139–62.

41. Shils, *Tradition*, pp. 13–14.

42. Shils, *Tradition*, pp. 4–5, 10–11, 46–54, 287–310.

43. Shils, *Tradition*, p. 198.

44. Anthony Giddens, "Living in a Post-Traditional Society," in Beck, Giddens, and Lash, *Reflexive Modernization*, pp. 56–109; Giddens, "Reith Lectures 1999: Runaway World," lecture 3, "Tradition"; John Walliss, "The Problem of Tradition in the Work of Anthony Giddens," *Culture and Religion* 2, no. 1 (2001): 81–98.

45. T. W. Adorno, "On Tradition," *Telos* 94 (1993/1994): 75–82, 75, translated from

the version of an article which first appeared in 1966 and is reprinted in Adorno, *Gesammelte Schriften*, vol. 10, part 1 (Frankfurt, 1977): 310–20.

46. Adorno, "On Tradition," p. 76.

47. Adorno, "On Tradition," p. 78.

48. Adorno, "On Tradition," pp. 79–82.

49. Stith Thompson, *The Folktale* (Berkeley, CA, 1946), esp. pp. 4–20, 406–12; Eugenia Shanklin, "Two Meanings and Uses of Tradition," *Journal of Anthropological Research* 37 (1981): 71–89; Terence Ranger, "The Invention of Tradition in Colonial Africa," in Eric Hobsbawm and Terence Ranger, eds., *The Invention of Tradition* (Cambridge, 1983), pp. 211–62; Alice Horner, "The Assumption of Tradition," PhD thesis, University of California, Berkeley, 1990; Nelson Graburn, "What Is Tradition?," *Museum Anthropology* 24, nos. 2/3 (2001): 6–11; Christopher B. Steiner, "The Tradition of African Art," in Mark Salber Phillips and Gordon Scochet, eds., *Questions of Tradition* (Toronto, 2004), pp. 88–109; John R. Campbell, "Who Are the Luo? Oral Tradition and Disciplinary Practices in Anthropology and History," *Journal of African Cultural Studies* 18 (2006): 73–87.

50. Hugh Trevor-Roper, "The Invention of Tradition: The Highland Tradition of Scotland," in Hobsbawm and Ranger, *The Invention of Tradition*, pp. 15–41.

51. Eric Hobsbawm, "Introduction," in Hobsbawm and Ranger, *The Invention of Tradition*, p. 2. Hobsbawm's point here is related to Marx's in *The Eighteenth Brumaire* (see note 16).

52. Hobsbawm, "Introduction," in Hobsbawm and Ranger, *Invention of Tradition*, p. 9.

53. According to Gregg Horowitz, "tradition" refers to the ways in which the past is taken up in the present; see the collection edited by Karen Lang, "Notes from the Field: Tradition," *Art Bulletin* 95 (2013): 518–43, 528.

54. Terence Ranger, "The Invention of Tradition Revisited," in Terence Ranger and Olufemi Vaughan, eds., *Legitimacy and the State in Twentieth-Century Africa* (Basingstoke, 1993), pp. 62–111.

55. Hans-Georg Gadamer, *Truth and Method*, 2nd ed., trans. rev. Joel Weinsheimer and Donald G. Marshall (London, 1989; first published as *Wahrheit und Methode*, 4th ed. [Tübingen, 1975]) (subsequent references in parentheses). I am grateful to Neil Kenny for insisting that I study this book.

56. Joel C. Weinsheimer, *Gadamer's Hermeneutics* (New Haven, CT, 1985), pp. 63–66. See also Steven Mailloux, "Articulation and Understanding: The Pragmatic Intimacy between Rhetoric and Hermeneutics," in Walter Jost and Michael J. Hyde eds, *Rhetoric and Hermeneutics in Our Time: A Reader* (New Haven, CT, 1997), pp. 378–94.

57. Weinsheimer, *Gadamer's Hermeneutics*, pp. 201–6.

58. Weinsheimer, *Gadamer's Hermeneutics*, pp. 164–84.

59. Gadamer's idea of learning through dialogue with tradition may be related to comments by Heidegger in *Being and Time*, trans. John Macquarrie and Edward Robinson (Oxford, 1978), pp. 183–92, 262, 311.

60. Weinsheimer, *Gadamer's Hermeneutics*, pp. 157–58, 183–84.

61. Weinsheimer, *Gadamer's Hermeneutics*, pp. 249–54.

62. Jürgen Habermas, *On the Logic of the Social Sciences*, trans. Shierry Weber Nicholsen and Jerry A. Stark (Cambridge, MA, 1988; first published as *Zur Logik der Sozialwissenschaften* [1967]), pp. 143–70; Paul Ricoeur, "Towards a Hermeneutics of Historical Consciousness," *Time and Narrative* 3 (1988): 216–29; Alan How, *The Habermas-Gadamer Debate and the Nature of the Social* (Aldershot, 1995); Robert Piercey, "Ricoeur's Account of Tradition and the Gadamer-Habermas Debate," *Human Studies* 27 (2004): 259–80, and extensive further bibliography.

63. Weinsheimer, *Gadamer's Hermeneutics*, pp. 102–5.

64. Matisse, "Letter to Raymond Escholier," 10 November 1936, in Jack D. Flam, ed., *Matisse on Art* (Oxford, 1978), document 14, p. 75: "In the thirty-seven years I have owned this canvas, I have come to know it quite well, though not entirely, I hope; it has sustained me morally in the critical moments of my venture as an artist; I have drawn from it my faith and my perseverance."

65. Curtius's whole chapter on classicism is an essential resource on the history of canon formation. Curtius, *European Literature and the Latin Middle Ages*, pp. 247–72.

Chapter 1. Petrarch, Scholarship, and Traditions of Love Poetry

1. Giuseppe Billanovich, *Petrarca letterato*, vol. 1, *Lo scrittoio del Petrarca* (Rome, 1947); Ernest Hatch Wilkins, *Life of Petrarch* (Chicago, 1961); Kenelm Foster, *Petrarch: Poet and Humanist* (Edinburgh, 1984); Nicholas Mann, *Petrarch* (Oxford, 1984); Peter Hainsworth, *Petrarch the Poet* (London, 1988); Petrarca, *Africa*, ed. Nicola Festa (Florence, 1926); *Rerum memorandum libri*, ed. Marco Petoletti (Florence, 2014).

2. Martin L. McLaughlin, *Literary Imitation in the Italian Renaissance* (Oxford, 1995), pp. 22–48.

3. A. Fontana, "La filologia romanza e il problema del rapport Petrarca-Trovatori," in Fritz Schalk, ed., *Petrarca: Beiträge zu Werk und Wirkung* (Frankfurt, 1975), pp. 55–70; Franco Suitner, *Petrarca e la tradizione stilnovistica* (Florence, 1977); Jennifer Petrie, *Petrarch: The Augustan Poets, the Italian Tradition, and the Canzoniere* (Dublin, 1983); Olivia Holmes, "Petrarch and the Vernacular Lyric Past," in Albert Russell Ascoli and Unn Falkeid, eds., *The Cambridge Companion to Petrarch* (Cambridge, 2015), pp. 154–66.

4. Curtius, *European Literature and the Latin Middle Ages*, p. 396; Ernest Hatch Wilkins, "A General Survey of Renaissance Petrarchism," *Comparative Literature* 2 (1950): 327–42; George Watson, *The English Petrarchans* (London, 1967); Leonard Forster, *The Icy Fire* (Cambridge, 1969); Carlo Dionisotti, "Fortuna del Petrarca nel Quattrocento," *Italia Medioevale e Umanistica* 17 (1974): 61–113; Thomas P. Roche, *Petrarch and the English Sonnet Sequences* (New York, 1989); Joseph B. Trapp, *Studies of Petrarch and His Influence* (London, 2003).

5. Petrarca, *Epistolae familiares*, ed. Vittorio Rossi and Umberto Bosco, 4 vols. (Florence, 1933–1942), vol. 1 (1933): books I–IV; vol. 2 (1934): books V–XI; vol. 3

(1937): books XII–XIX; vol. 4 (1942): books XX–XXIV; Petrarca, *Letters on Familiar Matters*, trans. Aldo Bernardo, 3 vols. (Albany, NY, 1975–Baltimore, 1985); Petrarca, *Le Senili*, ed. Elvira Nota, 3 vols. (Turin 2004–2010); Petrarca, *Letters of Old Age*, trans. Aldo Bernardo, Saul Levin, and Reta Bernardo, 2 vols. (Baltimore, 1992); Petrarca, *Selected Letters*, trans. Elaine Fantham, 2 vols. (Cambridge, MA, 2017); Petrarca, *My Secret Book*, ed. and trans. Nicholas Mann (Cambridge, MA, 2016).

6. Nicholas Mann, "From Laurel to Fig: Petrarch and the Structures of the Self," *Proceedings of the British Academy* 105 (2000): 17–42.

7. Mann, "From Laurel to Fig," pp. 34–37.

8. For example, Petrarca, *Familiares*, II.1, 6, V.18, VIII.5.

9. For example, Petrarca, *My Secret Book*, I.15.2, II.5.8–6.1, 14.10–11, 14, III.5.9, 9.1.

10. For example, Petrarca, *Familiares*, XII.8, XVIII.2, 3, 4, 12, XXI.10; Petrarca, *Seniles*, XV.7, XVI.1.

11. Petrarca, *Familiares*, VI.4.1–5, pp. 77–78; Petrarca, *Selected Letters*, vol. 2, pp. 10–17.

12. Petrarca, *Familiares*, VI.4.12–14, p. 80.

13. Petrarca, *Familiares*, XXII.2.22–26, pp. 108–9; Petrarca, *Selected Letters*, vol. 1, pp. 334–49. Nicholas Mann discusses this letter and XXIII.19 in his *Pétrarque: Les Voyages de l'esprit* (Grenoble, 2004), pp. 35–40, as does Martin McLaughlin in *Literary Imitation*, pp. 25–32.

14. Petrarca, *Familiares*, XXII.2.1–7, pp. 104–5.

15. Petrarca, *Familiares*, XXII.2.11–16, pp. 105–6.

16. Petrarca, *Familiares*, XXII.2.20, p. 108: "Sum quem priorum semitam, sed non semper aliena vestigia sequi iuvet; sum qui aliorum scriptis non furtim sed precario uti velim in tempore, sed dum liceat, meis malim; sum quem similitudo delectet, non identitas, et similitudo ipsa quoque non nimia, in qua sequacis lux ingenii emineat, non cecitas non paupertas." Petrarca, *Selected Letters*, trans. Fantham, vol. 1, p. 345.

17. Petrarca, *Familiares*, XXII.2.27, p. 109.

18. Petrarca, *Familiares*, XXIII.19.9–11, pp. 205–6; Petrarca, *Selected Letters*, vol. 1, pp. 348–57.

19. Petrarca, *Familiares*, XXIII.19.11–13, p. 206.

20. Petrarca, *Familiares*, XXIII.19.14–16, pp. 206–7.

21. For example, Petrarca, *Familiares*, XXII.13.

22. Hainsworth, *Petrarch the Poet*, pp. 34–41; Marco Santagata, *I frammenti dell'anima*, 2nd ed. (Bologna, 2004), pp. 117–53, 243–48, 257–60, 267–75, 318–32.

23. For example, Petrarca, *Familiares*, XXI.13; Petrarca, *Seniles*, V.2, XIII.11, XV.11, XVIII.1.

24. Translations of Petrarch's poems in this chapter are mine. For texts and translations of all the poems, see *Petrarch's Lyric Poems*, trans. and ed. Robert M. Durling (Cambridge, MA, 1976).

25. Petrarca, *Canzoniere*, ed. Marco Santagata, updated edition (Milan, 2004), pp. 1203–5; Virgil, *Eclogues*, 3.56–57, 9.40–42; Virgil, *Georgics*, 2.328–31.

26. Petrarca, *Epistolae familiares*, XX.12, XXII.2; V. Grassi, *Il "De consolatione Philosophiae,"* in Grassi, *Dante, Petrarca, e Chaucer* (Catania, 1923).

27. Petrarca, *Canzoniere*, ed. Santagata, p. 648.

28. Anne Carson, *EROS the Bittersweet* (Champaign, IL, 1998), pp. 1–9, 168–73.

29. For example, readings from Ovid, Dante, and Cecco d'Ascoli, as Santagata suggests in *Canzoniere*, pp. 649–51.

30. As Santagata suggests in *Canzoniere* (pp. 653–54), such earlier vernacular love poetry may have included Dante and Cavalcanti.

31. Horace, *Odes*, II.7, III.13, Virgil, *Eclogues*, I.1–5, III.55–57, V.1–7, *Aeneid*, VI. 638–41. Curtius, *European Literature and the Latin Middle Ages*, pp. 183–202, and Santagata in *Canzoniere*, pp. 592–600.

32. Nancy Vickers, "Re-membering Dante: Petrarch's 'Chiare, fresche e dolci acque,'" *Modern Language Notes* 96 (1981): 1–11.

33. I owe this point to Maria Devlin McNair. On this passage, see also Ullrich Langer, "Petrarch's Singular Love Lyric," in Ascoli and Falkeid, *The Cambridge Companion to Petrarch*, pp. 70–73.

34. Petrarca, *My Secret Book*, II.11.7, III.14–18.

35. Richard Lansing ed., *The Dante Encyclopedia* (New York, 2010), pp. 198–213; Marcella Roddewig, ed., *Die Göttliche Komödie: Vergleichende Bestandsaufnahme der Commedia-Handschriften* (Stuttgart, 1984).

36. Billanovich, *Petrarca letterato*, vol. 1, pp. 161–64.

37. Petrarca, *Familiares*, XXI.15.4, 7–8, 14, pp. 95–97; Petrarca, *Selected Letters*, vol. 1, pp. 314–29.

38. Petrarca, *Familiares*, XXI.15.21, p. 98: "Quam tandem veri faciem habet ut invideam illi qui in his etatem totam posuit, in quibus ego vix adolescentie florem primitiasque posuerim? ut quod illi artificium nescio an unicum, sed profecto supremum fuit, michi iocus atque solatium fuerit et ingenii rudimentum?" Petrarca, *Selected Letters*, trans. Fantham, vol. 1, p. 325 (slightly amended).

39. Petrarca, *Familiares*, XXI.15.12–13, p. 96: "Hoc unum non dissimulo, quoniam siquid in eo sermone a me dictum illius aut alterius cuiusquam dicto simile, sive idem forte cum aliquot sit inventum, non id furtim aut imitandi proposito, que duo semper in his maxime vulgaribus ut scopulos declinavi, sed vel casu fortuito factum esse, vel similitudine ingeniorum, ut Tullio videtur, iisdem vestigiis ab ignorante concursum. Hoc autem ita esse, siquid unquam michi crediturus es, crede; nichil est verius." Petrarca, *Selected Letters*, trans. Fantham, vol. 1, p. 321 (slightly amended).

40. Simon Gilson, *Dante and Renaissance Florence* (Cambridge, 2005), pp. 32–40, 51–52.

41. Petrarca, *Familiares*, XXI.15.13, 15–16.

42. Vickers, "Re-membering Dante."

43. Hainsworth, *Petrarch the Poet*, p. 80.

44. Hainsworth, *Petrarch*, pp. 88–89.

45. Hainsworth, *Petrarch*, p. 93.

46. Hainsworth, *Petrarch*, pp. 95, 98.

47. Hainsworth, *Petrarch*, pp. 99–100.

48. Peter Brand and Lino Pertile eds, *The Cambridge History of Italian Literature*, rev. ed. (Cambridge, 1999), pp. 161–63, 165, 251–57, 260–65; Gaspara Stampa, *The*

Complete Poems, ed. Troy Tower and Jane Tylus (Chicago, 2010), pp. 11–12, 20–24, 58–239. The literature on Petrarchism is immense, but guides and samples can be found in Wilkins, "A General Survey of Renaissance Petrarchism"; Watson, *The English Petrarchans*; Forster, *The Icy Fire*; Dionisotti, "Fortuna del Petrarca nel Quattrocento"; Roche, *Petrarch and the English Sonnet Sequences*; Trapp, *Studies of Petrarch and His Influence*; Cristina Montagnani, ed., *I Territori del Petrarchismo* (Rome, 2005); Loredana Chines, Floriana Calitti, and Roberto Giliucci, eds., *Il Petrarchismo: Un modello di poesia per l'Europa*, 2 vols. (Rome, 2006); "Petrarch's Afterlife," in Ascoli and Falkeid, *The Cambridge Companion to Petrarch*, pp. 179–218.

49. See, for example, Petrarca, *Familiares*, I.4, V.8, X.5, XXII.1; Petrarca, *Seniles*, IV.5, XV.3.

50. For example, John Donne, "The Ecstasy," "The Sun Rising," "To the Countess of Huntingdon" ("That unripe side of earth"). See Donald L. Guss, *John Donne, Petrarchist* (Detroit, 1966), and Sylvia Ruffo-Fiore, *Donne's Petrarchism: A Comparative View* (Florence, 1976).

Chapter 2. *Chaucer and Boccaccio's* Il Filostrato

1. Chaucer, *Troilus and Criseyde*, ed. Barry Windeatt (Harlow, 1984), IV.715–28 (subsequent references in parentheses).

2. Giovanni Boccaccio, *Caccia di Diana, Il Filostrato*, ed. Vittore Branca (Milan, 1964) (subsequent references in parentheses); Chaucer, *Troilus and Criseyde*, ed. Windeatt. The parallel Italian texts in the 1984 Windeatt edition make it particularly useful for comparisons. Translations in this chapter are mine.

3. Boccaccio, *Il Filostrato*, p. 325.

4. David Wallace, *Chaucer and the Early Writings of Boccaccio* (Woodbridge, 1985), p. 96.

5. Edgar Finley Shannon, *Chaucer and the Roman Poets* (Cambridge, MA, 1929); Robert A. Pratt, "Chaucer and the Hand That Fed Him," *Speculum* 41 (1966): 619–42; Bruce Harbert, "Chaucer and the Latin Classics," in Derek S. Brewer, ed., *Geoffrey Chaucer* (London, 1974), pp. 137–53; Donald R. Howard, *Chaucer: His Life, His Works, His World* (New York, 1987), pp. 41–43; Helen Cooper, "The Classical Background," in Steve Ellis, ed., *Chaucer: An Oxford Guide* (Oxford, 2005), pp. 255–71; K. P. Clarke, *Chaucer and Italian Textuality* (Oxford, 2011), pp. 9–46.

6. Wallace, *Chaucer and the Early Writings*, pp. 102–5; Robert O. Payne, *The Key of Remembrance* (New Haven, CT, 1963), p. 16 and passim; Martin Camargo, "Chaucer and the Oxford Renaissance of Anglo-Latin Rhetoric," *Studies in the Age of Chaucer* 34 (2012): 173–207.

7. Philip Knox, "The *Romance of the Rose* in Fourteenth-Century England," PhD thesis, University of Oxford, 2015, pp. 183–226, 237–40.

8. Charles Muscatine, *Chaucer and the French Tradition* (Berkeley, CA, 1957); Howard H. Schless, *Chaucer and Dante* (Norman, OK, 1984); James I. Wimsatt, *Chaucer and His French Contemporaries* (Toronto, 1991): Barry Windeatt, *Oxford Guides to Chaucer: Troilus and Criseyde* (Oxford, 1995); N. S. Thompson, *Chaucer, Boccaccio,*

and the Debate of Love (Oxford, 1996); William T. Rossiter, *Chaucer and Petrarch* (Woodbridge, 2010); Clarke, *Chaucer and Italian Textuality*, pp. 95–164.

9. Maria Gozzi, "Sulle fonti del *Filostrato*," *Studi sul Boccaccio* 5 (1968): 123–209.

10. Wallace, *Chaucer and the Early Writings*, p. 72.

11. Boccaccio, "Proemio" (Foreword), 26–34; Boccaccio, *Il Filostrato*, pp. 65–67.

12. Vittore Branca, "Introduzione" (Introduction), in Boccaccio, *Il Filostrato*, pp. 52–53; Branca, *Studi sui Cantari* (1936; reprint, Florence, 2014), pp. 5–54, 69–71, 75, 83–85; Wallace, *Chaucer and the Early Writings*, pp. 131–35. Branca's edition points out many parallels between *Il Filostrato* and Dante's *Vita nuova*.

13. For further examples, see Boccaccio, *Il Filostrato*, IV.18, VII.80.

14. For example, I.38, II.80.7–8, III.1–2, 74–89, IV.30–40, 163–66, V.19–21, 23–28, V.56–59, VII. 62–65.

15. Chaucer, who also could have learned this from Machaut, employs lyric interludes in *The Book of the Duchess* as well, as David Wallace points out to me.

16. Payne, *The Key of Remembrance*, p. 185. These are I.400–434, II.827–75, III.1422–42, 1450–70, 1702–8, 1744–71, IV.958–1082 (the predestination soliloquy, so perhaps not really a lyric), V.218–45, 540–53, 638–58.

17. James Wimsatt suggests that Chaucer here imitates the French three-stanza ballade; Wimsatt, "The French Lyric Element in *Troilus and Criseyde*," *Yearbook of English Studies* 15 (1985): 18–32; Piero Boitani, *The Tragic and the Sublime in Medieval Literature* (Cambridge, 1989), pp. 70–72. Kara Gaston analyzes the translation and compares Chaucer's approach to translation to Dante's in the *Convivio*; Gaston, "Save Our Tonges Difference: Translation, Literary History, and *Troilus and Criseyde*," *Chaucer Review* 48 (2014): 258–83.

18. Rossiter, *Chaucer and Petrarch*, pp. 109–31.

19. Rossiter, *Chaucer and Petrarch*, pp. 87–108; Gordon R. Silber, "Alleged Imitations of Petrarch in the *Filostrato*," *Modern Philology* 37 (1939): 113–24.

20. Chaucer, *Troilus and Criseyde*, ed. Windeatt, p. 249.

21. For example, IV.958–1078.

22. Will Rossiter tells me that he has sometimes had this thought.

23. Branca, "Introduzione," in Boccaccio, *Filostrato*, pp. 47–49; Alessia Ronchetti, "Da Beatrice a Fiammetta: Prime risposte boccacciane al modello autobiografico dantesco," *Critica del testo* 14, no. 1 (2011): 555–80, 565–76; "Between *Filocolo* and *Filostrato*: Boccaccio's Authorial Doubles and the Question of Amore per Diletto," *Italianist* 35 (2015): 318–33.

24. Wallace, *Chaucer and the Early Writings*, pp. 95–97. Wallace adds that "I not" is almost certainly a contraction of "I ne woot" (I do not know) thus expressing uncertainty about how to react to these other opinions.

25. E. T. Donaldson, "The Ending of *Troilus*," in Donaldson, *Speaking of Chaucer* (London, 1970), pp. 84–101.

26. Chaucer also copies Boccaccio's very brief narration of Troilus's death (V.1806).

27. Derek S. Brewer, "The Relationship of Chaucer to the English and European Traditions," in Brewer, ed., *Chaucer and Chaucerians* (London, 1966), pp. 1–38, 2–9.

28. Wallace, *Chaucer and the Early Writings*, pp. 78–91, 78.

29. Charles Muscatine, *Chaucer and the French Tradition* (Berkeley, CA, 1957).

30. Per Nykrog, *Les Fabliaux* (Copenhagen, 1957).

31. Jill Mann, *Chaucer and Medieval Estates Satire* (Cambridge, 1973), pp. 17–37.

32. Chaucer, *The Canterbury Tales*, in Larry D. Benson, ed., *The Riverside Chaucer* (Boston, 1987), General Prologue, fragment I, lines 168–88 (subsequent references in parentheses). In *The Riverside Chaucer*, *The Canterbury Tales*, which was incomplete at Chaucer's death, is presented as ten fragments. Hence, in citations I give the title of the tale (usually obvious from the context), the number of the fragment in Roman numerals, and the line numbers in Arabic numerals.

33. Ralph Hanna III and Traugott Lawler, "The Wife of Bath's Prologue," in R. Correale and M. Hamel, eds., *Sources and Analogues of the Canterbury Tales*, vol. 2 (Woodbridge, 2005), pp. 351–403.

34. Hanna and Lawler, "The Wife of Bath's Prologue," pp. 362–63.

35. Hanna and Lawler, "The Wife of Bath's Prologue," p. 373.

36. I am grateful to Maria Devlin McNair for this point.

37. The only earlier fabliau in English is *Dame Sirith*, found in the late thirteenth-century manuscript Bodleian Digby 86. I am grateful to Sarah Wood for this information.

38. Peter Beidler, "The Miller's Tale," in Correale and Hamel, *Sources and Analogues*, vol. 2, pp. 249–75.

39. David Anderson, *Before "The Knight's Tale": Imitation of Classical Epic in Boccaccio's "Teseida"* (Philadelphia, 1988); Clarke, *Chaucer and Italian Textuality*, pp. 77–85.

Chapter 3. Renaissance Epics: Ariosto, Tasso, and Spenser

1. I have used the editions of *Orlando Furioso* edited by Lanfranco Caretti (2 vols., Turin, 1992) and Emilio Bigi (Milan, 2012) and the prose translation by Guido Waldman (Oxford, 1974).

2. Daniel Javitch, *Proclaiming a Classic: The Canonization of* Orlando Furioso (Princeton, NJ, 1991), pp. 5, 10–20; C. P. Brand, *Ariosto* (Edinburgh, 1974), p. 184.

3. Brand, *Ariosto*, p. 60.

4. Italo Calvino, "Presentazione," in Ariosto, *Orlando Furioso*, ed. Caretti, vol. 1, pp. xliii–iv.

5. Pio Rajna, *Le fonti dell'Orlando Furioso*, 2nd ed. (Florence, 1900; reprint, 1975), pp. 5–23; Brand, *Ariosto*, pp. 46–53; Calvino, "Presentazione," pp. xxv–xxxiii; Juliann Vitullo, *The Chivalric Epic in Medieval Italy* (Gainesville, FL, 2000); Giovanni Palumbo, *La Chanson de Roland in Italia nel medioevo* (Rome, 2013).

6. Rajna, *Le fonti*, pp. 24–64; Brand, *Ariosto*, pp. 50–54; Jane E. Everson, *The Italian Romance Epic in the Age of Humanism* (Oxford, 2001).

7. See the index to Rajna, *Le fonti*, pp. 624–31; Maria Cristina Cabani, *Fra omaggio e parodia: Petrarca e petrarchismo nel Furioso* (Pisa, 1990); Colin Burrow, *Epic Ro-*

mance (Oxford, 1993), pp. 63–74; Daniel Javitch, "The Grafting of Virgilian Epic in *Orlando Furioso*," in Valeria Finucci, ed., *Renaissance Transactions: Ariosto and Tasso* (Durham, NC, 1999), pp. 56–76; Maria Cristina Cabani, *Ariosto, I volgari e I latini suoi* (Lucca, 2016).

8. Andrew Fichter, *Dynastic Epic in the Renaissance* (New Haven, CT, 1982), pp. 77–81; Albert Russell Ascoli, *Ariosto's Bitter Harmony* (Princeton, NJ, 1987), pp. 228–32, 311–31; Sergio Zatti, *The Quest for Epic* (Toronto, 2006), pp. 25–38, 50–54. I am grateful to Walter Stephens for this point.

9. Rajna, *Le fonti*, pp. 393–403.

10. Clare Carroll, *The Orlando Furioso: A Stoic Comedy* (Tempe, AZ, 1997), pp. 165–68.

11. *Orlando Furioso*, trans. Waldman, pp. 6–7 (slightly amended).

12. *Orlando Furioso*, trans. Waldman, p. 75 (slightly amended).

13. *Orlando Furioso*, trans. Waldman, pp. 218–19 (slightly amended).

14. *Orlando Furioso*, trans. Waldman, pp. 219–20 (slightly amended).

15. Rajna, *Le fonti*, pp. 164–88.

16. Rajna, *Le fonti*, pp. 200–205.

17. XXI.13–66, XXVIII, XLIII.6–46, 71–143; Rajna, *Le fonti*, pp. 329–44, 433–55, 570–89. For an exploration of dilation and its relationship to romance that is relevant here, see Patricia Parker, *Literary Fat Ladies* (London, 1987), pp. 8–16.

18. Daniel Javitch, "The Advertising of Fictionality in *Orlando Furioso*," in Donald Beecher, Massimo Ciavolella, and Roberto Fedi, eds., *Ariosto Today* (Toronto, 2003), pp. 106–25.

19. I have used the editions of Torquato Tasso, *Gerusalemme Liberata*, edited by Lanfranco Caretti (Turin, 1993) and by Franco Tomasi (Milan, 2009) (subsequent references in parentheses), as well as *The Liberation of Jerusalem*, the translation by Max Wickert (Oxford, 2009), and Franco Tomasi, ed., *Lettura della Gerusalemme Liberata* (Alessandria, 2005).

20. Tasso, *Gerusalemme Liberata*, ed. Caretti, pp. xxiii–vii, xlv–viii; Tasso, *Gerusalemme Liberata*, ed. Tomasi, pp. 10–14; Mark Davie, "Introduction," in Tasso, *The Liberation of Jerusalem*, trans. Wickert, pp. xiii–xvii.

21. Torquato Tasso, *Discorsi dell'arte poetica e del poema eroico*, ed. Luigi Poma (Bari, 1964), pp. 263–70. Graham Hough provides a very good summary in English in *A Preface to the Faerie Queene* (London, 1962), pp. 54–58.

22. Tasso, *Discorsi*, pp. 7, 14, 17–21.

23. Tasso, *Discorsi*, pp. 35–36.

24. Tasso, *Discorsi*, pp. 12–14, 38.

25. Tasso, *Discorsi*, pp. 40, 43, 47, 54.

26. David Quint, "Political Allegory in the *Gerusalemme Liberata*," in Quint, *Epic and Empire* (Princeton, NJ, 1993), pp. 213–47.

27. Tasso, *The Liberation of Jerusalem*, trans. Wickert, pp. 110–11.

28. Tasso had presented an earlier and more conventional version of the night raid in canto IX, including a beautiful boy beloved by Solimano (81–87).

29. Tasso, *The Liberation of Jerusalem*, trans. Wickert, p. 230.

30. For the sacred forest which Caesar cuts down at Marseilles and Erichtho's rites of prophecy using a corpse, see Lucan, *Pharsalia*, III.401–53, VI.620–830.

31. Tasso, *The Liberation of Jerusalem*, trans. Wickert, p. 290.

32. Tasso, *The Liberation of Jerusalem*, trans. Wickert, p. 293.

33. Tasso, *The Liberation of Jerusalem*, trans. Wickert, p. 295.

34. Tasso, *The Liberation of Jerusalem*, trans. Wickert, p. 398.

35. Tasso, *Gerusalemme Liberata*, ed. Tomasi, p. 1282, referring to Tasso, *Lettere poetiche*, ed. Carla Molinari (Parma, 1995), XX.4, XXI.2–3, XL.2.

36. Spenser, *The Faerie Queene*, ed. A. C. Hamilton, 2nd ed. (Harlow, 2007), p. 715 (subsequent references in parentheses in the text are to this edition). Recent work on Spenser is gathered in Andrew Hadfield, ed., *The Cambridge Companion to Spenser* (Cambridge, 2001), and Richard A. McCabe, ed., *The Oxford Handbook of Edmund Spenser* (Oxford, 2010).

37. Spenser, *Works*, ed. R. Morris (London, 1912), p. 710; Andrew Hadfield, *Edmund Spenser: A Life* (Oxford, 2012), pp. 97–98.

38. On Spenser's borrowings from Ariosto, see R. E. Neil Dodge, "Spenser's Imitations from Ariosto," *PMLA* 12 (1897): 151–204; Allan H. Gilbert, "Spenser's Imitations from Ariosto: Supplementary," *PMLA* 34 (1919): 225–32; Peter Marinelli, "Ariosto," in A. C. Hamilton, ed., *The Spenser Encyclopedia* (Toronto, 1990), pp. 56–57. In general, *The Spenser Encyclopedia* is the first reference on any issue in Spenser.

39. Ariosto, *Orlando Furioso*, II.55–56, IV.42, VIII.10–11; Paul Alpers, *The Poetry of the Faerie Queene* (Princeton, NJ, 1967), pp. 166–79.

40. Ariosto, *Orlando Furioso*, IV.51–VI.16; Alpers, *The Poetry of the Faerie Queene*, pp. 54–69.

41. Ariosto, *Orlando Furioso*, XXV, 20–70 (esp. 27–45); Alpers, *The Poetry of the Faerie Queene*, pp. 180–85.

42. Ariosto, *Orlando Furioso* XIX.17–33; Alpers, *The Poetry of the Faerie Queene*, pp. 185–94; Burrow, *Epic Romance*, pp. 110–15.

43. Matthew 4:3–4; *Faerie Queene*, III.5.15–25, and note to 15; Donald R. Howard, *The Three Temptations* (Princeton, NJ, 1966).

44. In general, see David Quint, "Tasso," in *The Spenser Encyclopedia*, pp. 678–79; H. H. Blanchard, "Imitations from Tasso in the *Faerie Queene*," *Studies in Philology* 22 (1925): 198–221; Alberto Castelli, *La Gerusalemme Liberata nella Inghilterra di Spenser* (Milan, 1936).

45. Spenser also uses Rinaldo's prayer at the Mount of Olives (XVIII.12–16), especially the stanza in which Rinaldo comes to understand the deceptiveness of earthly love and glory (13).

46. See Paul Alpers, "The Bower of Bliss," *The Spenser Encyclopedia*, pp. 164–67; A. Bartlett Giamatti, *The Earthly Paradise and the Renaissance Epic* (Princeton, NJ, 1966), pp. 251–86; Stephen Greenblatt, *Renaissance Self-Fashioning* (Chicago, 1980), pp. 173–79.

47. Paul Piehler, "*Romance of the Rose*," in *The Spenser Encyclopedia*, pp. 618–19, with bibliography; C. S. Lewis, *The Allegory of Love* (Oxford, 1936), pp. 339–46, R. Tuve, *Allegorical Imagery* (Princeton, NJ, 1966).

48. Thomas Hyde, "Busirane, House of," in *The Spenser Encyclopedia*, pp. 123–25, with bibliography.

Chapter 4. Reading and Community as a Support for the New: Elizabeth Gaskell's Mary Barton

1. Charles Kingsley, unsigned review of *Mary Barton*, *Fraser's Magazine* 39 (April 1849): 417–32, in Angus Easson, ed., *Elizabeth Gaskell: The Critical Heritage* (London, 1991), pp. 152–55, 153.

2. Kathleen Tillotson, *Novels of the Eighteen-Forties* (Oxford, 1956), pp. 202–10, 221–23; Raymond Williams, *Culture and Society 1780–1950* (Harmondsworth, 1963), pp. 99–103; W. A. Craik, *Elizabeth Gaskell and the English Provincial Novel* (London, 1975), pp. 1–7.

3. Peter Fritzsche, *Stranded in the Present: Modern Time and the Melancholy of History* (Cambridge, MA, 2004), pp. 31, 45, 55, 93, 116.

4. Jenny Uglow, *Elizabeth Gaskell: A Habit of Stories* (London, 1993), pp. 38–44, 152–55.

5. Uglow, *Elizabeth Gaskell*, p. 36.

6. Uglow, *Elizabeth Gaskell*, pp. 40–42.

7. J.A.V. Chapple and Arthur Pollard eds, *The Letters of Mrs. Gaskell* (Manchester, 1966) (hereafter *Letters*), p. 7.

8. Gaskell, *Letters*, p. 110; *Further Letters of Mrs. Gaskell*, ed. John Chapple and Alan Shelston (Manchester, 2003), p. 73.

9. Uglow, *Elizabeth Gaskell*, pp. 42–43; Gaskell, *Letters*, pp. 85, 92, 95, 121, 130.

10. Gaskell, *Letters*, p. 117.

11. Uglow, *Elizabeth Gaskell*, pp. 37–38, 152–55; Gaskell, preface to *Mary Barton*, p. 3.

12. Gaskell, *Letters*, p. 82.

13. Gaskell, *Letters*, p. 541.

14. Gaskell, *Letters*, p. 542.

15. From her letters it appears that Elizabeth Gaskell had not read this novel, though she knew of its existence. *Letters*, pp. 62, 63.

16. Angus Easson, *Elizabeth Gaskell* (London, 1979), pp. 62–72; Jill L. Matus, ed., *The Cambridge Companion to Elizabeth Gaskell* (Cambridge, 2007), p. 30.

17. Gaskell, *Letters*, p. 70.

18. Elizabeth Gaskell, *Mary Barton: A Tale of Manchester Life*, ed. Macdonald Daly (London, 2003), chap. 1, p. 11 (most subsequent references in parentheses).

19. John Burnett, *A Social History of Housing* (London, 1980), pp. 54–93, citing Peter Gaskell, *Manufacturing Population of England* (1833); Oz Frankel, "Blue Books and the Victorian Reader," *Victorian Studies* 46, no. 2 (2004): 308–18. I am grateful to Carolyn Steedman for this point and these references. On contrasting streets and rooms in the novel, see Deborah Epstein Nord, *Walking the Victorian Streets* (Ithaca, NY, 1995), pp. 147–49.

20. John Lucas quotes this passage at even greater length than I have and contrasts

it with the squalor of Davenport's cellar to argue that Gaskell understood the distinctions and resources of Manchester working-class life better than Engels. Carolyn Steedman uses the passage to reflect on the ways in which historians understand working-class interiors and their objects. John Lucas, "Engels, Mrs. Gaskell, and Manchester," in Lucas, *The Literature of Change*, 2nd ed. (Brighton, 1980), pp. 34–56, 51–52; Carolyn Steedman, "What a Rag Rug Means," *Journal of Material Culture* 3 (1998): 259–81.

21. Thomas Carlyle, *Past and Present*, ed. Richard D. Altick (New York, 1977), book 1, chap. 1, pp. 7–12; book 1, chap. 3, pp. 20–24.

22. Tillotson, *Novels of the Eighteen-Forties*, pp. 150–56, 205–12, 221–22; Gillian Beer, "Carlyle and Mary Barton: Problems of Utterance," in Frances Barker et al., eds., *1848: The Sociology of Literature* (Colchester, 1978), 242–55; Jane Spencer, "*Mary Barton* and Thomas Carlyle," *Gaskell Society Journal* 2 (1988): 1–12; Maurice Milne, "The 'Dark Expounder' and the 'Melodious Voice: Thomas Carlyle and Elizabeth Gaskell on Chartism," *Carlyle Society Occasional Papers* 20 (2007): 5–17. I owe this point to Gill Frith.

23. Hilary M. Schor, *Scheherezade in the Marketplace: Elizabeth Gaskell and the Victorian Novel* (New York, 1992), pp. 37–39; Nord, *Walking the Victorian Streets*, pp. 155–57.

24. Craik, *Elizabeth Gaskell and the English Provincial Novel*, p. 35.

25. Jonathan Rose, *The Intellectual Life of the British Working Classes* (New Haven, CT, 2001).

26. Homer, *Iliad*, 24, 486–506. Mr. Thornton's reading of Homer with Mr. Hale is a leitmotif of Gaskell's *North and South*, for example, in chapters 10, 15 and 20. Isobel Hurst, *Victorian Women Writers and the Classics* (Oxford, 2006), pp. 155–61.

27. Schor understands the hope of a more perfect communication between workers and men as one of the aims of the novel. *Scheherezade in the Marketplace*, pp. 17–18, 23.

28. Schor comments on the narrator's interventions in *Scheherezade in the Marketplace*, pp. 41–44.

29. Thomas Carlyle, letter of 8 November 1848, reprinted in Easson, *Elizabeth Gaskell: The Critical Heritage*, p. 72.

30. Patsy Stoneman, *Elizabeth Gaskell*, 2nd ed. (Manchester, 2006), pp. 55–56, 145–46; Patsy Stoneman, "Gaskell, Gender, and the Family," in Matus, *The Cambridge Companion to Elizabeth Gaskell*, pp. 137–38.

31. Gaskell, *Letters*, p. 108. The term "whh" means "which."

32. The case of the Bible is rather different, when, as we have seen, she uses a quotation from Luke 23:34 to bring about a crucial change in Carson's attitude (chap. 35, pp. 367–70).

33. Gaskell, *Letters*, p. 64.

34. Pauline Nestor, *Female Friendships and Communities* (Oxford, 1985), pp. 28–37.

35. Gaskell, *Letters*, p. 559.

36. Gaskell, *Letters*, p. 592.

37. Gordon S. Haight, *George Eliot: A Biography* (Oxford, 1968), p. 313; *The George Eliot Letters*, vol. 3, *1859–1861*, ed. Gordon S. Haight (New Haven, CT, 1954), pp. 198–99.

38. Uglow, *Elizabeth Gaskell*, pp. 461–67.

39. Gaskell, *Letters*, p. 116.

40. Gaskell, *Letters*, p. 65.

41. Margaret Smith, ed., *The Letters of Charlotte Brontë*, vol. 2 (Oxford, 2000), pp. 286, 296.

42. Gaskell, *Letters*, p. 345.

43. Uglow, *Elizabeth Gaskell*, p. 392; Easson, *Elizabeth Gaskell: The Critical Heritage*, pp. 372–73.

44. Gaskell, *Letters*, p. 349.

45. Christopher Ricks, "Victorian Lives: E. C. Gaskell's *Charlotte Brontë*," in Ricks, *Essays in Appreciation* (Oxford, 1996), pp. 114–45.

46. Easson, *Elizabeth Gaskell: The Critical Heritage*, pp. 373, 374.

47. Easson, *Elizabeth Gaskell: The Critical Heritage*, p. 387.

48. Linda H. Peterson, "Elizabeth Gaskell's *The Life of Charlotte Brontë*," in Matus, *The Cambridge Companion to Elizabeth Gaskell*, pp. 67–72.

49. Mary Taylor, "Letter to Gaskell 30/7/1857," in Easson, *Elizabeth Gaskell: The Critical Heritage*, p. 429.

50. Uglow, *Elizabeth Gaskell*, p. 411.

Chapter 5. European and African Literary Traditions in Ngũgĩ wa Thiong'o's Wizard of the Crow

1. Ngũgĩ wa Thiong'o, *Dreams in a Time of War* (London, 2010), pp. 218–21; Ngũgĩ wa Thiong'o, *Birth of a Dream Weaver* (London, 2016), pp. 37, 76, 84–85, 183–85; Ngũgĩ wa Thiong'o, *Writers in Politics*, rev. ed. (Oxford, 1997), p. 87.

2. Ngũgĩ, *Birth of a Dream Weaver*, pp. 131, 135, 139–40.

3. Ngũgĩ wa Thiong'o, *In the House of the Interpreter* (New York, 2012), pp. 165–67; Ngũgĩ, *Birth of a Dream Weaver*, p. 77; Ken Olende and Ngũgĩ wa Thiong'o, "Ngũgĩ wa Thiong'o Interviewed on His New Novel, *Wizard of the Crow*," *Socialist Worker*, 4 November 2006, https://socialistworker.co.uk/art/9867 (accessed 24 July 2017).

4. Simon Gikandi, *Ngũgĩ wa Thiong'o* (Cambridge, 2000), pp. 31–32, 128–29, 135–46, 256–58.

5. Ngũgĩ, *Birth of a Dream Weaver*, pp. 75–76; compare the description of the evolution of the idea of his first novel on pp. 89–95.

6. Ngũgĩ wa Thiong'o, *Wizard of the Crow* (New York, 2006) (subsequent references are to this edition and appear in parentheses). A Gikuyu edition (possibly of only the first two parts) appeared in 2004.

7. Olende and Ngũgĩ, "Ngũgĩ wa Thiong'o Interviewed on His New Novel, *Wizard of the Crow*."

8. Simon Gikandi, "The Postcolonial Wizard," *Transition* 98 (2008): 156–69, 165.

9. Gikandi, "The Postcolonial Wizard," pp. 163–64.

10. Brady Smith, "Wizards, Superwonders, and a Fictional African State: Money and the Ecology of the Grotesque in Ngũgĩ wa Thiong'o's *Wizard of the Crow*," *Research in African Literatures* 46, no. 3 (2015): 165–89, 185.

11. Ngũgĩ, *Birth of a Dream Weaver*, pp. 223–26.

12. Ngũgĩ, *In the House of the Interpreter*, pp. 164–65; Ngũgĩ, *Birth of a Dream Weaver*, pp. 84, 219; Ngũgĩ, *Writers in Politics*, pp. 70–87; R. L. Colson, "Arresting Time, Resisting Arrest: Narrative Time and the African Dictator in Ngũgĩ wa Thiong'o's *Wizard of the Crow*," *Research in African Literatures* 42, no. 1 (2011): pp. 133–53.

13. M. M. Bakhtin, "Epic and Novel," in Bakhtin, *The Dialogic Imagination* (Austin, TX, 1981), pp. 3–40; Warwick Research Collective, *Combined and Uneven Development: Towards a New Theory of World-Literature* (Liverpool, 2015), pp. 16–17.

14. Rose Mwangi, *Kikuyu Folktales: Their Nature and Value* (Nairobi, 1983), pp. 22–27, 86–89.

15. Mwangi, *Kikuyu Folktales*, pp. 23–24, 35.

16. Gikandi, "Postcolonial Wizard," p. 163; Mwangi, *Kikuyu Folktales*, pp. 72–75.

17. Gikandi, "Postcolonial Wizard," pp. 163, 161. Mwangi's collection, *Kikuyu Folktales*, does not include any stories about the Wizard of the Crow.

18. Mwangi, *Kikuyu Folktales*, pp. 36–43.

19. Mwangi, *Kikuyu Folktales*, pp. 17–21.

20. Exodus 7:8–12, where Moses's snakes devour those of the Pharaoh's magicians.

21. Genesis 11:1–9.

22. Matthew 21:1–11.

23. Matthew 27:11, Mark 15:2, Luke 23:3.

24. John 8:32; Shakespeare, *Henry IV, Part I*, III.1.58 (and proverbial).

25. Ngũgĩ wa Thiong'o, "Interview of 1980," in *Ngũgĩ wa Thiong'o Speaks: Interviews with the Kenyan Writer*, ed. Reinhard Sander and Bernth Lindfors (Oxford, 2006), p. 121.

26. Ian P. Macdonald, "The Cybogre Manifesto: Time, Utopia, and Globality in Ngũgĩ's *Wizard of the Crow*," *Research in African Literatures* 47, no. 1 (2016): pp. 57–75.

27. Neil Lazarus has suggested to me that this may be a hilarious attack on those postcolonial theorists ("decolonial theorists") who regard the idea of modernity as irretrievably Eurocentric and propose instead the notion of multiple or alternative modernities.

28. Ngũgĩ, *Birth of a Dreamweaver*, pp. 13, 59–61; Ngũgĩ, *In the House of the Interpreter*, pp. 13–14, 51.

29. Shakespeare, *Macbeth*, ed. G. K. Hunter (Harmondsworth, 1967), IV.1.79–80, 89–93; V.3.2–3, 6–7, 59–60; V.5, 34–35, 44–46; V.6, 12–14, 51–61.

30. Olende and Ngũgĩ, "Ngũgĩ wa Thiong'o Interviewed on His New Novel."

31. Gikandi, "Postcolonial Wizard," pp. 161, 167, 168; Raphael Dalleo, "Ngũgĩ wa Thiong'o's *Wizard of the Crow* and Postcolonial Pedagogy," *Research in African Literatures* 43, no. 2 (2012): pp. 138–54; Ngũgĩ, *A Grain of Wheat*, rev. ed. (Oxford, 1986), pp. 109, 245–47.

Conclusion: Writers' and Readers' Traditions

1. Curtius, *European Literature and the Latin Middle Ages*, pp. 14–16, 380–97.

2. Aby Warburg's lectures on Renaissance astrology and snake ritual similarly emphasize the need to look beyond the European tradition. Warburg, *The Renewal of Pagan Antiquity* (Los Angeles, 1999), pp. 563–697; Warburg, *Schlangenritual* (Berlin, 2011).

3. Benedict Anderson, *Imagined Communities*, rev. ed. (London, 1991), pp. 133–34, 141–49; Geoffrey Hosking, "Literature as 'Nation-Builder,'" in Hosking, *Russia: People and Empire 1552–1917* (London, 1997), pp. 286–311, xxi–xxvii.

4. When Curtius speaks of tradition as "a vast passing away and a renewal," he gives a series of reasons for the decay of traditions. Curtius, *European Literature and the Latin Middle Ages*, pp. 392–95; see also Shils, *Tradition*, pp. 213–61.

This bibliography is divided into two sections. "Primary Literary Texts" lists the texts cited for the principal authors discussed and their major sources. "Selected Secondary Texts" lists general books on literary tradition and the most significant of the secondary works on individual authors. All texts cited, including those not listed in the select bibliography, are given full bibliographical references in the footnotes on their first appearance in each chapter. Standard editions of classical texts (such as Homer and Virgil) and major reference works (such as *The Oxford English Dictionary*) are not listed here.

Primary Literary Texts

Alighieri, Dante, *La Divina Commedia*, edited by Giorgio Petrocchi (Turin, 1975).

Ariosto, Ludovico, *Orlando Furioso*, edited by Lanfranco Caretti, 2 vols. (Turin, 1992).

Ariosto, Ludovico, *Orlando Furioso*, edited by Emilio Bigi, new edition (Milan, 2012).

Ariosto, Ludovico, *Orlando Furioso*, translated by Guido Waldman (Oxford, 1974).

Boccaccio, Giovanni, *Caccia di Diana, Filostrato*, edited by Vittore Branca (Milan, 1964).

Carlyle, Thomas, *Past and Present*, edited by Richard D. Altick (New York, 1977).

Chaucer, Geoffrey, *The Riverside Chaucer*, edited by Larry D. Benson (Boston, 1987).

Chaucer, Geoffrey, *Troilus and Criseyde*, edited by Barry Windeatt (Harlow, 1984).

Gaskell, Elizabeth, *Further Letters of Mrs. Gaskell*, edited by John Chapple and Alan Shelston (Manchester, 2003).

Gaskell, Elizabeth, *The Letters of Mrs. Gaskell*, edited by J.A.V. Chapple and Arthur Pollard (Manchester, 1966).

Gaskell, Elizabeth, *Mary Barton*, edited by Macdonald Daly (London, 2003).

Guillaume de Lorris and Jean de Meun, *Le Roman de la rose*, edited by Armand Strubel (Paris, 1992).

Ngũgĩ wa Thiong'o, *Birth of a Dream Weaver* (London, 2016).

Ngũgĩ wa Thiong'o, *Dreams in a Time of War* (London, 2010).

Ngũgĩ wa Thiong'o, *A Grain of Wheat*, revised edition (Oxford, 1986).

Ngũgĩ wa Thiong'o, *In the House of the Interpreter* (New York, 2012).

Ngũgĩ wa Thiong'o, *Ngũgĩ wa Thiong'o Speaks*, edited by Reinhard Sander and Bernth Lindfors (Oxford, 2006).

Ngũgĩ wa Thiong'o, *Wizard of the Crow* (New York, 2006).

Ngũgĩ wa Thiong'o, *Writers in Politics*, revised edition (Oxford, 1997).

Olende, Ken, and Ngũgĩ wa Thiong'o, "Ngũgĩ wa Thiong'o Interviewed on His New Novel, *Wizard of the Crow*," *Socialist Worker*, 4 November 2006, https://socialistworker.co.uk/art/9867 (accessed 24 July 2017).

Petrarca, Francesco, *Canzoniere*, edited by Marco Santagata, updated edition (Milan, 2004).

Petrarca, Francesco, *Epistolae familiares*, edited by Vittorio Rossi and Umberto Bosco, 4 vols. (Florence, 1933–1942).

Petrarca, Francesco, *Le Senili*, edited by Elvira Nota, 3 vols. (Turin, 2004–2010).

Petrarca, Francesco, *Letters of Old Age*, translated by Aldo Bernardo, Saul Levin, and Reta Bernardo, 2 vols. (Baltimore, 1992).

Petrarca, Francesco, *Letters on Familiar Matters*, translated by Aldo Bernardo, 3 vols. (Albany, NY, 1975–; Baltimore, 1985).

Petrarca, Francesco, *My Secret Book*, edited and translated by Nicholas Mann (Cambridge MA, 2016).

Petrarca, Francesco, *Petrarch's Lyric Poems*, translated and edited by Robert M. Durling (Cambridge, MA, 1976).

Petrarca, Francesco, *Selected Letters*, translated by Elaine Fantham, 2 vols. (Cambridge, MA, 2017).

Spenser, Edmund, *The Faerie Queene*, edited by A. C. Hamilton, 2nd edition (Harlow, 2007).

Spenser, Edmund, *Works*, edited by R. Morris (London, 1912).

Tasso, Torquato, *Discorsi dell'arte poetica e del poema eroico*, edited by Luigi Poma (Bari, 1964).

Tasso, Torquato, *Gerusalemme Liberata*, edited by Lanfranco Caretti (Turin, 1993).

Tasso, Torquato, *Gerusalemme Liberata*, edited by Franco Tomasi (Milan, 2009).

Tasso, Torquato, *Lettere poetiche*, edited by Carla Molinari (Parma, 1995).

Tasso, Torquato, *The Liberation of Jerusalem*, translated by Max Wickert (Oxford, 2009).

Selected Secondary Texts

Adorno, T. W., *Minima Moralia: Reflections from Damaged Life*, translated by E.F.N. Jephcott (London, 1978).

Adorno, T. W., "On Tradition," *Telos* 94 (1993/1994): 75–82.

Alpers, Paul, *The Poetry of the Faerie Queene* (Princeton, NJ, 1967).

Anderson, Benedict, *Imagined Communities*, revised edition (London, 1991).

Ascoli, Albert Russell, and Unn Falkeid, eds., *The Cambridge Companion to Petrarch* (Cambridge, 2015).

Bakhtin, M. M., *The Dialogic Imagination*, translated by Caryl Emerson and Michael Holquist (Austin, TX, 1981).

Brewer, Derek S., "The Relationship of Chaucer to the English and European Traditions," in Brewer, ed., *Chaucer and Chaucerians* (London, 1966), pp. 1–38.

Burrow, Colin, *Epic Romance: Homer to Milton* (Oxford, 1993).

Campbell, John R., "Who Are the Luo? Oral Tradition and Disciplinary Practices in Anthropology and History," *Journal of African Cultural Studies* 18 (2006): 73–87.

Calvino, Italo, "Presentazione," in Ariosto, *Orlando Furioso*, edited by Lanfranco Caretti, vol. 1, pp. xxv–xlvi.

Carson, Anne, *EROS the Bittersweet* (Champaign, IL, 1998).

Clarke, K. P., *Chaucer and Italian Textuality* (Oxford, 2011).

Compagnon, Antoine, "Sainte-Beuve and the Canon," *Modern Language Notes* 110 (1995): 1188–99.

Curtius, Ernst Robert, *European Literature and the Latin Middle Ages* (Princeton, NJ, 1953).

Easson, Angus, ed., *Elizabeth Gaskell: The Critical Heritage* (London, 1991).

Eliot, T. S., "Tradition and the Individual Talent," in *Selected Essays* (London, 1972), pp. 13–22.

Ferrante, Elena, *Frantumaglia*, translated by Ann Goldstein (London, 2016).

Ferrante, Elena, *La Frantumaglia*, 2nd edition (Rome, 2016).

Fritzsche, Peter, *Stranded in the Present: Modern Time and the Melancholy of History* (Cambridge, MA, 2004).

Gadamer, Hans-Georg, *Truth and Method*, translated by Joel Weinsheimer and Donald G. Marshall, 2nd edition, revised (London, 1989).

Giddens, Anthony, "Living in a Post-Traditional Society," in Ulrich Beck, Anthony Giddens, and Scott Lash, *Reflexive Modernization: Politics, Tradition, and Aesthetics in the Modern Social Order* (Cambridge, 1994), pp. 56–109.

Giddens, Anthony, "Lecture 3: Tradition," "Reith Lectures 1999: Runaway World," 21 April 1999, downloads.bbc.co.uk/rmhttp/radio4/transcripts/1999_reith3.pdf (accessed 25 April 2017).

Gikandi, Simon, *Ngũgĩ wa Thiong'o* (Cambridge, 2000).

Graburn, Nelson, "What Is Tradition?," *Museum Anthropology* 24, nos. 2/3 (2001): 6–11.

Hadfield, Andrew, *Edmund Spenser: A Life* (Oxford, 2012).

Haight, Gordon, *George Eliot: A Biography* (Oxford, 1968).

Hainsworth, Peter, *Petrarch the Poet* (London, 1988).

Hamilton, A. C. ed., *The Spenser Encyclopedia* (Toronto, 1990).

Hobsbawm, Eric, and Terence Ranger, eds., *The Invention of Tradition* (Cambridge, 1983).

Hosking, Geoffrey, "Literature as 'Nation-Builder,'" in Hosking, *Russia: People and Empire 1552–1917* (London, 1997), pp. 286–311, xxi–xxvii.

Hough, Graham, *A Preface to* The Faerie Queene (London, 1962).

Javitch, Daniel, "The Advertising of Fictionality in *Orlando Furioso*," in Donald Beecher, Massimo Ciavolella, and Roberto Fedi, eds., *Ariosto Today* (Toronto, 2003), pp. 106–25.

Lang, Karen, ed., "Notes from the Field: Tradition," *Art Bulletin* 95 (2013): 518–43.

Leavis, F. R., *The Great Tradition: George Eliot, Henry James, Joseph Conrad* (London, 1973).

Levin, Harry, "The Tradition of Tradition," in Levin, *Contexts of Criticism* (Cambridge, MA, 1957), pp. 55–66.

MacIntyre, Alasdair, *Whose Justice? Which Rationality?* (London, 1988).

McCabe, Richard, ed., *The Oxford Handbook of Edmund Spenser* (Oxford, 2010).

McLaughlin, Martin, *Literary Imitation in the Italian Renaissance* (Oxford, 1995).

Mann, Nicholas, "From Laurel to Fig: Petrarch and the Structures of the Self," *Proceedings of the British Academy* 105 (2000): 17–42.

Mann, Nicholas, *Petrarch* (Oxford, 1984).

Marx, Karl, *The Eighteenth Brumaire of Louis Bonaparte* (Moscow, 1972).

Matus, Jill, ed., *The Cambridge Companion to Elizabeth Gaskell* (Cambridge, 2007).

Muscatine, Charles, *Chaucer and the French Tradition* (Berkeley, CA, 1957).

Mwangi, Rose, *Kikuyu Folktales: Their Nature and Value* (Nairobi, 1983).

Paine, Thomas, *Rights of Man*, in Paine, *Political Writings*, edited by Bruce Kuklick, revised edition (Cambridge, 2000).

Payne, Robert O., *The Key of Remembrance* (New Haven, CT, 1963).

Prendergast, Christopher, *The Classic: Sainte-Beuve and the Nineteenth-Century Culture Wars* (Oxford, 2007).

Quint, David, *Epic and Empire* (Princeton, NJ, 1993).

Rajna, Pio, *Le Fonti dell'Orlando Furioso*, 2nd edition (Florence, 1900; reprint, 1975).

Ranger, Terence, "The Invention of Tradition Revisited," in Terence Ranger and Olufemi Vaughan, eds., *Legitimacy and the State in Twentieth-Century Africa* (Basingstoke, 1993), pp. 62–111.

Reynolds, L. D., and N. G. Wilson, *Scribes and Scholars*, 4th edition (Oxford, 2013).

Rossiter, Will, *Chaucer and Petrarch* (Woodbridge, 2010).

Roud, Steve, and Julia Bishop, eds., *The New Penguin Book of English Folk Songs* (London, 2014).

Sainte-Beuve, Charles Augustin, "Qu'est-ce-que c'est la tradition littéraire?," in *Causeries du lundi*, 16 vols., 3rd edition (Paris, 1857–1870), vol. 15, pp. 356–82.

Sainte-Beuve, Charles Augustin, "Qu'est-ce qu'un classique?," in *Causeries du lundi*, vol. 3, pp. 38–55.

Salber Phillips, Mark, and Gordon Scochet, eds., *Questions of Tradition* (Toronto, 2004).

Santagata, Marco, *I frammenti dell'anima*, 2nd edition (Bologna, 2004).

Schor, Hilary, *Scheherezade in the Marketplace: Elizabeth Gaskell and the Victorian Novel* (New York, 1992).

Shanklin, Eugenia, "Two Meanings and Uses of Tradition," *Journal of Anthropological Research* 37 (1981): 71–89.

Shils, Edward, *Tradition* (London, 1981).

Stoneman, Patsy, *Elizabeth Gaskell*, 2nd edition (Manchester, 2006).

Tillotson, Kathleen, *Novels of the Eighteen-Forties* (Oxford, 1956).

Tomasi, Franco, ed., *Lettura della Gerusalemme Liberata* (Alessandria, 2005).

Thompson, Stith, *The Folktale* (Berkeley, CA, 1946).

Uglow, Jenny, *Elizabeth Gaskell: A Habit of Stories* (London, 1993).

Wallace, David, *Chaucer and the Early Writings of Boccaccio* (Woodbridge, 1985).

Warburg, Aby, *The Renewal of Pagan Antiquity* (Los Angeles, 1999).

Weber, Max, *Economy and Society*, 2 vols. (Berkeley, CA, 1978).

Weinsheimer, Joel, *Gadamer's Hermeneutics* (New Haven, CT, 1985).

Williams, Raymond, *Culture and Society 1780–1950* (Harmondsworth, 1963).

Williams, Raymond, *Keywords*, revised edition (New York, 1985).

Wimsatt, James, *Chaucer and His French Contemporaries* (Toronto, 1991).

Windeatt, Barry, *Oxford Guides to Chaucer: Troilus and Criseyde* (Oxford, 1995).

A NOTE ON THE TYPE

THIS BOOK has been composed in Miller, a Scotch Roman typeface designed by Matthew Carter and first released by Font Bureau in 1997. It resembles Monticello, the typeface developed for The Papers of Thomas Jefferson in the 1940s by C. H. Griffith and P. J. Conkwright and reinterpreted in digital form by Carter in 2003.

Pleasant Jefferson ("P. J.") Conkwright (1905–1986) was Typographer at Princeton University Press from 1939 to 1970. He was an acclaimed book designer and AIGA Medalist.

The ornament used throughout this book was designed by Pierre Simon Fournier (1712–1768) and was a favorite of Conkwright's, used in his design of the *Princeton University Library Chronicle.*